REALIST BIOGRAPHY AND EUROPEAN POLICY

Realist Biography and European Policy

An Innovative Approach
to European Policy Studies

edited by

Jeffrey David Turk

and

Adam Mrozowicki

LEUVEN UNIVERSITY PRESS

© 2013 by Leuven University Press / Universitaire Pers Leuven / Presses Universitaires de Louvain. Minderbroedersstraat 4, B-3000 Leuven (Belgium).

All rights reserved. Except in those cases expressly determined by law, no part of this publication may be multiplied, saved in an automated datafile or made public in any way whatsoever without the express prior written consent of the publishers.

ISBN 978 90 5867 971 0
D / 2013 / 1869 / 67
NUR: 754

Design: Jurgen Leemans
Cover design: Griet Van Haute
Cover illustration: Velázquez, *La Fábula de Aracne o Las Hilanderas* (Museo del Prado, 1657-58).

Foreword

I am very delighted to be able to write the foreword to this very timely and fascinating book at a time when its never been more pressing to understand how European Policy is made and at a time of the Euro's worst crisis in its history unfolding. This book brings together a remarkable group of cutting edge thinkers and their analytical tools. Its method can reveal so much more of what matters to people.

I became involved in this project from very early on in working with Jeff Turk when trying to choose a methodology for green economics. Jeff contributed an article to a special issue on philosophy in green economics in one of the early issues of the International Journal of Green Economics that I had just founded as the first academic journal in green economics.

In my own work I have been keen to include specificity as well as complexity as reflected in the real world. I have expressed nervousness at the abstraction or generalisation used so often in, for example, costing biodiversity loss – as it is not possible to generalise about the fate of a species – as each one is habitat specific and requires a certain set of conditions – as indeed people are each products of their own baggage.

Jeff invited me to speak at the workshop on Realist Biography and European Policy in Leuven, April 2010. I was very happy to speak there as it opened my eyes to the very exciting formulation of critical realist biographical methodology. The workshop was particularly interesting as it was held on the very same weekend when the volcano erupted in Iceland, spewing out noxious fumes all over Europe and it was indeed so bad that weekend that we when I walked around Leuven I had to keep a scarf over my mouth to keep out the sulphur smell and taste. It was one of those weekends where the power of nature became much more influential and immediate.

I first questioned mainstream research and analysis in economics about 10 years ago when I envisioned how a green economics analysis might differ from a mainstream economics outcome; and at the time the research community ridiculed my suggestion that green economics had something very useful to offer the mainstream analytical narrative. The rest as they say is history... The ideas and analyses I have worked so hard to bring to bring forth through the journal and my personal campaigning are now being adopted by nearly every government in the world.

But the reason I am so pleased to recommend this book to the reader is the particular opportunities the ideas have offered to me and my research. In the past it was considered a given assumption that truth, reality and analysis was in pure form only to be found in economics in using mathematics and quantitative and formulaic descriptions of the world. It seemed to me – as Tony Lawson, professor of econometrics at Cambridge puts it – that using solely mathematics for economics is like using a power drill to dust a window. So not only does this methodology not work but it also wrecks the windowsill whilst it is doing it!

I have found increasingly that:
a) there is a difference between reality as it actually exists and our views of it under certain lights – depending on where you are looking from and
b) every person sees and experiences the world in different ways, based on their personal experiences.

In particular I find when I am writing one of my speeches, even, a speech I write at 9 in the morning is a different speech from one I write at 10, as the influences on my experiences that I am most fully aware of are actually different even at different times. How much more different are perceptions of reality, truth and data between people and between peoples own different and very personal "baggage and experience". So in understanding how policy is made and how norms are created, to leave out realist biography and personal life stories of the very people we are seeking to understand or what motivates them when making policy to – is to miss 90% of what is relevant! Hence it has become clear to me and even to parts of the UK government that this methodology is of the utmost importance when seeking as I do in my work to make "waves of change" (one of the mottos of our institute). Ultimately humans remember and value things about people rather than things!

I am struck again and again how very important the critical realist perspective is in explaining the world, how it is becoming more and more popular and how the previous ceteris paribus approach of the mainstream failed dismally even to predict the huge economic recession and crisis looming even though people were very much personally struggling at the time. Had they used this type of approach it is highly probable much misery and suffering could have been avoided.

The book is therefore particularly interesting for those of us working in the European policy field, as it focuses on details of how policies for Europe have been made and how officials see the world. Indeed it is of particular interest to me in my work as an assembly member of the Green European Foundation where I have to make decisions about the green groups around all the member states of the European Union and in my international network. It is also a must read for anyone who is working at the European level and wants the latest cutting edge innovation in research methodology and where governments are heading at the moment.

For researchers and those interested in methodology for all kinds of social science who have not yet come across this methodology it is very important to keep up to date with this latest development. For policy makers, it is a vital tool in understanding how policy is actually made, the institutional constraints and how it all works in reality. What are the blocking points to change? This has never been a more pressing question as climate change has not been taken up by officials in the way the public would perhaps want and clearly need as we lurch dangerously towards 7 degrees of warming, potentially releasing a seriously destructive force of nature that threatens our very survival. This is definitely NOT the time for a Business as Usual Approach to methodology- but rather a time to adopt clearly appropriate and relevant techniques and tools to get us out of this mess, both financial and climatic! It is definitely time to explore the real world and to have a serious reality check of our methodology, data and what we consider the important "facts" and "assumptions" in a case to be.

Miriam Kennet, Director of the Green Economics Institute
Founder and Editor of the *International Journal of Green Economics*, the first ever academic journal in green economics – now in its 7th volume.

Reading, UK, December 2012

Contents

List of Figures	10
List of Tables	10
Acknowledgements	11
1. **Introduction: the Need for Realist Biography in European Policy Studies**	13
Adam Mrozowicki, Jeffrey David Turk & Markieta Domecka	
2. **Realism and Social Research: A Morphogenetic Approach**	43
Bob Carter	
3. **Biography-using Research (BNIM), Sostris, Institutional Regimes, and Critical Psycho-Societal Realism**	63
Tom Wengraf with Prue Chamberlayne	
4. **Biographical Costs of Transnational Mobility in the European Space**	93
Antonella Spanò, Elisabetta Perone & Markieta Domecka	
5. **Biographical Approach in the Study of Identities of Ethnic Minorities in Eastern Europe**	115
Lyudmila Nurse	
6. **Social Dialogue as a European Social Field: Setting up a "Critical Realist" Explanatory Framework of the Practices of the European Works Councils in Multinationals in Europe**	141
Valeria Pulignano & Norbert Kluge	
7. **Biographies and the Drafting of EU Environmental Policy in an Anthropological Framework**	167
Tatiana Bajuk Senčar & Jeffrey David Turk	
8. **Linking Structural and Agential Powers: A Realist Approach to Biographies, Careers and Reflexivity**	191
Markieta Domecka & Adam Mrozowicki	
Contributors	215
Index	221

List of Figures

Figure 1.1 Realist science: checking knowledge against the world   21
Figure 8.1 Career patterns in workers' and business milieus and the types of reflexivity   197

List of Tables

Table 3.1 Illustration of the twin tracks and three columns of the BNIM method   77
Table 5.1 Summary of the biographical cases   123
Table 6.1 Summary of the type and content of EWCs practices   160

Acknowledgements

This book is the result of the workshop: *Realist Biography and European Policy* hosted by the Centre for Sociological Research (CeSO) KU Leuven, 16-18 April 2010, and organised by CeSO and the Scientific Research Centre of the Slovenian Academy of Sciences and Arts, with the financial support of UACES (University Association for Contemporary European Studies): Exchanging Ideas on Europe. We would especially like to express our thanks to the CeSO group, including Valeria Pulignano, Geert van Hootegem, Vickie Dekocker and Marina Franckx for their flawless hosting of the event.

The workshop was the kick-off event of the informal Realist Biography Working Group, and this book is meant as an initial rallying point for its future activities. We would like to thank our keynote speakers for supporting us in this venture: Margaret Archer, Bob Carter, Robert Miller, Fritz Schütze, Tom Wengraf, Prue Chamberlayne, Valeria Pulignano and Miriam Kennet, as well as the numerous others who attended. While the eruption of Eyjafjallajökull prevented two of our speakers from attending, the event was still a success and we are grateful to all involved. All of the chapters of this book were authored or co-authored by someone involved in the workshop – either as keynote speaker, participant or organiser. We would like to thank our contributors for their time and fruitful interactions as well as their contributed chapters.

Lastly, we would like to thank Marike Schipper (Director), and Dr. Veerle De Laet (Acquisitions Editor) of Leuven University Press for their patience and support.

1. Introduction: the Need for Realist Biography in European Policy Studies

Adam Mrozowicki, Jeffrey David Turk & Markieta Domecka

This introductory chapter discusses the motivation for and use of realist biography in European policy studies, laying out the general framework for the rest of the book. It provides an introductory melding of the ideas of some of the key proponents of Critical Realism/Realist Social Theory and biographical methods and demonstrates how they can be developed leading to a toolbox for practical research in European policy studies and in the social sciences more generally. Both biographical methodology, as advanced by Schütze (1983) and Rosenthal (1995), and critical realism, in particular its variety proposed by Archer (2007), share common roots in philosophical pragmatism and sociological humanism, common interests in work stories and life stories, and similar analytical concepts, for instance biographical work and the processing of experience that takes the form of an internal conversation. For Archer,

> "a full understanding of how actors reflexively make their way through the world, dealing as they must with at least some of its social properties and powers, requires an exploration of their life and work histories." (Archer, 2007: 98)

This theoretical assertion offers a natural link with the tradition of biographical research, which has not been explored so far in the literature. While there are many books on the market which separately deal with biographical methods and methodological issues related to critical realism, no book so far has attempted to bring together these two theoretical traditions. The main goal of this collective volume is to fill this gap and demonstrate that the combination of critical realism and biographical methods is not only possible, but it can also be very beneficial for the exploration of newly emerging research fields at the European level.

One of the key features of this book is thus to place biographical research in an explicitly realist framework. Accordingly, we distinguish three component levels of science: (1) real world, (2) data and (3) our models and beliefs about the world that can emerge from and be grounded in empirical analysis, and which the data are used to check. Our task is to provide sufficient information to convince a presumed research community employing a similar realist framework that our findings about the data we collect and consider go beyond mere data-correlations, but can advance to having explanatory power at the level of the real world (Turk, 2009). Key to this approach is the problem of the perception of the subject matter under study – the issue of data acquisition for theory-checking in realist social science.

In order to firmly ground our models and beliefs in the real lived social world, we have to have an approach to data acquisition that makes this possible. We thus start with the hypothesis that there is an internal conversation (Archer, 2003) – people talking to themselves about their relation to society – that acts as a real causal mechanism mediating between social structures and human agency. It is this mediating mechanism in action that we wish to probe as accurately as possible as an important explanatory source for social dynamics at the various levels where it comes into play in European Union policy processes.

Inspired by the work of Schütze (1977; (2005 [1984]; 2008a; 2008b), as followed by Rosenthal (1995) and Wengraf (2001), we take the spontaneous, minimally directed autobiographical narratives from our informants as perhaps reflecting (not perfectly, but with some degree of accuracy) their internal conversations at play during the experiences they narrate. The notion of realist biography assumes that the actual life course influences the way that events and perceptions are recounted in the story, while the way the personal story is constructed is a reflection of the internal conversation (Archer, 2007), which in turn has real impact back on the world in which that person operates and on their action in that world. In other words, the realist biography concept suggests that life stories are something more than continuously fluid and situational narrative constructions. They offer a privileged way to reconstruct a real causal mechanism of reflexivity that influences human practices and processes in the real world.

This introductory chapter progresses in three parts:
- The first part separates the two terms "realism" and "biography" and shows how they fit together. First realism is argued as being a preferable philosophical framework as compared to the two competitors: empiricism and postmodernism. Then we show how biographical methods can work within a realist framework for social research. This section relates closely to the arguments entailed in the chapters by Carter (chapter 2) and Wengraf and Chamberlayne (chapter 3) in this book.
- In the second part we argue that the fields of European integration and European policy studies are ideal for the use of realist biography. We substantiate this thesis by addressing the need for further developing an actor-centred perspective in European studies that emerges both from existing literature in

the field and from chapters 3-8 in this volume. These chapters are explicit examples of the use of biographical methods.
• In the brief third section we address the content of the book and how the chapters of this volume contribute to a methodological toolbox for use in realist social science.

What is the realist framework, and why adopt it?

The problem we address here is not specific to European studies, but is a more general problem in the social sciences. However, because of the nature of the processes of European integration, the field of European policy studies is one particular area where the strengths of the approach espoused here can be expected to be particularly appropriate. Our approach is to combine the methods of biographical research with a solid realist foundation as a rigorous platform for social research. As noted by Carter (chapter 2 in this book), one of the strengths of realist sociology is precisely that it enables the formulation of clear methodological principles to inform social research. Substantiating this claim, we proceed in the following way: first we address the problem of realism (or the lack of it) in the social sciences. Then we consider why realist approaches are necessary. We then discuss biographical methods and show how they can be (and to what extent they are) compatible with a realist (social) science framework. Finally, in the last part we discuss some of the characteristics of European policy processes as they unfold in the real contemporary European context and we explain how and why realist biographical methods are particularly suitable for research in this area.

The first part of our task is to stake out the differences between the two main approaches to science (realism and empiricism) and between them and other approaches (such as postmodernism/radical constructivism) that radically challenge the very need for the development of a coherent and adequate scientific knowledge. We thus cluster science into three major types, but note that the postmodernist or radical constructivist type questions science altogether (while surreptitiously benefiting from it and exploiting its prestige). To help in this clustering, we use the exemplar fields of particle physics during the twentieth century for the realist (physical) science and economics during the same period for empiricist science. We do not engage much with the third type, since almost by definition it cannot lead to improved understanding of the social world, which is our purpose here.

In our explanation we will draw on the terminology of Searle (2010:17-18) for distinguishing ontological objectivity and subjectivity from epistemic objectivity and subjectivity. Ontological objectivity/subjectivity refers to the mode of existence of entities whereas epistemic objectivity/subjectivity refers to knowledge claims about those entities. Money is money through people collectively recognising it as money. While the bits of metal and water-marked sheets of paper do have ontologically objective existence as material objects, their status and functioning as money in human social systems is ontologically subjective. Money has subjective ontology but is epistemically objective.

All but the most extreme constructivists would probably agree that there is an objective reality that is the social world. But we have to be more specific. It is an epistemically objective reality whose mode of existence depends on people believing or at least tacitly accepting it. David Cameron is currently (2013) the (epistemically objective and therefore real) prime minister of the UK, not because of any ontologically objective properties inherent in his person, but because that is the status he is generally recognised as having through collectively recognised election procedures. Cameron's status as prime minister is very much different from the mass of an electron, which has ontological objectiveness independently of how that mass is understood or conventionally recognised by any particular group.

A very important and subtle point that will be developed below is that because of that difference in the mode of existence, the realist measurement techniques used in the physical sciences (particle physics in particular) are not possible and that the empiricist form of measurement used in the social sciences is unsatisfactory. So what does that leave us with? We do want to probe the socially real; so what measurement techniques do we think actually can be used? The answer we explore in this book is the following: the reason realist measurement techniques as used in physics are not appropriate for the social sciences is that those techniques are used for physical entities with given (ontologically objective) properties to be measured independently of how people think about them or act them out. Socially real phenomena do not have properties in the same way. We therefore do not try to measure the properties of social entities directly. We are limited to probing how people act them out – a probing which we do claim is possible. Socially real phenomena can be probed – we claim – but not using the same realist measurement techniques appropriate for physical entities.

What concerns us as realists is the danger of fleeing from realism altogether into high theory and empiricist methods. We would argue that this is more than just a possible outcome: it has already happened and is the current state of most social science, particularly economics.

What we are trying to do is bring realism back in, not through inappropriate measurement techniques, but through techniques appropriate to the entities we study. We hold that these are the types of techniques that biographical researchers use implicitly. Our basic supposition is that biographical methods allow us to probe in an epistemically objective way how real people act out an ontologically subjective social world. This is the principle goal of the book and the realist biography project in general.

To be very clear on this point: as opposed to the realist measurement methods of physics (where we measure ontologically objective properties) or empiricist measurement methods (which are unsatisfactory watered-down versions of the former that try to make measurement independent of ontological considerations so that the same techniques can be used in both physical and social science) we are arguing in favour of realist biographical methods (where we probe how people act out their ontologically subjective world). We argue that these latter methods offer an appropriate approach for epistemically objective social science with subjective ontology.

An important clarification is essential here. In no way do we argue that statistical techniques are inappropriate for the social sciences. This is not our target. What we criticise are empiricist techniques that do not go beyond mere data correlations. Statistics are essential for placing information, such as interview data, into broader perspective. It is essential for highlighting problems, such as increased mortality for certain social groups. What we are against is the systematic bias against data incorporating first person information in explaining outcomes in favour of social hydraulics type of modelling with statistical data (Archer, 2007) that is not traceable back to the ontologically subjective social world we study. We want to know how things happen at the level of what real people think and do. We have no a priori reasons for discarding numerical data. It just happens to be the case that people are language-using beings, which simply must be taken into account at some level – as realist biography clearly does – if we are to remain consistent with realism. Nevertheless descriptive statistics are essential in giving the context and are a necessary component of most biographical research in practice.

In order to help follow the argument, let us spell it out by bullet point and then expand it in more detail.

Realist biography as a scientific method: key assumptions

1. Our task is to put forth an approach for realist social science, which can provide us with improved understanding of how real people do things in this real world. We begin with particle physics as a solid model for a realist (physical) science that studies real things in the real world. Particle physics uses realist measurement as a reality check on theory.

2. Realist measurement requires the assumption that properties measured exist with true values. Measurement is the one key

domain that separates empiricism from realism. Realist measurement takes into explicit account the systematic uncertainty of a measurement, while empiricist measurement does not, which makes it a weaker form of measurement.

3. In order to estimate the systematic uncertainty of a measurement, the property measured must be assumed to have (and be consistent with having) a true value: the phenomena measured must be assumed to have intrinsic properties. The systematic uncertainty of a measurement is an estimate of how well a measurement with zero statistical uncertainty might still deviate from the true value of the measurand; and thus requires an analysis of the data acquisition process: a realist measurement cannot be ontologically (or epistemically) neutral.

4. Phenomena of social ontology do not have intrinsic properties – their properties derive from the social systems in which they emerge and are acted out. In Searle's (2010: 17-18) terms they are ontologically subjective, unlike the ontologically objective entities studied in physical science.

5. Therefore economics cannot and does not use realist measurement as a reality check on theory. Mainstream economics for instance (an important exemplar of social science) as a programme of abstract mathematical modelling without adequate concern for the data acquisition process (the relationship between data and real things in the world) is thus forced into empiricist measurement. But we do not need to give up on realism, just on an excessive reliance on mathematical models requiring quantitative measurement when such measurement is not possible under the constraints of realism.

6. Under a realist approach, the nature of phenomena with social ontology dictates that they be studied through the way they are acted out by real people in order to obtain a reality check on tentative knowledge claims. Realist biography is one such approach. Realist biography therefore requires attention to the real human phenomenon of collective intentionality because it underpins social ontology.

First we note that physics is not a good model for social science, but it does allow for a realist understanding of science. The main purpose here is thus not to show how social science should somehow use the methods of physics, but to show the difference between the empiricism of economics, which as the "queen of the social sciences" has spearheaded empiricism in social research as compared to the realism of physics as an archetypical natural science. The comparison highlights the importance of realist data acquisition as a prerequisite for realist social science – even though the different natures of the physical and social require different forms of data acquisition tuned to the respective subject matters.

As our primary source for explaining the difference between realist and empiricist approaches to measurement we use the text *Measurement in Economics: a Handbook* (Boumans, 2007). This book (hereinafter: *The Handbook*) claims to be "the first book that takes measurement in economics as its central focus" and "provides comprehensive and up-to-date surveys of recent developments in economic measurement". In his chapter of *The Handbook*, Mari gives a description as to what is involved in empiricist measurement, the point of which is to make measurement independent of the ontology of any particular research tradition:

> "…it is precisely the fact that measurement can be characterized in a purely structural way, therefore not considering any requirement on the usage of physical devices, that leaves the issue of measurability open to both physical and non-physical properties. Accordingly, measurement is *ontologically-agnostic*: in particular, it does not require measurands to have a 'true value', however this concept is defined, although it does not prevent and is usually compatible with this hypothesis." (Mari, 2007: 48; emphasis in the original)

In a telling footnote Mari explains:

> "My opinion is that Measurement Science is currently living a transition phase in which the historically dominant truth-based view is being more and more criticized and the model-based view is getting more and more support by the younger researchers. On the other hand, the truth-based view is a paradigm that benefits from a long tradition: the scientists and the technicians who spent their whole life [sic.] thinking and talking in terms of true values and errors are fiercely opposing the change." (Mari, 2007: 64)

Note that Mari uses the terms "truth-based" and "model-based" for what are in this introduction termed the "realist" and "empiricist" approaches to measurement, respectively.

As noted elsewhere in greater detail (Turk, 2005; 2009; 2011a), realist measurement (in Mari's terms "truth-based") is alive and well in particle physics. The allusion to empiricist ("model-based") measurement is rather his way of allowing for measurement in the social sciences, where he tries to circumvent the fact that realist measurement is not possible there due to the nature of the phenomena studied.

Note also that our criticism of what Mari terms "model-based" measurement can in no way be construed as a criticism of the use of models, which we consider essential in any science. It would perhaps be clearer to contrast "truth-based" approaches with "non-truth-based" approaches. Here the uncertainty of measurement is either taken as how close we estimate the measured value to be with respect to the true value (truth-based) or it is not. The former only works in the physical sciences where the entities measured are consistent with having true (ontologically objective) values. Again, this is not the case with the ontologically subjective entities of social science, so some other approach, such as realist biography, is required.

Therefore, contra Mari, we argue that social scientists should join with physicists in resisting the change away from realism towards empiricism, an undesirable change. Instead we present a rigorous approach for realist social science tuned to the underlying social ontology.

Accordingly we must deal with the fact that we cannot directly measure quantities of social ontology, since their properties are ontologically subjective and therefore lack the true values physical phenomena normally have. Instead we can only study the way these phenomena are acted out in a given social setting. Instead of asking what the properties of a given social phenomenon are and how it functions, we can only ask how that given phenomenon is acted out by the participants involved. Our method of realist biography is a way of doing just that using a realist conceptualisation of science. It is our way of dealing with the same question Searle (2010: 18) contributes to answering: "How can there be an epistemically objective set of statements about a reality which is ontologically subjective?"

We make use of the diagram of Figure 1.1, adapted from Turk (2009), to help illustrate the argument. The problem we address here is that of comparing tentative knowledge claims to what actually happens in the world. Since there is no direct knowledge about the world without perception, the issue of data and data acquisition is important. The diagram illustrates a realist conceptualisation of science. In empiricist approaches the issue of the procedures and methodologies of data acquisition is downplayed and models are only checked against data in an ontologically-neutral way. On the other hand, postmodernist/radical constructivist approaches only consider the top layer of the diagram, which is the top epistemic level, and claim that the rest is merely the social construction of the scientists, meaning that knowledge produced has little bearing on any hypothetical world beyond that constructed by the social scientists. We of course argue that all components of the diagram are necessary for realist science.

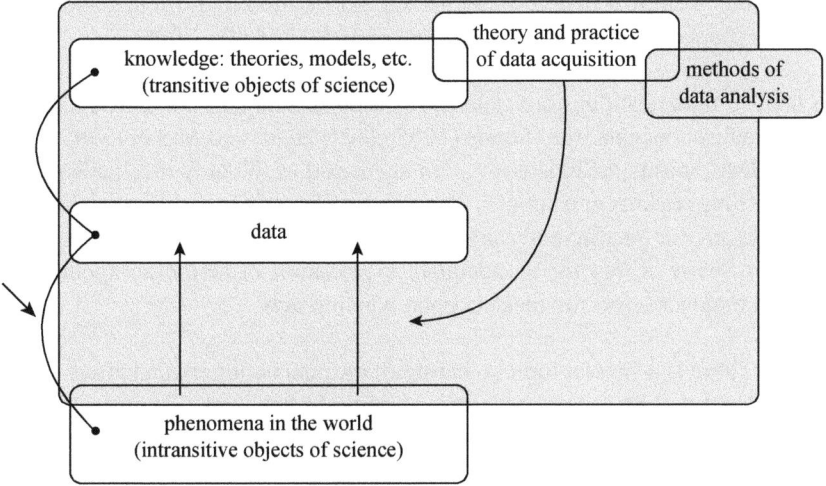

Figure 1.1 Realist science: checking knowledge against the world
Source: Modification of diagram from Turk (2009).

For the remainder of this introductory chapter, we mainly focus on the link between phenomena in the social world and the acquisition of data from those phenomena within a realist framework. First we stress the difference between data and world. Data depend on the theory of data acquisition employed in their acquisition. Phenomena even in the social world, while ontologically subjective on the part of the participants involved, are independent of any theory of data acquisition to be used. The specific (primary) tool we use to acquire data from an ontologically subjective real world is to make use of the real human attributes of the participants in the social phenomena in providing narratives that (in combination with each other and other available sources of information) allow us to check our tentative and improving knowledge against what happens in the real world as made tangible through those narratives.

This observation is consistent with the method of abduction introduced by Peirce (1974/1979) and discussed in the context of biographical method by Rosenthal (2004). Abduction enables us to explain unexpected facts through re-arranging our knowledge and making new connections between ideas. As noted by Kelle:

> "in making abductive inference, researchers depend on previous knowledge that provides them with the necessary categorical framework for the interpretation, description and explanation of the empirical world under study (...) The framework which guides empirical investigations should be modified, rebuilt and reshaped on the basis of empirical material." (Kelle, 2005: 31)

To help in understanding our data acquisition techniques, we introduce some further realist concepts from Searle (1995; 2001; 2010) and Archer (1995; 2003; 2007). Searle posits the existence of an agent-self as the only mechanism capable of turning reasons into actions. The agent-self operates within a gap in which actions taken are insufficiently predetermined by the given causes. The crucial point for Searle is that for an adequate explanation of action an agent-self is required that can select the reasons upon which it acts:

> "There is a special logical feature of rational action explanations. Construed as causal explanations, they do not work. The causes are typically not sufficient to explain the action. Yet they are perfectly adequate as they stand. Their intelligibility requires that we think of them not as citing causes that determine an event, but as citing the reasons that a conscious rational agent acted on. That agent is a self. Agency plus the apparatus of rationality equals selfhood." (Searle, 2001: 92)

For Searle (2001: 95), there are several necessary properties of these real human agent-selves. They are 1) conscious; 2) persist through time; 3) operate with reasons, under the constraints of rationality; 4) operating with reasons, are capable of deciding, initiating and carrying out actions, under the presupposition of freedom; and 5) are responsible for at least some of their behaviour. Note that Searle's understanding of practical human rationality as discussed above is in absolute opposition to the type of cost-benefit analysis usually associated with the term "rationality" such as in rational actor theory. Searle's version of practical human rationality is a reflexive deliberative process, which is squarely at odds with a simple exercise of instrumental rationality, which Searle describes as the "classical model" of rationality (Searle, 2001: 5).

One last concept we take from Searle is that of "collective intentionality". This is a very common form of first-person plural intentionality found among real people and exemplified in such statements as "We are doing such and such," "We intend to do such and such," and "We believe such and such (Searle, 2010: 43)." The important point Searle makes about collective intentionality is that:

> "...it cannot be required of each individual's intentionality that he know what the intentionality on the part of others is. In complex forms of teamwork or collective behavior, one typically does not know what the others are doing in detail. All one needs to believe is that they share one's collective goal and intend to do their part in achieving the goal." (Searle, 2010: 45)

The reason that this is important for realist biography is that there are two crucial settings of collective intentionality in our data acquisition procedure. The first setting is in the real collective intentional world in which the phenomenon we study is situated. The second is in the separate interview setting where a participant from the first setting gives a sensible account of her actions according to her understanding of her part in the common undertaking of the interview.

It is in going from the first setting of collective intentionality to the second that Searle's above five properties of agent-selves come into play. It is these properties of real people that allow us to acquire data in the second setting that allow us to probe the first. It is thus through data acquired in such a fashion that we can cross-check our tentative knowledge claims with real phenomena in the social world, which is sustained through collective intentionality.

We find Searle's analysis of the reflexive practical rationality of real human agent-selves compatible with the operation of reflexivity in Archer's (1995; 2003; 2007) realist social theory. For Archer (2000: 7), reflexivity is a personal emergent power, irreducible to a social and cultural context, and is causally co-responsible for human conduct. It is embedded in our continuous sense of the self, resulting from our embodied practices in the world that are held to be constitutive for our sociality. The main properties of reflexivity are its interiority, its first-person perspective, and its causal efficacy vis-à-vis social forms (Archer, 2007: 63-64). The modality through which reflexivity is exercised is the internal conversation. By means of an inner dialogue with themselves, people delineate and prioritise their concerns, survey objective circumstances, and make judgements about courses of action (Archer, 2003: 142). The mediating role of reflexivity in the relationship between agency and social structures is well illustrated by the three-stage model of human action proposed by Archer (2007). The model asserts that:

> "(1) Structural and cultural properties objectively shape the situations that agents confront involuntarily, and inter alia possess generative powers of constraint and enablement in relation to (2)

subjects' own constellation of concerns, as subjectively defined in relation to three orders of natural reality: nature, practice and the social. (3) Courses of action are produced through the reflexive deliberations of subjects who subjectively determine their practical projects in relation to their objective circumstances." (Archer, 2007: 17; emphasis in the original)

Thus according to Archer:

"[The] final stage of mediation is indispensable because, without it, we have no explanatory purchase on what exactly agents do. The absence of this purchase means settling for empirical generalisations about what 'most of the people do most of the time'. Sociologists often settle for even less: 'Under circumstance x, a statistically significant number of agents do y.' This spells a return to a quest for Humean constant conjunctions and, in consequence, a resignation to being *unable* to adduce a causal mechanism." (Archer, 2007: 21; emphasis in the original)

Both authors are thus very useful for grounding the process of data acquisition in realist biography. Certainly, we cannot uncover "real" social structures by interviewing people in-depth about them. Yet, in accordance with the critical realist stance, we do need such (fallible) people's accounts to understand the powers of agency in mitigating structural and cultural conditionings. An epistemological consequence of this stance was clearly stated by Bhaskar (1998a: xvi), who claimed that for critical realists

"in contrast to the hermeneutical perspective…actors' accounts are both corrigible and limited by the existence of unacknowledged conditions, unintended consequences, tactic skills and unconscious motivations; but in opposition to the positivist view, actors' accounts form the indispensable starting point of social inquiry." Bhaskar (1998a: xvi)

A key issue in realist accounts is the focus on real causal mechanisms, which may lie dormant and become expressed only in certain circumstances. They may thus not always be expressed as a universal phenomenon in all cases. Therefore a process-oriented type of methodology (Maxwell, 2004) that infers from narrative interviews the constraints and enablements that actors perceive they work under. Thus with interview data, we can use a form of process-tracing (Bennett, 2010; Checkel, 2008; George and Bennett, 2005) to reach and test results. Here the causal processes involved in individual cases are probed, rather than looking for statistical correlations between large numbers of cases.

One trap we would like to note and avoid is that we do not wish to bypass the intentionality of our informants, making direct inferences between the narrative data collected and phenomena in the world. Since the social phenomena we study are manifested through human intentionality, should we try to remove human intentionality from the phenomenon, there would be no phenomenon left to study. Therefore, while we follow a form of process-tracing in analysing causal chains from inputs to outcomes, part of that analysis follows the rational processes available in the logic of the story-telling of the informants.

In typical process-tracing, '[t]he researcher looks for the observable implications of hypothesized explanations, often examining evidence at a finer level of detail or a lower level of analysis than that initially posited in the relevant theory. The goal is to establish whether the events or processes within the case fit those predicted by alternative explanations' (Bennett, 2010: 208).

Arguably, the tradition of biographical approach offers a privileged, but still largely unexplored link between the ontological assumptions of critical realism and the practice of empirical research. Of course there is a long history of biographical research even without the explicitly realist framework presented here (Chamberlayne, Bornat, and Wengraf, 2000; Miller, 2005). Our neglect of that body of research so far in this analysis does not in any way imply that the scientific foundations of that work have been erroneous, weak or misguided. Our purpose was rather first to provide a solid realist framework for social science and then show how the solid corpus of biographical research already seems at home within it. It is not our intent to criticize one body of research on the grounds of another, but rather show the close affinities between the two. By developing a perspective of realist biography, we hope to contribute to a long-established epistemological discussion in the field of biographical studies. Important threads of this discussion are presented in detail in the chapter by Wengraf and Chamberlayne (chapter 3) in this book, which both address problems involved in "empiricist" and "constructivist" reading of biographical accounts.

Biographical approaches, having their roots in early Chicago School tradition[1], in the epistemological, ontological and also in the practical sense of

---

[1] Starting in the 1920s with *The Polish Peasant in Europe and America* by Thomas and Znaniecki biographical research was then developed in the work by Ernest W. Burgess, Robert E. Park, Clifford R. Shaw and others. In Europe biographical approach was established through the great input by Florian Znaniecki and Józef Chałasiński in Poland, Fritz Schütze and his collaborators in Germany, Daniel Bertaux in France, and many others. There have been also some efforts aimed at institutionalising this stream of research. In 1978 Daniel Bertaux initiated "Biography and Society" group within the International Sociological Association and in 1979 Martin Kohli and others founded the German working group "Biographieforschung", which was later accepted by the German Sociological Association.

Robert Park's advice for sociologists to get their hands dirty in the real world (cf. Becker, 1999: 3), during the last three decades have become increasingly prevalent in the social sciences as a way of addressing the dynamics of social change from the perspectives of those affected (cf. Chamberlayne et al., 2000). Broadly understood biographical methods are mainly concerned about the subjective perspective of the individuals under study and the interaction between individual actions and broader social processes. Firstly, these are individual actions, strategies, experiences, meanings and interpretations, which are treated as a starting point for the construction of theoretical generalizations. Secondly, a great significance is ascribed to the role of the individual, human agency, reflexivity and subjectivity in social processes, which is connected with the conviction that sociological analysis cannot be reduced only to macro sociological regularities. Biographical analysis is focused first on the course of individual life as a fragment of social reality and then on the way the story of one's life is constructed and re-constructed. The aim is to discover patterns in life courses, to understand both individual actions and social processes, to explain the interdependence between human agency and social structures. On the one hand, the researcher reconstructs the course of events, as narrated, that forms the individual life history, and on the other hand, s/he takes into account the subjective interpretation of those events. The individual experience of structural influences is only one part of the focus. Equal importance is given to the agential power exercised by individuals over the structures. According to Schütze, social reality is not only experienced and bestowed with meaning by individuals, but "it is produced, is supported and kept in force, is endured with pain and suffered, is protested at and turned over or even destroyed as well as it is gradually changed by individual actors with their personal life histories and involved biographical development" (Schütze, 2008b: 2). Thus, the analysis of people's autobiographical narrations is not only a way to understand the subjective, but it is also a way to shed light on the working of structures and their interaction.

Early sociological analyses of spoken biographies, exemplified best by Shaw's (1930) research on a delinquent boy "The Jack-Roller", have been criticised for maintaining an assumption "that accurate, truthful, valid, consistent interpretations of events can be given" (Denzin, 1992: 37). Addressing this criticism, the question of the relationship between life accounts (told stories) and subject's experiences (lived lives) arose as one of the main concerns in methodological debates within the biographical approach (Bertaux, 2005; Kochuyt, 2005; Rosenthal, 2004). On the one hand, Bertaux (2003: 45) assumed that life stories can give us an access to realities irreducible to representations, "made up of signs and subjective meanings as much as of material or structural realities". Bertaux (2005: 130) called his approach "realist", since it was based on the assumption that "socio-historical realities existed independently of the conscious minds of actors and that it was possible to obtain relatively objective knowledge about them." However, he also argued that:

> "through multiple testimonies and a cumulative intersubjectivity, we could arrive at objective knowledge concerning the social phenomena being studied, as the exterior reality of subjects: events, facts, situations, interaction, actions and practices concretely encountered" (Bertaux, 2005: 133)

Instead of the realist notion of casual mechanism, Bertaux seems to defend here the Humean conjunction of observable phenomena as the key to the "real". Obviously, this is not compatible with a critical realist stance. Importantly, also on the grounds of biographical sociology the approach by Bertaux (2005), JP Ross (2000) and other 'biographical realists', or rather 'biographical empiricists', claiming that biography reflects **directly** people's thoughts, plans and actions was repeatedly criticised. According to Schütze, the assumption that narratives would simply depict social and personal reality like a mirror leads to some misunderstanding regarding the empirical grounding of biographical analysis (Schütze, 2008a: 12). Even more problematic is an approach that emerged in the wake of a more general constructivist turn in biographical research. According to Riessman (2002), as one of the proponents of the constructivist stance, biographies are performative products, deeply conditioned by interview's situation in which narrators "do not 'reveal' an essential self as much as they perform a preferred self, selected from the multiplicity of selves" (Riessman, 2002). However, from a critical realist perspective, it is unconvincing to reduce the questions about mechanisms generating biographical processes and the ways of narrating about them to epistemological questions. As argued by Bhaskar (1998a: 27), to assert otherwise would be to fall into "epistemic fallacy" which "consists in the view that statements about being can be reduced to or analysed in terms of statements about knowledge."

Arguably, life stories are indeed socially embedded constructions about past life events, selected from the present perspective of informants. However, since "the present arises out of the past and the future" (Rosenthal, 2004: 50) not all biographical reconstructions are admissible. Moreover, assuming that the production of a narrative is just a performance, which varies according to changing interview situation deprives autobiographical narration its pivotal epistemic power (cf. Schütze, 2008a: 12). Therefore, autobiographical story telling "should not be seen just as a freewheeling and flexible course of textual invention of the narrator" (Schütze, 2008a: 14). It does not mean, however, that there are no performative aspects in the autobiographical narration. Undoubtedly, we can find some attempts of presenting oneself in the most favourable light or avoiding a detailed account of painful experiences, but such attempts can be identified during the interview and further during the analysis and taken into account in the interpretation. An argument against the 'freewheeling narrator' comes also from critical realism with its focus on human concerns and reflexivity. As Margaret Archer convincingly demonstrated, we are not subjectively free to make what we want of the past, constructing our biographies along such story lines we please. "We bring to the present the objective results of our previous commitments. The 'deposited' features are real and impose serious limitations upon narrative freedom because any re-telling of the past has to account for them" (Archer, 2003: 126).

The approach, which fits much better into the perspective defended in this book than the "empiricist" and "constructivist" alternatives illustrated by the positions of Bertaux and Riessman, arises then from the pioneering work of Schütze (1977, 1983). According to Schütze, a spontaneously told life story is a sequential ordering of process structures (Schütze, 1983: 284) that describes the storytellers' attitudes towards the most important parts of their life. Life stories cannot be reinvented all over again, because the narrator cannot tell them in a completely free manner. On the interactive level, s/he is subjected to communicative constraints which guarantee a mutual understanding between the speaker and listener: specifically a constraint (or drive) to condense (i.e. to focus life story on its overall logic), a constraint to close the narrative forms once tackled in life account, and a constraint to go into details (Kallmeyer and Schütze, 1977). On the level of content, the freedom of self-presentation is limited by the cognitive figures of improvised narrative story, safeguarding the life story from interactive influences (Schütze, 2005 [1984]). For instance, every biographical story must include its subject, the subjects of presented experiences, the chains of narration connecting events and experiences, and the social frames (situations, social milieux and social worlds) of their presentation. Additionally, the overall form of a biography expresses the tangle of process structures to which narrators refer presenting their life stories (ibidem).

The autobiographical narrative interview, the tool used by various biographical approaches, starts with a single eliciting question that is designed to encourage an interviewee to tell the history of his or her life. When the narrative starts, the researcher does not intervene, but provides only non-committal, mostly non-verbal responses. In most cases we can observe how the narrator becomes guided by his/her own recollections, re-living past experiences, changing the past tense into present, indirect to direct speech performing whole dialogues and describing in great detail relevant people, places, and situations. The researcher waits with additional questions till the end of the narrative part of the interview. It has been observed that asking some questions earlier often breaks the red thread of narration and brings argumentation instead. It needs to be emphasised at the beginning of the interview that this is the interviewee's life history which is the core interest for the researcher. Although some questions will be asked later, they are not more relevant than the life history itself. When the narrative part is finished with a coda, which may take a following form: "That's it, this is my life", some questions are asked in relation to topics already introduced by the narrator. At this point, the aim is to exhaust the additional narrative potential. It is only in the third, more probing stage that the researcher explicitly asks questions on issues relating to the core of his study. S/he may activate the communicative scheme of description asking about the social frames, routines, and structural conditions. Only at the very last phase of the interview the argumentative 'why' questions are asked, which activate the self-theoretical reflections.

Biographical analysis as developed by Fritz Schütze and his collaborators involves the reconstruction of the subjective perspective of actors, the objectifiable courses of action, and the interplay between both. For the analysis of biographical data Schütze proposes "pragmatic refraction" (Schütze, 2008a) which means that verbal expressions are not taken at face value but they are "analytically related to their contexts of experiential background, their context of production and use as well as to their contexts of later application, social function and meaningful overall (biographical or actional) structure" (Schütze, 2008a: 14). The analysis begins with text sort differentiation, which examines how the autobiographical text has been produced interactively (Schütze, 2008b: 15). The narrative, descriptive, and argumentative parts are identified. Moreover, different types of restrictions, communicative mistakes and mutual misunderstandings involved in the production of autobiographical materials are taken into account (Schütze, 2008b: 16). Sequential structural description is the next analytical step. It focuses on formal features, especially presentation and demonstration markers, of the main narrative. The careful analysis of formal features gives a picture of the biographical processes and the identity development involved (Schütze, 2008b: 18-19). Importantly, through the textual and socio-biographical contextualization it is possible to depict analytically even unnoticed, faded-out, ambivalent or enigmatic social and biographical processes (Schütze, 2008b: 20). A sub-step of structural description consists of putting together the pieces of information extracted from different parts of interview dealing with the same event and the same process of identity change. In this way it is possible to fill the "gaps" of difficult experiences initially faded out in the main story line, and then referred to in the questioning part, as in case of background constructions (Schütze, 2008b: 22). The next step of analysis consists of distinguishing elementary biographical process structures, such as biographical and institutional action schemes, trajectories of suffering and metamorphoses. Through biographical action schemes individuals attempt to actively shape the courses of their lives and on the basis of institutional action schemes people follow normatively defined courses of life, such as organisational career patterns, family life cycles and others. Trajectories of suffering describe the process in which people are not capable of actively shaping their lives as they are under a strong influence of several destabilising conditions (described also as "cumulative mess"). It is possible, however, to overcome the trajectories through biographical work. It becomes possible then to enter the process of metamorphosis, by which a new important, often unexpected, inner development starts in one's biography (Schütze, 2008a: 26-27). The reconstruction of the overall biographical structuring, the gestalt, as a sequence of biographical process structures is a part of analytical abstraction. It also focuses on the interlink of biographical processes and other social phenomena and collective changes as revealed in the case. Some of these interlinks engender agency and the autonomous development of personal identity, and others support it (cf. Schütze, 2008b: 24). At this stage also the self-theoretical insights and rationalisations of the narrator are taken into account, as realised through argumentative strings of text: commentaries to narrative presentations, turning point experiences, pre-coda evaluations, etc. (Schütze, 2008b: 42). An attempt is also made to detect what is "case distinctive" and what are general features, which are theoretically remarkable (Schütze, 2008b: 24). As a result of analytical abstraction a grid structure of analytical categories is developed.

Biographical analysis as developed by Rosenthal (2004), named biographical case reconstruction, starts with a sequential approach to biographical data aimed at the reconstruction of the sequences of live events independently of narrator's interpretations. Thematic analysis, which follows, is focused on the reconstruction of the mechanism governing the selection of the narrated biographical themes. In the third step, the reconstruction of the lived life as experienced by a subject takes place, and is centred on the microanalysis of selected text segments. After which, the results of the sequential analysis are confronted with narrator's own interpretations. A similar approach is taken by the Biographic-Narrative Interpretive Method (BNIM; cf. Wengraf, 2001), which explicitly separates two strands of analysis: 1) the actual unfolding of the biographical trajectory of the participant-interviewee (the living of the lived life) and 2) the way that the narrative is told (the telling of the told story) (see chapter 3 by Wengraf and Chamberlayne in this book). It then analyses the influences of the two parts on each other for the complete case. This is useful for our purposes in that it makes highlights the distinction between the narrative as data and an actual life in the social world. While these are clearly not the same things, there is a close analytically accessible relationship between them. Such approaches are particularly appealing for realist biography. Firstly, because they put great emphasis on the self-reflexive biographical work. Secondly, subjectivity is given great importance there but at the actual core of analysis is the embeddedness of the autobiographical histories in the broader social structures. And thirdly, people's perspectives, concerns and interpretations are taken seriously and become incorporated into researcher's own interpretations and conceptualisations. The two concepts linking critical realism and biographical approach are those of reflexivity and biographical work. Reflexivity, as understood by Archer, is an intrinsic property of human beings. It is the exercise of mental ability shared by all people to consider themselves in relation to their social contexts and vice versa (Archer, 2007: 4). It is "the mental activity which, in private, leads to self-knowledge: about what to do, what to think and what to say" (Archer, 2003: 26). Both concepts, reflexivity and biographical work in the sense of Anselm Strauss (1993), can be translated substantively into descriptive language such as "thinking over", "struggling with", "fighting out with himself", and "finally getting a new slant on himself" (cf. Strauss, 1993: 98). Implicit in the pragmatist theoretical action scheme, shared by the biographical approach and critical realism, there is the idea of work – imagining, trying out, assessing actions or lines of action involves "working things out" to use a common phrase. Work is entailed in the process of unblocking the blocked action, and moving along into the future (Strauss, 1993: 52). However, in the sense given to reflexivity by Archer, there is one more dimension to it: a causal power. Through reflexivity people exercise their causal powers and determine their future courses of action. In other words, reflexivity is the means by which people make their way through the world (Archer, 2007: 5). It is reflexivity which enables transformation of actors into "active agents" who are able to exercise some governance in their lives; who develop and define their ultimate concerns, elaborate projects and attempt to accomplish them in order to advance or protect what they care about most (Archer, 2007: 7). Any attempt to pursue a project entails two sets of causal powers: those pertaining to agents, and those pertaining to surrounding reality: objects, artefacts, structural and cultural properties. Once the causal powers are activated by the projects, they will obstruct or facilitate their accomplishment. Importantly, the actual outcomes are matters of secondary determination, governed by people's inner deliberations about existing enablements and constraints (Archer, 2007: 7-8). "Reflexivity needs not to be consigned to the free-form construction, deconstruction and reconstruction of life narratives; it can be examined as the causally powerful relationship between deliberation and action in people's social lives" (Archer, 2007: 37).

Biographical work means biographical reorientation: a reflective reconsidering of one's inner states and one's overall personal identity (Schütze, 2008a: 6). It is this type of work which is done by autobiographical recollection and reflection about alternative interpretations of one's life course. These are self-critical attempts of understanding one's own misconceptions of oneself and self-erected impediments as well as the impediments superimposed by others and by structural conditions. Biographical work also involves imagining future courses of action that support the overall *gestalt* of the unfolding biographical identity (Schütze, 2008a: 6). It is basically an inner activity of the mind constituted by conversation with significant others and oneself (Schütze, 2008a: 7); and as such goes hand in hand with reflexivity and internal conversation as defined by Archer (2003; 2007). However, there is one important difference between these notions. Whereas reflexivity remains first of all a cognitive concept, biographical work is both a cognitive and emotional (even psychoanalytical) process including doubt, fear, anguish, suffering or relief[2]. In smoothly ongoing life situations biographical work is just a quick deliberation and recollection connected to the focus on other activities. In crisis situations, biographical work may become the explicit and central action scheme of cognitively and emotionally ordering one's own life (Schütze, 2008a: 7). Biographical work is carried out in the service if an actor's biography, including its review, maintenance, repair, and alteration (Strauss, 1993: 98). Doing biographical work involves seeing oneself as a developing entity that matters (Schütze, 2008b: 43). The power of reflexivity and biographical work allow maintaining a continuous sense of self: knowing oneself to be oneself over time, despite different life experiences and life contexts. Both the biographical approach and critical realism have it clear that this continuous sense of self cannot be eliminated as "phenomenological froth" (Archer, 2003: 46). The subjective powers of reflexivity and biographical work are a condition for development of a self-directed agent as they mediate the role objective structural powers play in influencing social action.

A final topic we discuss in this section on realism and methods is validity. As part of any work of science – social or otherwise – the analysis does not end with an explanation of the procedure followed by a report of the results, but the validity of the results should also be evaluated (Adcock and Collier, 2001; Maxwell, 2012: chapter 8). Any methodology chosen is bound to have shortcomings; and its use will require some defending. On the other hand, social science itself is pointless if the methods are indefensible or if the results of the method chosen used cannot be demonstrated to have some relevance to the social world studied. We associate this relevance with "validity". In their seminal work, Shadish, Cook and Campbell (2002: 513) broadly define validity as the "truth of, or correctness of, or degree of support for an inference." Rather than leave it to the reader to judge the validity of the reported results, it is the responsibility of social scientists to provide an honest assessment of the validity of their own work, which then aids readers in reaching their own conclusions as well as providing a basis for comparison to other research. It is therefore necessary to

---

[2] We would like to thank Antonella Spanò for turning our attention to this important difference.

provide some analysis of the possible shortcomings of the results – sources and magnitudes of threats to validity (Maxwell, 2005: 106-109).

We take as our starting point Adcock and Collier's (2001) foundational plea for a shared standard of validity for qualitative and quantitative research. Our contribution is intended to help in this standardisation. Drawing on Searle's (2010: 17-18) distinction between objective and subjective ontology, our view of validity is that it is a gauge of the epistemic objectivity of our results in relation to the ontologically subjective social phenomena we study. In other words, the intentionality-relative nature of the phenomena limits the outcome to epistemically valid statements about the ontologically subjective world. The trick is thus to have an epistemically objective methodology that has purchase in the ontologically subjective world we study. Our question here is then: How valid (epistemically objective) are our results in that limited context?

Referring back to the article of Adcock and Collier (2001: 531-532) and to our discussion of measurement above, validity is normally associated with measurement error and reliability. Measurement error is separated into statistical and systematic components, where the statistical component is associated with reliability of a measurement. The two ways of associating validity and reliability are that (1) validity can be exclusively thought of in terms of bias, in which case it corresponds to systematic uncertainty. Alternatively, (2) validity can be an encompassing term to include both systematic and statistical components of uncertainty. We prefer the second usage for the following reasons: Clearly, if we are concerned with epistemically objective statements about phenomena that are ontologically subjective, we cannot associate validity with bias from an ontologically objective value. However, since that is the standard of measurement in the physical sciences (where ontological objectivity can be assumed), it is better to avoid the confusion by not using the uncertainty approach to validity in the social sciences. Instead, we define validity as the encompassing term of epistemic objectivity relative to the collective intentional system of the social system under study. In this case it will be difficult to tease out statistical and systematic components with reference to ontologically subjective values, since grounding ourselves in ontological subjectivity will normally itself be the largest source of uncertainty. Discerning what an epistemically objective value of something is with respect to the multiple subjectivities involved makes the task severely complicated. Nevertheless, this is the task we have.

Furthermore, we are dealing with a small set of overlapping subjectivities in what we study. In this case, it does not make sense to make too much of an issue of the separation of statistical and systematic components, since our concern with teasing out epistemically objective statements relative to the subjectivities involved overrides such secondary issues. Instead we prefer to follow Maxwell's (2012: chapter 8) alternative example of breaking validity down into the three overlapping categories of descriptive, interpretive and theoretical validity in social research. (Bajuk Senčar and Turk show an example of this in chapter 7 of this volume.) In this case, validity remains an encompassing term which takes into account all of the different possible threats to it from the various sources. This remains an important issue that should be taken up as a strong point of realist social research as compared to either empiricist or post-modernist approaches, which either could not (in the case of empiricism) or would not even try to reach the same standards.

Why is realist biography useful for European policy studies?

The sui generis nature of the institutions of the European Union (EU) and their unique processes of policy making and implementation make the political processes of the European Union an ideal area for the use of realist biography. Indeed, the integration process and the development of the institutions of the European Union are already receiving increased attention, particularly in light of the latest three enlargements that nearly doubled the number of member states and brought in an enormous diversity of historical backgrounds (Best, Christiansen, and Settembri, 2008; Shore, 2000; Stevens and Stevens, 2001; Thedvall, 2006; Checkel, 2007; Wiener and Diez, 2004; Rosamond, 2000). One of the peculiar features of European Union decision-making is the unique system of "comitology" that has emerged whereby legislative powers are shared through a collection of different committees (Bergström, 2005; Christiansen and Larsson, 2007; Blom-Hansen and Brandsma, 2009). Recent scholarship has indeed noted the remarkable resilience of this institutional framework to the shock of enlargement:

> "In light of this challenge, the ability of the system not only to cope, but to continue to function in a largely unchanged manner, is remarkable. But perhaps it should not come as a surprise – the very purpose of *institutionalizing* cooperation among states in the way practised by the EU is to create a decision-making system that is flexible enough to respond to change, while being stable enough to persist in face of 'external shocks'. By this standard, not only is it evident that enlargement is one of the most successful experiences of the EU, but indeed so is the institutional adaptation that has occurred alongside it" (Christiansen, Best, and Settembri, 2008: 244; emphasis in the original).

The actual functioning and continuity of these types of institutions under rapid development with new actors continuously coming in are ideal situations for the use of realist biography. In order to explore the "Europe in the making", it is necessary to acknowledge that not only the institutions shape actors, but also the biographies of the actors leave their imprint on the institutions within which they operate (Eyal, Szelenyi, Townsley 2000: 15). To assert that "biographies matter" can fill the existing gaps in the dominant practice in European studies. Existing research has been predominantly focused on the question of how the actions of social actors are affected and co-determined by the effects of European Union policies. Much less explored has been the problem of how the emergence, reproduction and change of institutional arrangements in Europe are influenced by the actions and interactions of variety of European social actors. The latter actor-sensitive research agenda emerges very clearly from recent discussions in the fields of organisation theory and comparative institutional analysis, which inspires much of European policy studies. As noted by Lawrence, Suddaby and Leca (2009: 1), "institutional approaches to organisation theory have traditionally focused attention on the relationship between among organizations and the fields in which they operate, providing strong accounts of the processes through which institutions govern actions". Instead, they propose to focus attention on "institutional work" defined as "the practical actions through which institutions are created, maintained, and disrupted" (ibid). The need for an actor-centred perspective is also clear in recent publications in comparative institutional analysis. In their *Handbook of Comparative Institutional Analysis*, Morgan et al. openly suggest that:

> "...institutions are now less likely to be discussed as exogenous constraints on actors and more as resources, which actors can draw on depending on the context. Further, it is increasingly clear that institutions in a society may offer different resources that seem dominant at a particular time and it is through combining and reorganising institutional resources that the possibility for institutional change and experimentation arises." (Morgan et al., 2010:5)

These authors acknowledge the need to "understand how actors can be both the products of structures and the origin of changes in structure" (Morgan et al., 2010: 5). However, they do not propose a coherent methodological approach to explore the influence of social actors on the emergence of institutions and social structures. In this respect, the notion of realist biography can provide a valid supplement to the existing methodological approaches in research inspired by institutional theories.

Similarly, but from the perspective of European research on welfare regimes, Stubbs emphasises limited attention paid by existing literature to:

> "... an emerging 'cultural' perspective on welfare, which focuses much more on the social relations of welfare; the role of biographies, subjectivities and memories; and the need for forms of reflexivity and attention to the minutiae of everyday life constructed within, and itself constructive of, 'welfare' as a lived experience" (Stubbs, 2002: 326)

More generally, the chapters in this book demonstrate that an analysis focused on the effects of European-level policies is insufficient to understand why so many of them fail in bringing about expected changes at the level of both European institutions and the social consciousness of Europeans. For instance, Wengraf and Chamberlayne (chapter 3) observe that centrally-driven welfare policies adopted at the European Union level "overlook and bypass" resources that are embedded in biographical experiences of European citizens. Similarly, a clear finding of the Euroidentities project, discussed by Spanò, Perone and Domecka (chapter 4), is that human reflexivity must be taken into account in order to understand how the new opportunities for transnational experience in the European Union can lead to personal entrapment instead of flourishing. In her chapter (chapter 5), Lyudmila Nurse shows that quantitative studies that lack the information available through biographical research can miss key aspects of fluid identities under transformation, and thus policies based on macro-level quantitative indicators can be misguided. The usefulness of realist biography concept for understanding the dynamics of career patterns and developing more adequate policy tools in the areas of labour market policies and occupational counselling in Europe is a central theme of the chapter by Domecka and Mrozowicki (chapter 8).

Reflecting such criticisms, the realist biography approach advanced in this book explicitly places social actors in the centre of empirical analysis of European-level processes and practices. It assumes that the degree of success in formulating, negotiating and implementing European policies cannot be assessed without hearing the voices of those responsible for managing these policies and the addressees of these management practices. The need to develop an actor-centred approach in the European studies has been recently emphasised by Georgakakis and Weisbein:

> "focusing on people involved in EU processes can take us beyond classical dichotomies, such as structure/agency, individual/ collective, rational/unconscious in order to understand what social agents involved in EU processes think and do considering their position in wider structures of interaction and domination" (Georgakakis and Weisbein, 2010:93).

The actor-centred perspective can be particularly useful to study not only how the "varieties of capitalism" (Hall and Soskice, 2001) in Europe are created from above by policy-makers, but also how the properties of differentiated capitalist regimes are negotiated, maintained and resisted in the variety of local practices by European citizens and, more generally, those affected by European Union policies. A similar conclusion arises from Pulignano and Kluge's chapter (chapter 6) in this book. Advocating the need to go beyond one-sided institutionalist analysis of European social dialogue, they argue that it is necessary to "examine more deeply the dynamics which have historically contributed to characterize its evolution through the narratives of its protagonists." To this end, the realist biography concept and associated methodology can aid in understanding the actual practices of social actors that underlie institutional dynamics in contemporary Europe.

Furthermore, the notion of realist biography makes it possible to address some of the emergent methodological problems in the field of European studies. One of the key debates in this field, and indeed the focus of one particular book (Christiansen, Jørgensen, and Wiener, 2001), is the introduction of the social constructivism debate from international relations theory into the study of the European Union. Accordingly we argue that the nature of human social systems demands serious attention to methodological issues concerning the roles of the immediate participants to the policy processes under study, which is why we propose rigorously grounded realist biography as a research tool. Again, in order to avoid either slipping into empiricism or letting moderate constructivism fall off into postmodernism, we insist on the realist framework in our approach. Chapter 7 by Bajuk Senčar and Turk takes such an approach to the study of a focal group of participants involved in the drafting of EU policy at a unique historical juncture between the enlargement of the European Union and its global engagement as an actor in the fight against climate change.

The outline of the book: towards a methodological toolbox

This book emerged out of the international workshop "Realist biography and European policy" held at the Catholic University of Leuven on 16-18 April 2010. It comprises eight chapters connecting the themes of realism, biographical methods and European studies. This first introductory chapter and the second chapter by Bob Carter provide an overview of the critical realism's ontological assumptions and their methodological consequences. Carter reviews the core ideas of a realist approach – analytical dualism, causal mechanisms, stratified social ontology and emergence. He argues that all of them entail important methodological commitments which, whilst not restricting realist research to particular research methods, do compel a distinctive view of such methods and a critical approach to their customary application. He substantiates his claims by examining examples of realist research: in the development of case study approaches; in the analysis of biographical interviews using corpus linguistic analysis; and in the refinement of theoretical concepts in researching ethnicity and race.

Chapters 3-5 discuss the examples of three European projects (Sostris, Euroidentities and ENRI-EAST) which successfully adopted biographical framework to analyse European level phenomena, processes and practices, enabling the reader to understand better practical challenges and heuristic advantages connected with biographical research. The chapter written by Tom Wengraf and Prue Chamberlayne describes a significant part of the history of the UK biographical methods connected with the "Sostris" project, which was a landmark study in the use of biographical methods for policy-related research funded by the European Commission as a mainstream pan-European project. The contribution by Spanò, Perone and Domecka derives from the most recent application of biographical methods to the analysis of the European identity development, the "Euroidentities" project. They focus on the different scenarios of transnational mobility, as a strategy actively promoted and facilitated by European legislation, and show how they are connected with the amount and composition of resources held and type of reflexivity practised. In addition, the chapter by Lyudmila Nurse is based on work carried out within the FP7 ENRI-EAST: Interplay of European, National and Regional identities project.

The remaining three chapters demonstrate how a critical realist framework and biographical methodologies can be combined into innovative heuristic tools to explore the current dynamics of the "Europe in the making". In their contribution, Pulignano and Kluge identify the need for an agency-centred perspective in the analysis of European industrial relations. Reviewing a complex history of the European social dialogue and existing research in the field, they argue that in order to understand more clearly what social dialogue is in concrete in Europe it is necessary to make sense of the meaning attributed to it by the social actors operating at the European Union level (in particular employers and trade unions). How European studies can benefit from the realist biography framework is illustrated in the contribution of Bajuk Senčar and Turk, which presents the results of the project "Anthropology of European Integration" that adopted the proposed framework. The project examines the Slovene officials involved in European environmental policy negotiations during the Slovenian Presidency of the European Union. This chapter further elaborates on the measurement and validity issue raised earlier in this Introduction as important in realist research, particularly in historically-situated realist biography. Lastly, Domecka and Mrozowicki analyse reflexivity and the career paths of workers and managers under the sweeping changes in Poland and develop a generic typology of career patters showing its (European) policy implications.

These chapters demonstrate the utility of biographical methods and how they can be made to work within an explicitly realist framework. The examples from policy-oriented studies clearly demonstrate the usefulness of the realist biography concept for European policy studies. Along with background articles, the chapters offer practical guidelines for researchers involved in actor-centred and biographical research on the European level. Thus, we are convinced that together they contribute greatly towards the development of a coherent methodological toolbox for realist social research.

On the basis of biographical analysis we can understand not only what happened and what kind of changes were experienced, but also how a coherent and continuous sense of self has been maintained despite all the changes. According to Atkinson, "in the telling of a life story, we get a good sense of how and why the various parts of a life are connected and what gives the person meaning in life. There may be no better way to answer the question of how people get from where they began to where they are now in life than through their life stories" (Atkinson, 1998: 20).

Acknowledgement

This chapter has been greatly improved through discussions with Tom Wengraf. We are also thankful to Valeria Pulignano for her very useful comments on the first draft of this text.

Works Cited

Adcock, R., and Collier, D. (2001). 'Measurement validity: A shared standard for qualitative and quantitative research'. *American Political Science Review*, 95 (3), 529-546.

Archer, M. S. (1995). *Realist Social Theory: The Morphogenetic Approach*. Cambridge, UK: Cambridge University Press.

Archer, M. S. (2003). *Structure, Agency and the Internal Conversation*. Cambridge, UK: Cambridge University Press.

Archer, M. S. (2007). *Making Our Way Through the World: Human Reflexivity and Social Mobility*. Cambridge, UK: Cambridge University Press.

Atkinson, R. (1998) *The Life Story Interview*, Qualitative Research Methods, Vol. 44, SAGE Publications.Becker, H. (1999) 'The Chicago School, So-Called', *Qualitative Sociology,* Vol. 22 (1): 3-12.

Bennett, A. (2010). 'Process-tracing and causal inference'. In H. Brady, and D. Collier (eds.), *Rethinking Social Inquiry: Diverse Tools, Shared Standards* (2nd ed., pp. 207-219). Lanham, MD, USA: Rowman & Littlefield.

Bergström, C. F. (2005). *Comitology: Delegation of Powers in the European Union and the Committee System*. Oxford: Oxford University Press.

Bertaux, D. (2003). 'The usefulness of life stories for a realist and meaningful sociology'. In R. Humphrey, R. Miller, and E. Zdravomyslova (eds.), *Biographical Research in Eastern Europe. Altered Lives and Broken Biographies* (pp. 39-51). Aldershot, Hampshire: Ashgate.

Bertaux, D. (2005). "A response to Thierry Kochuyt's 'Biographical and empirsist illusions: A reply to recent criticism'". In R. Miller (ed.), *Biographical Research Methods* (pp. 129-139). London: Sage Publications.

Best, E., Christiansen, T., and Settembri, P. (eds.) (2008). *The Institutions of the Enlarged European Union*. Cheltenham, UK: Edward Elgar.

Bhaskar, R. (1998a). 'General introduction'. In M. Archer, R. Bhaskar, A. Collier, T. Lawson, and A. Norrie (eds.), *Critical Realism. Essential Readings*. (p. ix-xxiv). London and New York: Routledge.

Bhaskar, R. (1998b [1975]). 'Philosophy and scientific realism' (from 'A realist theory of science'). In M. Archer, R. Bhaskar, A. Collier, T. Lawson, and A. Norrie (eds.), *Critical Realism. Essential Readings*. (pp. 16-47). London and New York: Routledge.

Blom-Hansen, J., and Brandsma, G. J. (2009). 'The EU comitology system: Intergovernmental bargaining and deliberative supranationalism?' *Journal of Common Market Studies*, 47 (4), 719-740.

Boumans, M. (ed.) (2007). *Measurement in Economics: a Handbook*. London: Elsevier.

Chamberlayne, P., Bornat, J., and Wengraf, T. (eds.) (2000). *The Turn to Biographical Methods in Social Science*. London: Routledge.

Checkel, J. T. (ed.) (2007). *International Institutions and Socialization in Europe*. Cambridge, UK: Cambridge University Press.

Checkel, J. T. (2008). 'Process tracing'. In A. Klotz, and D. Prakash (eds.), *Qualitative Methods in International Relations: A Pluralist Guide* (pp. 114-127). Basingstoke, Hampshire, UK: Palgrave Macmillan.

Christiansen, T., and Larsson, T. (eds.) (2007). *The Role of Committees in the Policy-Process of the European Union*. Cheltenham, UK: Edward Elgar.

Christiansen, T., Best, E., and Settembri, P. (2008). 'Conclusion'. In E. Best, T. Christiansen, and P. Settembri (eds.), *The Institutions of the Enlarged European Union* (pp. 243-252). Cheltenham, UK: Edward Elgar.

Christiansen, T., Jørgensen, K. E., and Wiener, A. (eds.) (2001). *The Social Construction of Europe*. London: Sage.

Denzin, N. K. (1992). *Symbolic Interactionism and Cultural Studies*. Oxford and Cambridge: Blackwell.

Eyal, G., Szelényi, I., and Townsley, E. (2000). *Making Capitalism Without Capitalists. The New Ruling Elites in Eastern Europe*. London, New York: Verso.

Fischer-Rosenthal, W. (2000). 'Biographical work and biographical structuring in present-day societies'. In P. Chamberlayne, J. Bornat, and T. Wengraf (eds.) *The Turn to Biographical Methods in Social Science*. London: Routledge.

Georgakakis, D., and Weisbein, J. (2010). 'From above and from below: A political sociology of European actors'. *Comparative European Politics* 8 (1): 93-109.

George, A., and Bennett, A. (2005). *Case Studies and Theory Development in the Social Sciences*. Cambridge, MA, USA: MIT Press.

Hall, P. A., and Soskice, D. (2001). 'An Introduction to Varieties of Capitalism'. In P. A. Hall, and D. Soskice (eds.), *Varieties of Capitalism. The Institutional Foundations of Comparative Advantage* (pp. 1-68). Oxford: Oxford University Press.

Kallmeyer, W., and Schütze, F. (1977). 'Zur Konstitution von Kommunikationsschemata der Sachverhaltdarstellung'. In D. Wegner (ed.), *Gesprächanalyse* (pp. 159-274). Hamburg: Buske Verlag.
Kelle, U. (2005). '"Emergence" vs. "forcing" of empirical data? A crucial problem of "grounded theory" Reconsidered'. *Forum Qualitative Sozialforschung / Forum: Qualitative Social Research* [On-Line Journal], 6(2).
Kochuyt, T. (2005). 'Biographical and empiricist illusions: A reply to recent criticism'. In R. Miller (ed.), *Biographical Research Methods* (pp. 125-128). London: Sage Publications.
Lawrence, T. B., Suddaby, R., Leca, B. (2009). *Institutional Work. Actors and Agency in Institutional Studies of Organizations.* Cambridge: Cambridge University Press.
Mari, L. (2007). 'Measurability'. In M. Boumans (ed.), *Measurement in Economics: a Handbook* (pp. 41-77). Amsterdam: Academic Press.
Maxwell, J. A. (2004). 'Causal explanation, qualitative research, and scientific inquiry in education'. *Educational Researcher*, 33 (2), pp. 3–11.
Maxwell, J. A. (2005). *Qualitative Research Design: An Interactive Approach* (2nd ed.). Thousand Oaks, CA: Sage.
Maxwell, J. A. (2012). *A Realist Approach for Qualitative Research*. London: Sage.
Miller, R. L. (ed.) (2005). *Biographical Research Methods* (Vols. I-IV). London, UK: Sage.
Morgan, G., Campbell, J.L, Crouch, C., Pedersen, O.K., Whitley, R. (2010). *The Oxford Handbook of Comparative Institutional Analysis.* Oxford: Oxford University Press.
Peirce, C. S. (1974/1979). *Collected Papers.* Published by Charles Hartshore, Paul Weiss and Arthur Burks. Cambridge (Mass.): The Belknap Press of Harvard University Press.
Rosamond, B. (2000). *Theories of European Integration.* New York: St. Martin's Press.
Riessman, C. K. (2002). 'Analysis of personal narratives'. In J. F. Gubrium, and J. A. Holstein (eds.), *The Handbook of Interview Research: Context and Method.* London: Sage.
Rosenthal, G. (1995). *Erlebte und erzählte Lebensgeschichte. Gestalt und Struktur biographischer Selbstbeschreibungen.* Frankfurt am Main: Campus
Rosenthal, G. (2004). 'Biographical research'. In C. Seale, G. Gobo, J. F. Gubrium, and D. Silverman (eds.), *Qualitative Research Practice* (pp. 48-64). London: Sage.
Ross, J. P. (2000) 'Reality or nothing! False and repressed memories and autobiography'. In Chamberlain, M. ed. *Trauma and Life Story. Memory and Narrative*,2. http://www.valt.helsinki.fi/staff/jproos/falsememory.htm [available on 20/08/2013].
Schütze, F. (1983). 'Biographieforschung und narratives Interview'. *Neue Praxis*, 3, 283-294.
Schütze, F. (1977). 'Die Technik des narrativen Interviews in Interaktionsfeldstudien'. *Arbeitsberichte und Forschungsmaterialien* Nr. 1 der Universität Bielefeld, Fakultät für Soziologie.
Schütze, F. (2005 [1984]). 'Cognitive Figures of Autobiographical Extempore Narration'. In R. Miller (ed.), *Biographical Research Methods* (pp. 289-338). SAGE Publications.
Schütze, F. (2008a) 'Biography Analysis on the Empirical Base of the Autobiographical Narratives: How to Analyse Autobiographical Narrative Interviews', Part I, INVITE – Biographical Counselling in Rehabilitative Vocational Training. Further Educational Curriculum. EU Leonardo da Vinci Programme. http://www.uni-magdeburg.de/zsm/projekt/biographical/1/B2.1.pdf [available on 20/08/2013].
Schütze, F. (2008b) 'Biography Analysis on the Empirical Base of the Autobiographical Narratives: How to Analyse Autobiographical Narrative Interviews', Part II, INVITE – Biographical Counselling in Rehabilitative Vocational Training. Further

Educational Curriculum. EU Leonardo da Vinci Programme. www.uni-magdeburg. de/zsm/projekt/biographical/1/B2.2.pdf [available on 20/08/2013].

Searle, J. R. (2010). *Making the Social World: The Structure of Human Civilization.* Oxford, UK: Oxford University Press.

Searle, J. R. (2001). *Rationality in Action.* Cambridge, MA, USA: MIT Press.

Searle, J. R. (1995). *The Construction of Social Reality.* New York: The Free Press.

Shadish, W., Cook, T., and Campbell, D. (2002). *Experimental and Quasi Experimental Designs for Generalized Causal Inference.* Boston: Houghton Mifflin.

Shaw, C. R. (1930). *The Jack-Roller: A Delinquent Boy's Own Story*: Phoenix Books.

Shore, C. (2000). *Building Europe: the Cultural Politics of European Integration.* London and New York: Routledge.

Stevens, A., and Stevens, H. (2001). *Brussels Bureaucrats? the Administration of the European Union.* New York: Palgrave Press.

Stubbs, P. (2002). 'Globalisation, memory and welfare regimes in transition: Towards an anthropology of transnational policy transfers'. *International Journal of Social Welfare*, 11(4), pp. 321-330.

Thedvall, R. (2006). *Eurocrats at Work: Negotiating Transparency in Postnational Employment Policy.* Stockholm: Intellecta Docusys.

Turk, J. D. (2005). 'The non-treatment of systematic uncertainty in economics'. In M. Moussa, and G. Brown (eds.), *Engaging Realism: Proceedings of the International Association for Critical Realism 2005 Annual Conference.* Universities of Wollongong and Western Sydney. ISBN No. 1-74108-130-1.

Turk, J. D. (2009). 'Traction in the world: economics and narrative interviews'. *International Journal of Green Economics*, 3 (1), 77-92.

Turk, J. D. (2011). 'Science is measurement: muons, money and the Nobel Prize. *International Journal of Pluralism and Economics Education*, 2(3): pp. 291-305.

Wengraf, T. (2001). *Qualitative Research Interviewing: Biographic Narratives And Semi-Structured Methods.* London: Sage.

Wiener, A., and Diez, T. (eds.) (2004). *Theories of European integration.* Oxford, UK: Oxford University Press.

2. Realism and Social Research: A Morphogenetic Approach

Bob Carter

Debates about the future of social science, and the purpose and relevance of social research, have intensified over the last decade or so (see, for example, Savage and Burrows, 2007; Latour 2007; 2010; Osborne and Rose, 2008). These debates have been driven by several developments, not necessarily related. Firstly, one of the consequences of the putative cultural and linguistic turns in social thought has been an elevation of the discursive and a corresponding inattention to the place and role of structured social relations in social research. Narratives, meanings, and interpretations remain key elements in any account of the social world but they are not exhaustive of what constitutes that world. Secondly, the past decade or so has seen the emergence of approaches, such as actor-network theory, associated particularly with the work of Latour (2007; 2010), and 'material semiotics', associated with, amongst others, the work of Law (2008), Haraway (2003; 2008) and Bennett (2010), which have sought to demolish the notion of 'the social' altogether. Although there are important differences between these writers, they share an emphasis on performativity – the notion that realities are enacted, or performed, and are therefore relatively evanescent – and on an affective view of action and agency, one which regards these terms as indistinguishable and defined by the ability of any thing to have an effect.

Sociological realism of the kind I wish to defend stands in contrast to both of these efforts to reconfigure the social. Whilst it is not prescriptive with regard to research methods (unlike some of the approaches mentioned above), it does favour caution when employing particular methods because of its firm insistence on a relational social ontology and the importance of causal explanations in the social world.

The chapter will develop as follows. Part One will set out the distinctive features of a sociological realism, namely its stratified social ontology, with its incorporation of emergence; its insistence on an analytical dualism of structure and agency; and its commitment to causal explanation. Part Two will consider the methodological implications of sociological realism and Part Three will apply it to an account of ethnicity as a biographical resource.

Part One: Sociological realism and morphogenesis

The central principle of sociological realism is its insistence that the world is made up of different kinds of things, each with distinctive properties and powers (see Bhaskar, 1979; 1989; see also Layder, 1990; Archer, 1995; Sayer, 1992). In this view, people and the social relations that are the product of their interactions, are analytically distinguishable from each other (of course, phenomenologically they cannot be distinguished in this way: we do not encounter entities such as 'people' or 'social relations', only actual persons interacting with us in social situations). This analytical dualism allows an exploration of the interplay between people and social relations, of how people find themselves in particular contexts or circumstances which they may, in various degrees, experience as either irksome or commodious (or, just as commonly, a mixture of both these states). They will therefore have an interest in changing their circumstances in order to make them less irksome or in maintaining them in order to continue to benefit from them. In either case their efforts, either to make things different or to keep things as they are, will also change them (there will be more later on this notion of 'double morphogenesis', the idea that in changing our circumstances we also change ourselves). At the heart of analytical dualism, therefore, is the relationship of structure and agency, the interplay, as Archer (1995) has it, between 'the parts' of the social system and 'the people' whose interaction generates it.

A consistent analytical dualism takes us a good deal further than this, however. Firstly, as mentioned earlier, the basis of this dualism rests on the ontological claim that 'the parts' (structured social relations) and 'the people' are different kinds of entities with different properties and powers. Human beings, for example, have the properties of self-consciousness and reflexivity; they can act on the basis of reasons because they have language (this does not mean that they always do so); they have an advanced capacity for social co-operation and organisation because of their capacities for manipulating symbolic forms of communication; and they have needs, interests, desires and ambitions. In contrast, structured social relations (for short, social structure, provided we bear in mind that the term is describing a nexus of relations among people and not a reified entity) have other sorts of properties and powers, such as persistence, durability and a relative imperviousness to discursive penetration. These two sorts of entity, people and structures, are not reducible to each other and, because they have different sorts of properties and powers, are not merely aspects of the same phenomenon as is sometimes argued by structuration theorists (for example, Giddens, 1984).

Secondly, by insisting on distinguishing ontologically between structure and agency, analytical dualism allows a nuanced account of their interplay in which the notion of emergence is central. There are several ways in which the term emergence may be understood (they are handily summarised in Elder-Vass,

2010), but in the realist sense I am suggesting here an emergent property is one that is produced by the relations between the parts of an entity; it is therefore irreducible to any of its individual constituent parts and its properties would not be possessed by the whole without the structuring relations between these constituents. A common example is that of water, an emergent property arising from the combination of oxygen and hydrogen in a particular way: water has properties and powers of its own and these are clearly different from the individual properties of either oxygen or hydrogen. An example of a cultural emergent property is language, which arises from the combination of human embodied practice and its attendant sociality, with the biological capacities of the human organism (vocal chords, particular arrangement of teeth, tongue and mouth and so on). Once emergent, languages are irreducible to individual speakers (see Sealey and Carter, 2004) and develop powers and properties of their own, such as collocational patterns which shape the interpretation of individual utterances.

If properties are emergent in the sense outlined above, then their irreducibility entails two further ontological features: they will have a relative autonomy from their constituent parts; and, because of this, they will also have causal efficacy. The simple stratified ontology that we began with has now been extended into an 'ontology of persons and relational structures, each with their respective emergent properties and powers, contingently combining to produce second and third-order emergent properties' (Carter and New, 2004:7). Such a view entails an acknowledgement that the world is an 'open' system of contingently combining entities and their emergent properties and powers.

Emergence and analytical dualism imparts to sociological realism a distinctive explanatory task. In a stratified and open world, explanation of phenomena has to move between phenomenal, experienced reality (often the reality most accessible to discursive understanding of both the commonsensical and formally theorized type) and the more 'epistemologically distant' reality of emergent properties and powers and the durable structured social relations that are a product of these. Realist analysis then is inescapably and simultaneously synchronic, examining current contexts and relations, and diachronic, seeking to account for how these contexts and relations came to persist from an earlier period of social interaction. This returns us to the structure-agency analytical dualism which we are now in a position to explore more subtly using the morphogenetic approach developed consistently within the realist tradition by Archer.

Archer's work (1988; 1995; 2000; 2003; 2007; 2012) rests squarely on analytical dualism and emergence. Her morphogenetic model distinguishes analytically between three elements of the social world: structure, culture and people. Each of these elements has its distinctive properties and powers, each is irreducible to any of the others and each develops emergent properties and powers specific to it. Thus, as has already been noted, languages are a cultural emergent property, but speech, like reflexivity, is a personal emergent property. Structures can persist and shape the contexts of generations of people, but, unlike persons, they cannot reflect or talk, or have ambitions or needs. Social research for Archer requires a means of examining the interplay between structure, culture and agency, one that recognises them as irreducible, autonomous and causally efficacious in their own right.

Archer's morphogenetic analysis begins with the identification of a historical starting point (T1 in Archer's terminology), identified by the researcher and determined by their particular interests and research questions. Any T1 will be configured by an antecedent distribution of material and cultural resources. One of the properties of structure is precisely its temporal priority to any determinate sequence of social action, which means that each new generation finds itself involuntaristically placed within this prior distribution. The causal effects of this objective placement on individuals, as Porpora puts it, 'are manifested in certain structured interests, resources, powers and constraints and predicaments that are built into each position by the web of relationships. These comprise the material circumstances in which people must act and which motivate them to act in certain ways' (1989:200).

Examining how the structural and cultural context is shaped for people before examining what they do in it, or what they can do about it, is a methodological procedure deriving from analytical dualism. The next stage of that procedure (T2) is to examine, and causally account for, what people do in response to their respective placements within an anterior distribution of resources. Realism, because of its analytical dualism, necessarily rejects two common responses to the relations between structures and action: the structuralist response, in which people are compelled to behave in certain ways (the degree of compulsion varies with the form of structuralism proposed); and the voluntarist response, in which people act without constraint (the degree of freedom varies with the form of voluntarism proposed). Interplay between the properties and powers of analytically distinct entities, and subsequently, the emergent properties and powers of this interplay, is the guiding methodological principle of realism. Here the notion of agency becomes central.

One of the difficulties associated with conventional understandings of the 'structure-agency' debate, even amongst realists, is not so much with the notion of structure but with the notion of agency. For many writers, agency is simply synonymous with action, so that references to human agency simply refer to the ability of human beings to act in the world, to 'make a difference' as Giddens (1984) puts it. Occasionally, agency is taken to refer to action on the part of groups or collectives, so that, for example, Elder-Vass distinguishes between political agency and individual agency. Political agency concerns the power to bring about change in collective life, whilst individual agency concerns the 'specific powers of human individuals' (Elder-Vass, 2010:88). Actor network theory, in contrast, has extended this notion of agency to include the nonhuman. Thus not only other animals, but also material objects have agency – 'children, raindrops, bullet trains, politicians, and numerals. All entities are on exactly the same ontological footing. An atom is no more or less real than the Deutsche Bank...' (Harman, 2009: 14). Despite these contrasts, all these writers share in common the belief that the distinction between action and agency is otiose or insignificant.

Archer takes a different view. To begin with, the notion of individual agency is for her an oxymoron, since agents are defined as collectivities sharing the same life chances. 'When we talk about 'social agents', Archer insists, 'we are of course referring to people, but not to everything about people since it [agency] is always and only employed in the plural' (Archer, 1995:257). Human beings act (along with other animals and, according to actor network theory, material objects), but this is not what Archer refers to as their agency. Agency is only concerned with action in or as part of a collectivity. These collectivities are historically contingent, are a product of the anterior distributions of resources (because they are comprised of people sharing the same situation) and are modified by people's efforts to either transform this distribution or maintain it. Importantly, then, we are agents before we become actors; relations of inequality and privilege are acquired by being born in a particular place at a particular time. Agency, on this account, is ineluctably relational, plural, and a product initially of the objective life chances given us at birth. It is also an incomplete account of people since it is concerned with only one aspect of social action. Therefore Archer distinguishes between agents and actors, and between both of these and personhood.

Actors and persons, for Archer, are singular, but also analytically distinguishable. Actors are defined as role incumbents and personhood refers to the psycho-biographically unique individual human being. Thus just as the concept of social agency was insufficient to account for people and their actions, so efforts to account for social action or to conceptualise the social actor without reference to their properties as social agents will also be incomplete. Lastly, human beings are not only agents and actors, but persons, with their own combination of personal properties and powers – biological, psychological, physical – and all three dimensions need to be incorporated into research. Archers summarises the task thus:

> The conditional influence of society works through the objective life chances which are dealt to us at birth. For the collectivities into which we are involuntaristically grouped affect the 'social actors' whom we are constrained or enabled to become voluntaristically. Yet someone has to do this becoming (which is neither fully random, nor fully regular) and thus it was essential not to

conflate 'human beings' and their capacities with social beings. Equally, it has to be allowed that it is the latter who, in combination, transform what it is socially possible for humans to become over time by their constantly elaborating on society's role array. (Archer, 1995:293)

The T2 stage of the morphogenetic cycle is precisely the exploration and causal analysis of the structure-agency interplay understood in this refined sense. Placed within an antecedent set of contextual conditions, people reflexively deliberate on what is important to them, on what is possible, on what matters (see Sayer, 2011). They will then make judgements about whether these are worth struggling for, worth paying a price for, whether they are wholly unrealisable or potentially possible and so on. Only when people act do the agentic aspects of their situation become relevant and they discover that pursuing this particular project in these particular conditions is either enabled or constrained.

The final stage of Archer's morphogenetic cycle, T3, provides an assessment of the success or otherwise of people's efforts to alter their situations and of how these efforts, in turn, will have entailed self-transformation (or what Archer refers to as 'double morphogenesis'):at the level of the person (through a recognition of what sorts of personal cost one is prepared to pay to change a situation); at the level of the social actor (new roles – 'an educated woman', for example – may have become available); and at the level of agency, since new relations may now obtain between different sorts of collectivities, or the same collectivities may now exist in new relations.

This is a necessarily condensed summary of what is distinctive about a realist approach. It has favoured the work of Archer as providing a consistent methodological complement to realism as a more general theoretical and philosophical orientation, one that stresses the role of reflexivity in mediating the interplay of structure, culture and agency in social life. Before providing examples of how the approach might be applied, it will be useful to identify some key implications for research methods that follow from the morphogenetic model.

Part Two: Realism and research method: methodological implications

As we have previously noted, the sort of realism advocated here is not especially prescriptive with regard to methods; there is not a set of realist research methods that are entailed by adopting realism. However, because of its insistence on social outcomes as always the product of the interplay between structure, culture and agency, realism does point to limitations in many conventional research methods and favours certain approaches to doing research. So research methods such as interviews or various forms of ethnographic method, whose primary purpose is to elicit or examine people's understandings or interpretations of social situations or public issues, are regarded as necessarily partial in so far as they are less appropriate for exploring the structural and cultural contexts shaping these interpretations. They miss, in other words, crucial dimensions of the structuring of understanding, and therefore are less reliable in grasping the emergent features of social interaction, those that arise from the engagement of people with anterior contexts of interests and resources. Certainly, such methods are important sources of data about human beings and their doings, about how they manage and negotiate the social world, but such data for the realist will always be partial unless incorporated in a range of other methods capable of eliciting data about other aspects of the social world (see Sealey, 2007 for a discussion of realist ethnography and also Layder, 1998).

Conversely, more obviously 'quantitative' methods such as surveys and various modes of statistical analysis may provide excellent depictions of the patterned and regular nature of much of social life, and particularly its distribution of what Layder terms 'contextual resources', but their awkwardness in accounting for the interpretive, reflexive character of social life requires supplementation.

A consistent commitment to analytical dualism will also distance the realist from reductionism of various sorts, since an emphasis on the interplay of structure, culture and agency will rule out accounts of the social world which insist that reality is discursively produced (as in some forms of social constructivism) just as it will rule out accounts which insist that reality is a product of structural forces (as in some forms of mechanistic Marxism, for example). It is perhaps stating the obvious, but from the realist perspective it is people, not institutions, historical forces or discourses, who make history, although not in conditions of their own choosing. We are thus concerned with research methods and strategies capable of grasping emergent properties and generative relations. It follows from this that the world the researcher is seeking to interpret and understand will be an open and complex one characterized by high levels of historical contingency. Research whose methods are exclusively actor focused, or research that reduces the world either to structures or to discourses, is ill equipped to investigate such a world.

In short, realism is ecumenical in its view of research methods, whilst insisting that neither 'quantitative' nor 'qualitative' approaches are sufficient in themselves (although different research projects may emphasize one or the other). This, it should be noted, is not a case for 'the more methods the merrier' or for multi-method research, arguments for which are often based on the notion that more methods are better than one. It is rather an argument that research should be methodologically informed and problem-driven and it is the contention here that realism and its methodological complement of morphogenesis do precisely this.

Realism's open-endedness on the matter of methods has given rise to debate about what realist empirical research might look like. After all, if the world has an existence independent of our theories about it, what sorts of knowledge of it can be generated by social research? This is an especially pressing matter in view of the concept dependence of many social phenomena. Sayer (2000) has pointed out that actions, texts and institutions have to be understood, read and interpreted if we are to identify their material effects and how these are produced. For Sayer, therefore, the production of any sort of knowledge is a social practice, whose conditions will influence its content. For the realist, this means that empirical data (though not empirical reality) is always constructed theoretically, or, in Pawson's pithy formulation, 'all measurement is an act of translation' (Pawson, 1989:287).

This insight sets realism firmly against research models, common in the social sciences and elsewhere, based on variables. Byrne (1998; 2004), in particular, has argued persuasively for an affinity between case-based strategies and realist approaches, noting that whilst 'Modelling reality using quantitative methods is an important part of any scientific practice...Such modelling must employ methods which in some way correspond to, represent, the reality being modelled' (Byrne, 2004:63). Such methods must take account of the non-linear character of the social world produced by generative mechanisms and emergent properties interacting in an open system.

A further distinctive emphasis in realist research is the commitment to causal explanation. The concern with generative mechanisms and emergence entails a consistent focus on the 'how' questions of causality, on the search for the causal mechanisms generating the relational links accounting for how and why something happened. In contradistinction to some other forms of post-positivist thought, notably actor network theory as expressed in the work of, say, Latour and Law, realism's depth ontology affirms a 'belief in the causal power of unobservables – such as states, markets or social classes – [which] does not depend on the rationality or truth of any given theory but upon practical evidence of its causal impact on the relationships in which it is embedded' (Somers, 1998: 743-744). This is a model of causality, then, which stresses the importance of the empirical, both as an element of reality but also as the key resource for providing evidence of the unobservable and causally efficacious elements of that reality. Once more, whilst not being prescriptive in terms of method, the recognition of the unobservable nature of causal mechanisms and their key role in generating phenomenal reality runs counter to research strategies that are either empiricist (only observable data may count as evidence) or that deny the relevance of the empirical (it is merely a reflection of structural relations or invariant human properties; for a discussion of the limits of rational choice theory as an example of this approach see Somers, 1998).

Instead, for realists the business of identifying causal mechanisms and developing causal explanations is managed through two complementary processes: the identification of causal mechanisms producing or generating an empirically regular and observable phenomenon (what Lawson, 1997, has termed 'demi-regularities' or 'demi-regs' for short), a process realists term retroduction; and the identification of how these particular mechanisms interact with each other to produce the contingent outcome that we are seeking to explain, a process realists term retrodiction (Lawson, 1997; see also Elder-Vass, 2010). Taken together, retroduction and retrodiction enable the development of genealogical histories of emergence whereby the interaction of causal powers and mechanisms produces second and third level emergent properties – themselves autonomous, irreducible and therefore causally efficacious – which in turn become a part of any causal explanation. The realist, morphogenetic approach then is one of multiple determinations, an inescapable corollary of emergence in an open system characterized by a stratified ontology.

Part Three: Doing realist research

How would research informed by realist principles be designed and carried out? Space does not permit an extensive investigation of realist research (and there have been a number of recent texts which deal with this in more detail; see in particular, Layder, 1998; Pawson 2007; Ragin and Byrne 2010; Maxwell 2012), so here I want to explore how a realist might approach the study of one particular form of social identification, namely ethnicity.

Is it possible to define an object of study for ethnicity? What status do we give to notions such as 'ethnic groups' and 'ethnic conflict' in sociological accounts of the social world? How might we account for the contexts in which people opt for certain forms of identification rather than others?

Researching ethnicity

The realism advanced here, and its methodological complement, Archer's morphogenesis, recognizes that, as Somers has it, 'the partial concept-dependence of social life puts limits on the general realist premise of the absolute mind-independent status of the social world; yet some degree of concept-dependence does not in any way subvert the premise of a social world that exists independently of our beliefs about it' (Somers, 1998:766). Instead, the contention is that realism encourages a greater degree of methodological reflexivity precisely because it acknowledges the limits alluded to by Somers, and so places an obligation on the researcher to insist that cases, which are theoretical constructions, are descriptively relevant to the reality they seek to analyze. How is this to be done?

All 'groups' are the product of descriptions of some kind which valorize particular kinds of human differences, making these differences matter. Hacking expresses it thus: 'Sometimes, our sciences create kinds of people that in a certain sense did not exist before. I call this "making up people".' (Hacking, 2006: 23). So, in developing the group categories we are going to study, we need to be aware of this process of 'making up', especially as naming in this way is not a one-way process: names interact with the named. A good illustration of the difficulties that can arise when conceptual categories are devised without due diligence can be found in research into 'race' and ethnicity.

Research using notions of ethnicity regularly finds itself making a number of assumptions. Firstly, there is the assumption that ethnic differences, however defined, are meaningful and sufficiently stable to allow for the identification of various ethnic groups. Secondly, it is assumed that the researcher's sampling criteria can be used to define groups for the purposes of the research. Thirdly, it is assumed that the differences putatively identified as 'ethnic' (such as religion, language, country of origin, cultural practices and so on; there are many, varied and frequently inconsistent ways of 'making up' people) are explanatorily significant, that is their 'ethnicity' is in some sense a significant factor accounting for what it is about them that we are trying to explain. If these are common problems associated with researching ethnicity, how might a realist approach contribute?

Let's start by offering some observations on a theme central to this volume, namely biography. In particular, we might examine ethnicity as a biographical resource. Biographical resources, from a realist perspective, are ideational and refer to the propositional ('there are ethnic groups and these can be identified for purposes of measurement') and affective ('I am proud to be Chinese') stock of available ways of making sense of who you are. This availability will depend on all sorts of things: not only contingent factors of what ideational resources one is exposed to in the family, the media and through social interactions, but also more durable factors enabling access to different sorts of ideational resources such as level of education and class background.

Two significant sources of ideas about ethnicity in western and northern Europe are policy initiatives and social research (the two often being closely allied – if a government is concerned about the 'poor performance' of 'ethnic minority' children in national schools and wishes to intervene to manage this, it will usually begin by commissioning academic research to investigate the extent of 'underperformance' amongst different ethnic groups). A methodologically unreflexive approach to casing in this instance has a number of effects. The first we have already mentioned: the assumption that there are 'ethnic groups' whose ethnicity is identifiable and capable of being compared to the ethnicity of other groups (a feature which often encourages politicians to establish such groups as the basis for the distribution of funding and resources). There are other effects, though, notably the reliance on lay definitions of ethnicity (especially where, as in the UK census, people are invited to self-define their 'ethnicity'). The inconsistency of these lay definitions, especially where they conflict with other sorts of definitions which are socially more powerful (as in the recent debates about the wearing of the hijab in France, Netherlands and Belgium), or more medically relevant (see Carter and Dyson, 2011), can give rise to new political tensions and policies (on integration and social cohesion, for example) which themselves rely on reified notions of ethnicity and ethnic identity.

For the realist, part of the problem here is that research (and sometimes sociological) definitions of ethnicity rely on popular or lay definitions. This compromises a critical approach to the concept by relying on a sort of experiential empiricism in which our knowledge of the social world is reduced to our knowledge of people's accounts of it. One of the consequences is a proliferation of ethnicized forms of politics and the affirmation and reproduction of ethnicity as a biographical resource. That is to say, ideas about ethnicity become a practically adequate means of making sense of oneself and one's relations to others and, in so far as this is the case, become elements in what Archer (2003) terms one's 'internal conversations' ('can I really be Flemish and wear a headscarf to work?').

Methodologically, this 'feedback loop' has to be incorporated into research. This does not mean that researchers should not ask questions about the ways in which people might care to respond to an interviewer when asked about their ethnic identification, but an approach grounded in a stratified social ontology would want to go much further. It would seek to grasp those conditions under which ethnicity as a biographical resource becomes implicated in broader systems of social action and expectation, embracing, inter alia, the competition for resources and the defence of privileges and prerogatives. This would entail, for example, recognizing that ethnic solidarity, with its intensification of ethnicity as a biographical resource, is, in Ruane and Todd's words, an 'emergent property of a system constituted by the intersection of practical categories and power relations' (Ruane and Todd, 2004). Analyzing this requires re-inserting 'ethnicity' into a general theory of social action and social structure (see Carter and Fenton, 2010 for further discussion of this point).

At this point, therefore, our research programme would need to go beyond an exercise in classification and comparison, since a case study involving the study of ethnicity or ethnic groups would also need to incorporate the question of how historically systems of naming take on political and social significance. How are they constructed and deployed and for whom do they become salient? The central question for the realist thus becomes: in which contexts and under what conditions does ethnicity (in its propositional and affective forms) become a significant resource for some people in understanding themselves and the social world?

In order to provide an answer to these questions, realists use two principal strategies: retroduction and the development of genealogical histories of emergence. Retroduction is a mode of inference characterized, in Lawson's words, 'by the move from knowledge of some phenomenon existing at any one level of reality, to a knowledge of mechanisms, at a deeper level or stratum of reality, which contributed to the generation of the original phenomenon of interest' (Lawson, 1997:26). Having identified certain empirical regularities – in this case the routine use of ideas about ethnicity in academic and policy discourses – retroduction is the task of identifying theoretically the causal mechanisms responsible for these regularities (see also Tilly, 2005).

Usually, there will be a number of these. In the case of ethnicity, for example, such mechanisms might include: at the social level, the imperative for classification of human populations deriving from contemporary models of governance (what Rose, 2006 has termed 'biopolitics'); at an institutional level the need for an organization, such as a university, to demonstrate that it is 'widening participation' by increasing recruitment from 'ethnic minorities' in order to avoid financial penalties; at a personal level the need to avoid shame and 'fit in' amongst peers by exaggerating an identification with those defined as significant others. Additionally, these mechanisms (and there may be others) will be interacting with each other in an 'open system', that is a social world not subject to deterministic laws and so both complex and contingent. Mechanisms, as Pawson (1997) has noted, always operate in a context to produce a specific outcome. Attention to context is therefore paramount and the morphogenetic approach, with its concern with diachronic emergence, is thus the second key element in the realist methodological armoury. At this stage, it might be appropriate to provide a concrete example of these rather abstract propositions at work.

Ewa Morawska's work on migration (2001; 2003; 2011) unusually combines an explicit commitment to theoretical relevance with detailed empirical study. Her recent work examining migration from the Polish village of Maszkienice in southeastern Poland in the mid-1880s provides a good example of an account of social action which is thoroughly consistent with the morphogenetic realism advocated here. (Although it should be pointed out that Morawska herself seeks to demonstrate that 'there is no unresolvable theoretical disagreement between the morphogenetic and time sensitive structuration approaches' (Morawska, 2011:1).) I shall therefore take the liberty of using Morawska's empirical study to illustrate how a realist might account for the phenomena of migration in this particular instance.

In her study, Morawska seeks to explain why some people chose to migrate from the village of Maszkienice to the US before the onset of mass transatlantic travel in subsequent decades. This explanandum provides the time sequence for empirical investigation. At T1 (in this case corresponding to the period preceding the mid 1880s), we have antecedent conditions which generate contextual discontinuity, such that life as it has been lived up to now in Maszkienice becomes less tolerable for certain people. This initiates T2 (in this case roughly from the mid 1880s onwards), the period of socio-cultural interaction in which some inhabitants of Maszkienice reflexively monitor their circumstances and decide that they would be improved by migration to the US. This results in T3 (in this case, the period at the end of the 19th century when Polish migration to the US has become an established means of resolving the difficulties of agrarian life), during which some things will have changed as a result of what takes place during T2 (the demographics of the village population, for example, or the credibility of migration as a source of personal or familial betterment) whilst others will have remained the same (life continues to be hard and restricted for those subsisting on the land). Across all three moments (T1 to T3), we will have to trace the operation of relevant causal mechanisms, their interaction in open, contingent contexts and the interaction between these mechanisms and the emergent properties that they generate.

Thus, Morawska begins her analysis by examining the contextual conditions generating the redistribution of roles and interests that will act as an initial impulsion prompting some villagers into a novel form of reflexive mediation, one in which they consider an innovative social action, namely migration to the US. The conditions that Morawska identifies are, at the most general level, the process of accelerated urbanization and industrialization in 19th century Eastern Europe, a process mediated in Poland by the extensive remnants of feudal social forms and political institutions. This, combined with the abolition of serfdom and alienation of noble estates (Morawska, 2011), left significant numbers of people, especially 'landless peasants and rural petty traders and craftsmen', in destitution. These anterior conditions at T1 prime a range of social actors to consider new options by disrupting the traditional and habitual availability of cultural, political and economic resources. Reflexivity – the conscious weighing up of options and the reviewing of choices – becomes an imperative in these circumstances.

Morawska points to more local factors that also contribute to the disruption of the taken-for-granted phenomenal world of the Maszkienice villagers. The southeastern part of Poland endured a particular underdevelopment because of 'its semi-colonial status under the political domination of Austria' (Morawska, 2011:8). In these circumstances, where to stay is to endure intolerable poverty, many considered, and acted upon, the choice to move elsewhere. Thus begins

T2, where some people seek to realize a personal project of migration. The key questions then will be who moves and where they move to.

In considering this, once again we have to uncover relevant contextual conditions, but at T2, where we are considering socio-cultural interaction, more attention has to be given to people as opposed to the emphasis in T1 which is more on the 'parts', the structural conditions providing the contexts within which people act. However, in distributing roles and resources, these conditions also profoundly shape agency, and thus the ability of people to realize projects through the exercise of their personal powers and properties. Decisions about where to go depend not only on the available means of transport and the necessity of obtaining a passport, but also, in Morawska's words, on the 'the micro-level local socio-cultural structures made up of the existing information and social support networks and the accustomed migration culture that directed income-seeking travellers into particular destinations' (Morawska, 2011:8). Up until the mid 1880s (prior to the start of our T2) those who decided that their conditions were no longer tolerable moved to neighbouring countries such as Austria and Hungary. When employment agents from the US arrived in the early 1880s, they had little success. Migration to the US was a risky option compared to migration to the customary destinations where a good deal of practical knowledge and success was to hand.

The shift in the ideational repertoire that makes migrating to the US an option for some comes about through the contingent success of two 'outsiders' who through happenstance decide against the usual destination and to dig coal in Pennsylvania instead. Their decision to do this is, as Morawska makes clear, a direct result of their 'outsider' status, which subjects them to a double sense of discontinuity: the one they share with everybody else in their position as young, poor agrarian workers (an aspect of their social agency – they are in this situation precisely because they are peasants with a particular relationship to those who own the land); and the one they endure as these particular individuals, isolated, looked down upon by the rest of the village. Reflexively, there are a number of ways they can deal with this; the way they choose is to go somewhere where they will not be known, giving them the opportunity, by freeing them from the constraints of village life, to mobilize fresh stores of reflexive resources and fashion for themselves new social and personal identities.

Conditions and material rewards for our migrants are superior in the US, so that when they return home after some two and a half years their impact is immediate: the US becomes an attractive rival as a migration destination to the neighbouring parts of Europe. In effect, our two successful migrants shift the field of agency inhabited by the villagers of Maszkienice: migration to the US is eventually installed as a realistic and credible choice of migration destination. Consequently, by the end of our T2, migration patterns are beginning to shift with more migrants heading for the US and fewer staying in Europe. This brings us to T3, the final stage in the morphogenetic cycle, which requires an assessment of the changes brought about in T2.

All action takes place in conditions not chosen by the participants themselves. This is a key principle of analytical dualism and directs our attention to the phenomenon well known to most of us, that we rarely get what we want. This is partly because anterior conditions, and their effects, are only partially known to us, but also because acting within those conditions generates fresh emergent properties whose irreducibility to individual actions imparts to them a causal impact of their own. So, for example, once migration to the US increased significantly in volume it generated the development of what Morawska terms a '(trans)local information system'. This emergent property of the combining factors outlined above becomes established as part of the cultural and ideational resources available to subsequent villagers, exerting a significant pull factor on their decisions about where to migrate and so modifying their social agency (migrating to America is now a realistic option for a male agrarian worker in Maszkienice when it was not before).

Other emergent properties of the changed patterns of migration between Maszkienice and the United States identified by Morawska include new patterns of normative regulation between the migrants, struggling to make sense of a new ideational environment, and the villagers left behind who seek to maintain the continued relevance of village mores. In the cultural elaboration that resulted from the effort to accommodate the experience of migration to the US, and the comparative prosperity it brought to those who succeeded in establishing themselves, the reflexive resources and possibilities for the villagers and for the migrants were significantly modified. Gender relations, ideas of success, religious commitment and notions of what it meant to be from Maszkienice and what it meant to be Polish, shifted under the impact. Many ideas came to seem irrelevant to some, whilst for others new understandings had to be forged and the practices of everyday life adapted and amended.

This summary of the situation at the end of this particular morphogenetic cycle (it may well be the start of another morphogenetic cycle, of course: our T3 may become another researcher's T1) allows an assessment of morphogenesis and morphostasis. In the final part of the chapter, however, I want briefly to concentrate on one aspect of the outcomes at T3, namely the cultural elaboration of social and personal identity. In particular I want to consider the question, put earlier, about how realist research might examine under which circumstances some people come to use notions of 'ethnic' identification as a key reflexive resource.

Realism, ethnic ideas and biographical method

Tilly has suggested that identities are social arrangements that have four components: 'a boundary separating me from you or us from them; a set of relations within the boundary; a set of relations across the boundary; a set of stories about the boundary and the relations' (Tilly, 2005:209). Prominent in Tilly's analysis are ideational entrepreneurs (such as the early migrants from Maszkienice to the US), who 'draw together credible stories from available cultural materials, similarly create we-they boundaries, activate both stories and boundaries as a function of current political circumstances, and maneouvre to suppress competing models'. Tilly's approach emphasizes the key role of reflexivity in ideational entrepreneurship, as people maneouvre and compete to 'alter stories, boundaries, and their social reinforcements' (Tilly, 2005:211). A necessary element of realist research methods, therefore, has to be a means of studying reflexivity.

Now, there are a variety of methods used in social research, broadly associated with qualitative or interpretive notions of research, whose methodological justification is that they provide access to actor meanings or understandings of their situation. There are in depth interviews, participant observation, visual methodologies such as photo-elicitation, and a range of ethnographic methods. It should be apparent from the preceding account that morphogenetic realism is not prescriptive in terms of methods; although it frequently draws attention to the partiality of many methods (see, for example, Sealey, 2007; Pawson and Tilley, 2007; Layder, 1998; Sayer, 1992), it is ecumenical in its use of them.

There is, however, a research method that explicitly draws on realism in its efforts to study reflexivity and the development of biographical resources namely the biographical method developed by Chamberlayne, Wengraf and others (Chamberlayne, Bornat and Wengraf, 2000). This method has been most systematically developed by Wengraf in his Biographic-Narrative Interpretive Method (BNIM). The method is dealt with more fully elsewhere in this volume, but its relevance to a discussion of realist research methods is its novel distinction between the lived life and the told story. The former refers to the 'uncontroversial hard biographical data that can be abstracted from the interview material and any other helpful source' which is deemed pertinent regardless of 'whether or how they are referred to in the interview'. The latter refers to the 'way that the person presents him or herself – both in their initial narrative and in their answers to specific questions – by selecting certain events in their life (and omitting others) and by handling them in a certain way (and not in another)' (Chamberlayne et.al., 2000: 144). BNIM, therefore, recognizes a central insight of the morphogenetic approach, namely that subjects' self-understanding emerges from their socially situated biographical existence. BNIM would thus appear to overcome the objection of being partial and limited often leveled by realists at the interview as a research method.

Conclusion

Realism has sometimes been accused of being too abstract, too concerned with philosophical questions about the nature of the real, and of therefore being largely irrelevant to the practical concerns of the jobbing researcher seeking empirical knowledge of social phenomena. However, morphogenetic realism, associated particularly with the work of Archer, provides a clear methodological complement to realist theory. Ecumenical in methods, inescapably historical, its foursquare commitment to analytical dualism, and the stratified social ontology derived from this, gives it a supple approach to research problems. The retroductive search for generative causal mechanisms and the retrodictive identification of their interplay in specific and contingent conjunctures means that realist research lends itself strongly to interdisciplinary work (in this regard see, amongst others Byrne, 1998; 2004; Uprichard, 2010; Sealey and Carter, 2004). The morphogenetic model is also particularly suited to case based study (see, for example, Byrne and Ragin, 2010; Archer, 2007; Tilly, 2005). Finally, realist approaches are well placed to take advantage of the turn to biography and biographical method in social research, as the contributions to the present volume amply demonstrate.

References

Archer, M.S. (1988). *Culture and Agency: The Place of Culture in Social Theory*. Cambridge: Cambridge University Press.
Archer, M.S. (1995). *Realist Social Theory: A Morphogenetic Approach*. Cambridge: Cambridge University Press.
Archer, M.S. (2000). *Being Human: The Problem of Agency*. Cambridge: Cambridge University Press.
Archer, M.S. (2003). *Structure, Agency and the Internal Conversation*. Cambridge: Cambridge University Press.
Archer, M.S. (2007). *Making Our Way Through the World: Human Reflexivity and Social Mobility*. Cambridge: Cambridge University Press.
Archer, M.S. (2012). *The Reflexive Imperative*. Cambridge: Cambridge University Press.
Bennett, J. (2010). *Vibrant Matter: A Political Ecology of Things*. Durham, NC: Duke University Press.
Bhaskar, R. (1979). *The Possibility of Naturalism: A Philosophical Critique of the Contemporary Human Sciences*. Brighton: Harvester Press.
Bhaskar, R. (1989). *Reclaiming Reality: A Critical Introduction to Contemporary Philosophy*. London: Verso.

Byrne, D. (1998). *Complexity Theory and the Social Sciences*. London: Routledge.
Byrne, D. (2004). 'Complex and contingent causation – the implications of complex realism for quantitative modelling: the case of housing and health'. in Carter, B., and New, C. (eds.) *Making Realism Work: Realist Social Theory and Empirical Research*. London: Routledge.
Byrne, D. (1998). *Complexity Theory and the Social Sciences*. London: Routledge
Byrne, D., and Ragin, C.C. (eds.) (2010) *The Sage Handbook of Case-Based Methods* London: Sage.
Carter, B., and New, C. (eds.) (2004). *Making Realism Work: Realist Social Theory and Empirical Research*. London: Routledge.
Carter, B., and Fenton, S. (2010). 'From re-thinking ethnicity to not thinking ethnicity'. *Journal for the Theory of Social Behavior* 40 (1): 1-18.
Carter, B., and Dyson, S.M. (2011). 'Territory, ancestry and descent: The politics of sickle cell disease'. *Sociology* 45 (6): 963-976.
Chamberlayne, P., Bornat, J., and Wengraf, T. (eds.) (2000). *The Turn to Biographical Methods in Social Science: Comparative Issues and Examples*. Abingdon: Routledge
Elder-Vass, D. (2010). *The Causal Power of Social Structures*. Cambridge: Cambridge University Press.
Giddens, A. (1984). *The Constitution of Society: Outline of the Theory of Structuration*. Cambridge: Polity Press.
Hacking, I. (2006). 'Making Up People' *London Review of Books* 28(16): 23-26.
Haraway, D. (2003). *The Companion Species Manifesto: Dogs, People and Significant Otherness*. Chicago: Prickly Paradigm Press.
Haraway, D. (2008). *When Species Meet*. Minneapolis: University of Minnesota.
Harman, G. (2009). *Prince of Networks: Bruno Latour and Metaphysics*. Melbourne: Re.press.
Latour, B. (2007). *Reassembling the Social: An Introduction to Actor-Network-Theory*. Oxford: Oxford University Press.
Latour, B. (2010). *On The Modern Cult of the Factish Gods*. Durham, NC: Duke University Press.
Law, J. (2008). 'On sociology and STS'. *The Sociological Review* 56 (4): 623-649.
Lawson, T. (1997). *Economics and Reality*. London: Routledge.
Layder, D. (1990). *The Realist Image in Social Science*. London: Macmillan.
Layder, D. (1998). *Sociological Practice: Linking Theory and Social Research*. London: Sage.
Maxwell, J.A. (2012). *A Realist Approach for Qualitative Research*. London: Sage.
Morawska, E. (2001). 'Immigrants, transnationalism and ethnicization: a comparison of this great wave and the last'. in Gerstle, G., and Mollenkopf J. (eds.) *E Pluribus Unum: Contemporary and Historical Perspectives on Immigrant Political Incorporation*. New York: Russell Sage Foundation.
Morawska, E. (2003). *For Bread with Butter: Life-Worlds of East Central Europeans in Johnstown, Pennsylvania 1890-1940*. Cambridge: Cambridge University Press
Morawska, E. (2011). 'Studying international migration in the long(er) and short(er) duree: Contesting some and reconciling other disagreements between the structuration and morphogenetic approaches' Paper presented at the *Workshop on Social Theory and Migration: Dialogues on Critical Realism and Migration Research*, Wolfson College, Oxford, April 2011.

Osborne, T., and Rose, N. (2008). 'Populating sociology: Carr-Saunders and the problem of population'. *The Sociological Review* 56 (4): 552-578.
Pawson, R. (1989). *A Measure for Measures: A Manifesto for Empirical Sociology*. London: Routledge.
Pawson, R., and Tilley, N. (1997). *Realistic Evaluation*. London: Sage.
Porpora, D.V. (1989). 'Four concepts of social structure'. *Journal for the Theory of Social Behaviour* 19 (2): 195-211.
Rose, N. (2006). *The Politics of Life Itself: Biomedicine, Power and Subjectivity in the Twenty First Century*. Princeton, NJ: Princeton University Press.
Ruane, J. and Todd, J. (2004). 'The roots of intense ethnic conflict may not in fact be ethnic: categories, communities and path dependence'. *Archive of European Sociology* XLV (2): 209-232.
Savage, M., and Burrows, R. (2007). 'The coming crisis of empirical sociology'. *Sociology* 41 (5): 855-899.
Sayer, Andrew. 1992. Method in Social Science: A Realist Approach. 2nd ed. London: Routledge.
Sayer, A. (2000). 'System, lifeworld and gender: associational versus counterfactual thinking'. *Sociology* 34 (4): 707-725.
Sayer, A. (2011). *Why Things Matter To People: Social Science, Values and Ethical Life*. Cambridge: Cambridge University Press
Sealey, A. (2007). 'Linguistic ethnography in realist perspective'. *Journal of Sociolinguistics* 11: 641–660.
Sealey, A., and Carter, B. (2004). *Applied Linguistics as Social Science*. London: Continuum.
Somers, M.R. (1998). 'We're no angels: Realism, rational choice and relationality in the social sciences'. *American Journal of Sociology* 104 (3): 722-784.
Tilly, C. (2005). *Identities, Boundaries and Social Ties*. Boulder, Colorado: Paradigm.
Uprichard, E. (2010). 'Introducing cluster analysis: what can it teach us about the case?' in Byrne, D., and Ragin, C.C. (eds.) *The Sage Handbook of Case-Based Methods*. London: Sage

3. Biography-using Research (BNIM), Sostris, Institutional Regimes, and Critical Psycho-Societal Realism

Tom Wengraf with Prue Chamberlayne[1]

> ... *those views will never change I have no regrets whatsoever regarding the eighty four eighty five strike and if it came around again and the opportunity was there I would not change a thing [one second pause].... only the fact that if I had greater knowledge then perhaps I would when I say I wouldn't change things I would approach it differently with my eyes a bit more wide open*

(Harold, ex-miner, narrative interview for the SOSTRIS project, 1997)

Critical Realism in search of a biographical method

Roy Bhaskar, the founder of Critical Realism, declared firmly that for critical realists, the accounts of actors form the starting point of CR inquiry:

> ...in contrast to the hermeneutical perspective...actors' accounts [*and deliberations, TW*] are both corrigible and limited by the existence of unacknowledged conditions, unintended consequences, tacit skills and *unconscious motivations*; but in opposition to the positivist view, actors' accounts form the indispensable starting point of social inquiry. (Bhaskar, 1998: xvi, *Italics and material in square brackets added TW*).

On the other hand, though indispensable, such life-stories (autobiographical accounts) are starting points, not finishing points. For Critical Realists (and many other research traditions, though not all) all 'life stories' can be seen as eminently seductive and persuasive. They are inevitably partial and told from

---

[1] This chapter by Wengraf draws on previous papers by both authors. We would like to thank the editors of this volume, and particularly Jeffrey Turk, for helping us complete the task.

a partial local and historical standpoint. The teller of the told story selects out certain events or mentions but minimises their importance; gives saliency and a central position to others; sometimes even invents. The teller of the told story is a fallible and 'interested' narrator and persuader.

To avoid being over-persuaded and implicitly seduced by the interviewee and by their story-telling, for a critical and a realist understanding it is crucial, therefore, that the researcher/interpreter separately gathers together and considers as much hard biographical and contextual data as they can in order to understand the 'dated situated subjectivity' of the story-teller and of the history that they lived. This involves an approach that needs to be characterised by both psychological and sociological sophistication: some form of psycho-social thinking. But it starts from thinking about actors' accounts.

Bhaskar is clear on this: for Critical Realist researchers to avoid what he calls positivism, "actors' accounts form the indispensable starting point of social inquiry". What is then *done* with these 'indispensable starting points' *after* the starting point? This is crucial as to whether they are both 'arrived at' and 'processed' in a way congruent with Critical Realism or not.[2]

In this chapter, we outline a current (i.e. UK and 2012) perspective on what we take to be psycho-societal (P/Societal) thinking and biographical methods on the one hand and their potential relation with what we take to be Critical Realist (CR) thinking and research on the other. Within this emergent current perspective, we then look at an early trans-European EU-funded biography-based research that took place now over a decade ago (Sostris 1996-2002), and at an expanded post-Sostris methodology (2003-5) for studying a community centre in the East End of London. Finally, we suggest some conclusions and possible directions for a critical psycho-societal realism using (but not confined to) biographical methods.[3]

---

[2] Formal discourse analysis which ignored everything outside the text is clearly not congruent with CR. 'Social constructionism' which does not investigate the local-global external world outside the speaking subject and in their history is also in practice non-congruent with CR. Not starting with the 'indispensable starting points' is *also* not congruent with CR.

[3] This paper dealing with a European research tradition (biographical method) and partly an EU project (Sostris) is written from a necessarily-limited viewpoint, that of a British researcher. To cover the ground and to argue the change for a particular type of research programme, many complexities in previous and current actual practice have had to be ignored. Our apologies to those concerned. We have cited only people for whom we have great respect and from whom there is much to be learned.

What was Sostris?

This chapter started from two papers, prepared for the Leuven Conference, one by Chamberlayne on a 3-year research project (1996-99) called 'Sostris' (Social Strategies in Risk Society) funded by the EU targeted socio-economic research programme 4 on social exclusion; the other on 'Critical Realism and the Psycho-societal' by Wengraf.

Sostris was a seven -country study covering Britain, France, Germany (especially the former German Democratic Republic area), Greece, Italy, Spain and Sweden. The first two years of the project were devoted entirely to biographic-narrative interviews with samples of individuals at risk in each of six categories. Four had to do with the labour market directly: unemployment among unqualified school leavers; unemployment among young graduates; loss of work for workers in declining traditional industries; the early retired. The two other categories – single parenthood; and migration or membership of an ethnic minority – highlighted dimensions of gender, race, and civic status. Overall some 250 or so interviews were undertaken. The final third year of the project was concerned with finding and exploring the work of 'innovative social agencies' in each country developing new institutional practices in working with individuals facing social exclusion.

Understanding both the achievements and the defects of Sostris as an EU pioneer research project may have something to contribute to understanding and supporting future research projects using biographic-narrative interviewing in general and particularly doing so on a cross-national (and cross-disciplinary) basis.

A Critical Realist (CR) approach can help to develop an understanding of the history of Sostris, clarifying the issues and potentials of what some of us then called 'socio-biography' (and what could now be called, a 'psycho-societal') approach to social research based on biographic-narrative research. In turn, such an understanding of Sostris can enrich the concept of what a psycho-societally thought-through project based on biographic narratives might contribute to current and future 'turns' in what has been called Critical Realism. We argue that inquiry into internal and external 'historical mutations of institutional regime' of individuals and societies using biographical research is a pivotal entry into the understanding of inner and outer worlds.

Current approaches: psycho-social psychologism and critical realist sociologism

We suggest that Critical Realism as currently articulated has tended towards the one-sidedly sociological and that Psychosocial studies as currently articulated has tended towards the one-sidedly psychological. A new model of the Psycho-societal and a re-balanced model of Critical Realism will be put forward.

Critical Realism we consider to be a profoundly useful research philosophy but one which, in our experience, has been so far interpreted primarily in an excessively sociological manner, and therefore needs qualification. Its potential and its dangers may be fairly represented by the following argument of a British social theorist and researcher, Margaret Archer, about the reflexive deliberation of agents.

> What is distinctive about social realism, but needs to be developed, is that the reflexive deliberations of agents do indeed have their own 'intrinsic' effects in modifying the lives of subjects themselves, but also 'extrinsic' effects, by *modifying the cultural and structural properties (CEPs and SEPs) of their societies.* There is only one story because we make our lives, at least in part, by deliberating *upon the structural and cultural contexts in which we find ourselves*, often involuntarily. It is our deliberations which determine what we will make of the constraints and enablements which we confront.... (Archer, 2003: 52), *italics added.*

It is worth noting that the last sentence of the above quotation of the last sentence – "*it is our deliberations which determine…*" marks a simplifying slippage from the more complex position of the previous sentence – "*We make our lives, at least in part, by deliberating*". Because the previous sentence leaves it completely unsaid what the other 'part or parts' might be, the simplifying slippage is all-too-easy to make; the qualification to which we've added italics, too easy to forget. The last sentence's explicit model of the 'internally-deliberating-actor' tends to generate a 'sociologism' which is implicitly psychologically unrealistic[4].

It may be that the "other parts or part" implied by Archer's "*we make our lives, at least in part, by deliberating*" might be a conceptual space where "tacit skills" and (above all) "unconscious motivations" (which might be expected to have a researchable effect on Archer's 'conscious deliberations') could be provided. However the failure of this rightfully-influential Critical Realist thinker's failure to provide them (and her action to remove that fleeting requisite conceptual space in her following sentence for things deemed, as we have seen, essential by Bhaskar) has been unhelpful and has promoted psychological unrealism.

---

[4] A more developed but otherwise similar critique has just been published by Ian Burkitt where he writes "The position of theorists of reflexivity is Cartesian: a knowledgeable agent stands at an emotional distance from the social world and makes reflexive choices on the basis of their knowledge…fear, anxiety and trust may influence reflexivity, but [for reflexivity theorists, TW] they are not the source of reflexivity (Burkitt 2012: 461)".

A sociologistic 'realism' which is psychologically unrealistic will not do. A truly critical 'Critical Realism' has to criticise and beware of the dangers of an anti-psychological unrealism.

Let us now consider another development, this time in psychology in the UK and maybe elsewhere, the recent emergence of something called 'psycho-social studies'. Professor Wendy Hollway of the Open University and a key figure in the 'Critical Psychology' movement explained in an early statement of the 'psycho-social' perspective:

> "In this perspective, we are psycho-social:
> - because we are products of a unique life history of anxiety- and desire- provoking life events and the manner in which they have been transformed in internal reality;
> - because such defensive activities affect and are affected by material conditions and discourses (systems of meaning which pre-exist any given individual);
> - because unconscious defences are intersubjective processes (i.e. they affect and are affected by others with whom we are in communication); and
> - because of the real events in the external, social world which are discursively, desirously and defensively appropriated (Hollway, 2004: 7)." (typography modified, TW)

Hollway's formulations were a great leap forward, but are now (like Archer's) no longer sufficient. What about the "real events in the external, social world" which are *not* known to the actor, or which are ignored or denied; what about real people elsewhere in the planetary world, people with whom we are not in communication but with whom we have objective relations (through the world market, through climate deterioration and biosphere destruction, through economic sanctions and through drone warfare)?

The previous citation from Bhaskar shows him to have been strongly concerned with 'unacknowledged conditions, unintended consequences'. CR cannot accept an understanding of the dynamics of the world external to the 'discursive, desiring and defensive' subjectivity as if it could be conceptually reduced to supplying subjectivity with "conditions", "events" and "discourses".

Hollway does recognise 'material conditions' but the tacit social relations and their dynamics in the world market (e.g. child slavery in the Congo to produce rare minerals for our mobile phones) are more than just 'material conditions' and 'events that happen to happen in our immediate external world' which may or may not be 'discursively appropriated'. What about systematic inadvertent practices and their systematically unrecognised consequences?

What about our Critical Realist and sociological interest in (world-wide, trans-national, regional and state and local) "social structures, their powers and liabilities, mechanisms and tendencies" as Archer summarises so well? What about a "life-historical developmental account" of societies (not just of (situated) selves) and even a life-historical developmental account of (moments of) the world-system currently in extreme crisis?

We cannot say that the 'societal-historical' is absent from Hollway's programmatic statement, but any concern for its local world-historical dynamics certainly seems not fleshed out equally and sufficiently: the 'social' in this concept of the 'psycho-social' appears primarily as the 'immediately social' of social psychology. Both the larger-external-societal and the longer-historical seem decisively rear-grounded. The text's 'psycho-social' psychology appears sociologically and historically naïve.

How do we move to construct a Bhaskar-based 'Critical Realism' which suffers from neither unhistorical-presentism, nor implicit psychological naiveté (Archer), nor implicit historical and sociological naiveté (Hollway)? A sophisticated rationalist sociologism (plus an unsophisticated psychology), or a sophisticated complex psychology (plus an unhistorical and unsophisticated sociology) – both relatively unhistorical – is not good enough.

How do we proceed? Should we just put them together, or side by side?

Paul Hoggett, Professor at the University of the West of England, calls for accounts of the 'internal' and 'external' worlds to be seen as being governed by what he calls 'separate rules of structure formation', even though they "overlap" and are "mutually constituting" (a contradiction not obviously easy to handle):

> I also firmly believe that the internal and external worlds, while overlapping and mutually constituting, are also irreducible to one another. Each is governed by its own rules of structure formation. For the inner world, these rules are part of what we call our psycho-logic. One of the great contributions of psychoanalysis has been to contribute to our understanding of these rules –condensation, displacement, repression, splitting, projection, identification, and so on. These constitute the rules of structure formation of our inner world (...) I would go so far as to say that they can be discerned at work in all human societies; they are, in this sense, constitutive of what it means to be human. Similarly, I believe that the external world has its own rules of structure formation, rules that govern economy and society. Marx's notion of the law of expanded reproduction of the capitalist mode of production (Luxemburg and Bukharin, 1972) would be an example. Such rules of structure formation, though generative, are not visible; their

existence has to be inferred. And this requires a going beneath and beyond the surface (Hoggett, 2008: 383).

This 'separate worlds' formulation has the advantage of the support of separate research programmes and conceptual models of (let us say) actually-existing psycho-analysis and political economy (and academic departments and learned/professional societies) and of mapping onto the Archer and Hollway 'separations'. However the disadvantage is the acceptance of an ontological notion of quite different realities with separate rules of structure formation. This is too high a price to pay. Except as a first approximation, it does not cross over but instead entrenches the psycho-societal divide.

Adding a psychologism to a sociologism (or juxtaposing them) is not the way forward and CR's general approach illuminates powerfully why this is the case.

My own view is less extreme than that of Hoggett. My *ontological* view is that there is only one Reality (a view shared by Critical Realism), and so the notion of "two different worlds" can be (perhaps only for a limited historical period in a given culture) a temporarily useful *epistemological* handling-device but only as a provisional vision, and no more than that. The 'two-worlds' idea is dangerous if thought of as more than that, as if it was an account of what Reality is ontologically like.

If we start – but only start – by (very provisionally) following Hoggett (but only epistemologically) into imagining *two mutual-constituting and overlapping worlds that are irreducible to each other, each* with their own 'rules of structure formation', then *the following things become (usefully) sayable and thinkable and researchable*:

- The part-model of the 'psyche' can be simple (simplifying) or sophisticated
- The part-model of the 'societal' can be simple (simplifying) or sophisticated
- Both or either of the above can be seen historically or unhistorically
- The practice in any given account of the relating of the two part-models can be simple (simplifying) or sophisticated

In the current state of historical reality and mono-disciplinary specialisation, our view is that the one ontological reality does at the moment require to be addressed epistemologically by at least *two different 'part-models' at high and comparable levels of sophistication in a sophisticated co-use of them both*. Our argument is that we mostly have (as a result of single-discipline, one-part-model, training and PhD departmental awards, and other emergent 'external world' structures and apparatuses) either (i) *complex dynamic sociologies spoiled by a simplifying commonsense psychology*; (ii) *complex dynamic psychologies spoiled by a simplifying commonsense sociology*. In addition, we mostly have them seriously weakened by an *unhistorical* – or *insufficiently historical* – approach to their objects of study which make their research products *historically naïve with an implicit simplifying commonsense history.*

Archer's social realism and Hollway's psycho-social realism as described above hold much promise as separate research programmes. However, each is inadequate for the 'world' that is not their primary focus: the notion of the internally-deliberating individual getting it wrong only for social reasons' (sociologist Archer); the notion of the non-immediate, external societal world as being merely conditions/event/discourse-providing (psychologist Hollway). Hoggett's solution is also unacceptable to Critical Realism if only because of its false ontological reification of 'worlds' that can be treated as 'separate' only epistemologically and conceptually. And because their secondary focus (the shadow part-model that their mono-discipline and mono-training generates at a commonsense level) is inadequate, the primary focus both of such current Critical Realisms and Psychosocial Studies are both substantively weakened and become perverse and misleading. Degrees of 'historical inadequacy' make matters worse.

What would overcome the weaknesses of both programmes as currently formulated?

Towards a fully psychosocietal and historical critical realism

We need a combined Critical Realist programme, integrating but going beyond the immediately social of 'Psychosocial Studies' towards the larger macro-structures of the 'societal', and towards a concept of the psychology of collectivities and individuals which includes Archer's 'deliberating' but has a more intra-psychic understanding of the limitations of conscious rationality: *not a psychosocial but a psycho-societal realism* (for the neglected contribution of four grand masters of late19th and early 20th century research to such psycho-societal thinking, see Cavalletto's superb 2007).

How should we proceed? We postulate a 'Critical Psycho-Societal Realism' as an emergent or future research programme – in Kuhn's (1962) terms a 'paradigm' – which needs confident conceptual elaboration, methodological development, and sustained theory-rectifying empirical work. In the spirit of Bhaskar's original concept of Critical Realism (see earlier citation and Wengraf, 2010), I shall postulate that there is only one single Reality – which can be better grasped by a notion of the 'Psycho-Societal' and that the different 'worlds' postulated with or without inverted commas (as for example in Paul Hoggett's account) to avoid error must never ever be seen as self-contained separated ontological realities – even if they may or may not be sometimes seen as more or less useful epistemological abstractions in flawed academic departments.[5]

A sketch of one such unified approach can be found in an exemplary single four-level map between the *societal macro-order* and the *states of mind within and between individuals*, constructed by Lynn Froggett (2002) in her *Love, Hate and Welfare*. Concerned with the 'imagined subject of welfare settlements', her argument is more general:

> Froggett (2002) [maps] out a theoretical and conceptual terrain on which the imagined subject of specific social welfare settlements can be depicted. She argues that this subject is analytically positioned between four interpenetrating domains of analysis: the macro political and economic order; *institutional* cultures that reproduce the social relations of welfare; *interpersonal* relationships implicated in caring and helping; and the *states of mind* and socially structured defences invoked by these relationships. She concludes that the imaginative and practical linking of these domains is continually attempted, and sometimes achieved... and may be illuminated by biographical research methodology (Froggett and Wengraf, 2004: 96 italics added).

For our purposes, this is a less one-sided account than the socio-centric model of Archer or the intra/inter-psychic-centric models of Hollway. It can be seen as an exemplary starting point for an approach which is (not psycho-social, as normally used, but) fully Psycho-Societal.

As we suggest in the next section, our experience of the strengths and weaknesses of Sostris – above all my sense of the direction that it and then the emergent research on the Bromley-by-Bow centre both prefigured – has made us want to argue for the key role of one of Froggett's above four 'domains'.

For us, the key role for developing a symmetrical and historical psycho-societal approach relating the four domains most fruitfully is at a reworked version of the second domain in her list: in the exploration of constants and variations in *institutional regimes and the 'regimes of practice'* they attempt to implement, modify, or prevent.

We shall just give a recent example of this from an article by Tom Wengraf and Lynn Froggett (Froggett and Wengraf, 2004), arising from the post-Sostris

---

[5] Indeed, we would argue that Reality is better postulated as being 'bio-psycho-societal-spiritual' and that Planet Earth and its alternative futures needs to be thought about within such a unified system of thinking and inquiry. In this text, our concern is to develop the notion of a Critical Psycho-Societal Realism without prejudice to any further elaboration of such a more general paradigm.

Bromley-by-Bow research project. In a case study focusing upon a particular person 'Nila' at a Healthy Living Centre in East London, we wrote:

> .... we use the word social to indicate the social setting ('the Centre') in which our research is being carried out. In other words it refers to its network of proximate relationships. These social relationships are in turn reflective of, or reactive to, wider societal relations of class, ethnicity, gender, generation and other societally-produced ascriptions. They intersect with overtly normative and political discourses such as those of leadership, citizenship and community and [*also with*] with powerful global relations of military, economic, political and cultural projection, domination, accommodation and resistance. Such relationships directly affect the interviewee's experience of the Centre and its staff, users and volunteers.
>
> They also form the main topic of the interview. Nila's experience of the Centre is mediated, as we shall show, by her inner world dynamics and their biographical roots. For example, to locate Nila in the area of London where she has grown up and in which the Centre is located, the multiple ethnic minorities from former British colonies and their difficult co-existence with white ex-docker communities needs to be understood in the context of the history of the British Empire, the post-colonial, the changing of transport technologies and the neoliberal ambivalence about empowering the poor that the neoliberal order produces at home and abroad. What happened [*and happens*] globally impacted then [*and goes on impacting now*] on the constitution and then of the functioning [*mutating regimes*] of institutions such as the [Bromley-by-Bow Healthy Living] Centre, which can therefore act as an observatory for intersections of inner world and outer world dynamics. (Froggett and Wengraf, 2004, modified and italics and material in square brackets added TW).

Institutions (organisations) in CR terms are defined as 'corporate' or 'collective agents' (or agencies). It should be stressed that they are born out of the desire of individuals to increase their individual leverage/power/agency in a field of power. Such 'corporate agents' might be global blocs (e.g. "the West" and its military and financial instruments of global subordination), 'whole societies', individual families or networks, enterprises, trade associations, federal states, trade unions, political parties, churches, etc. Within such 'collective agents', sub-collectives and individuals struggle incessantly to preserve or improve their own position. At certain moments and at certain levels, a new 'equilibrium' or 'historical settlement' occurs and the field of forces is significantly modified: the regime mutates or is replaced.[6]

The citation from Froggett and Wengraf (2004) above unfortunately fails to make fully explicit the importance of such a focusing upon historical regimes, their mutations and transitions. The notion of 'societal regime change' may make it easier to understand the importance of understanding outer-world dynamics in a fully sociological fashion. It may also suggest how 'regimes' may be seen as operative in the inner world as well.

'Societal regime change' has historically been less intuitively grasped in the UK and the anglophone world; more intuitively grasped in the rest of Continental Europe and in the rest of the decolonising/recolonising world. However, the neoliberal military turn and the intensifying 'great bankocratic money-grab' by ruling kleptocratic circles (2008-?) have given even in the UK a significant number of people and even researchers a better understanding of how, even when (for example Higher Education) institutions can look the same, the regime of and within those institutions and the 'felt lived experience' of those in different positions within and between institutional regimes, can be very different (a little earlier think Iceland; now think Spain, think Greece, think Europe, think the UK National Health Service forty years ago, now, in forty or in four years time). Biographical research into the experience of those who live through such historical changes can help capture these mutations of regime and mutations of subjectivity.

BNIM and Sostris Phase One: a 1990s biography-based inquiry

We need to grasp the Sostris moment as within and part of a historical transition. In CR terms, it may be seen as a dated temporary 'social structure' (or 'a configuration of dated situated practices', as Pierre Bourdieu might have said) constraining and enabling the subjectivity and inter-subjectivity of participants whose actions sometimes and in some ways modify and also sometimes and in some ways perpetuate their inheritance. As one of us wrote in 2002:

> What became most important for us in Sostris, and difficult for sociologists and social policy experts to do, is to assume that *we do not already know*, for a given moment, what the overall social structure or social policy context *really is, or really is*

---

[6] Immanuel Wallerstein's concept of 'the world system' was crucial in promoting popularising such 'world-thinking' more than two generations ago (see e.g. Wallerstein, 2004). This can also be seen as an appropriation of the work of Antonio Gramsci (e.g. 1971).

*becoming.... * At the level of the individual case.... We are *waiting for the case, for several cases – to tell us* (Wengraf, 2002: 313 slightly modified).

The historical transition of the 1990s was one in which a primary metaphor through which the societies of the time were perceived was that of the development of two aspects of 'world tendencies: that of 'risk society' (Beck) and that of 'individualisation' (Giddens). A key methodological foundation (or legitimation) was a turn towards 'action' embodied for us initially in the 'structuration/ structure-action' framework of Giddens. Later on, the UK Sostris group came across work by Archer which helped us maintain a more historical perspective on action and structure and stressed the importance of the 'agency' and 'reflexivity' of historical actors (Archer, 1995).

One way of seeing what was happening was that, on the basis of the fostered collapse of the Soviet Communist model and the determined and continuing uneven erosion by all political parties in Great Britain and elsewhere of the social democratic and welfare model/regime, the condition of insecure and micro-managed proletarian was being extended from the manual working classes to large sectors of the middle classes, including many of the state professions (by now, including academics) The deliberate multiplication of insecurities was seeing the construction of the 'insecurity state' within the forms of the earlier and attacked 'welfare state'.

What we now (2010- ?) are likely to call the destruction of welfare, the advance of neoliberal globalisation and the de-protection of non-elites was then (1980-90) primarily seen as the development of something called 'individualisation' which was occurring in a number of increasingly 'risky' risk societies. During this period, the European Union sponsored enquiries and research into what was then called 'social exclusion in risk societies', notably those in the then 'EU'. The term 'social exclusion and 'risk society' unusefully avoided reference to class, poverty, and exploitation under capitalism, but did enable 'moments of poverty and inadequate societal support in the life cycle and in particular areas' to be more clearly addressed. The goal of such research was to work for a modification of social policy and of welfare regimes to be more fitted for what was definitely but vaguely being identified as 'new conditions' in Western Europe. This occurred in a struggle between different EU directorates: some were neoliberal and economistic in their orientation; others were concerned with the promotion of social solidarity and European citizenships and social rights.

Social research transition were also being reconfigured: systems and statistical abstractions were being given slightly less dominance and qualitative research into the lived experience of people and groups was being allowed more access to funded research. There was a turn to qualitative research either as complementing quantitative and institutional macro-system studies, or (less helpfully) as simply displacing them. Particularly in the anglophone world, many researchers detected an undeclared war of positivist-statistical research in psychology, economics and elsewhere against qualitative interpretive understandings, and declared an explicit 'paradigm counter-war' of their own. In what were seen as 'paradigm wars' in many disciplines between (old) 'quantitative researchers' and (new) 'qualitative researchers', researchers were expected to declare or at least practice allegiance to one or other camp. What is now called 'mixed methods' was not the flavour of the day. In the 2000s, this has fortunately started to change.... hopefully, the notion of 'psycho-societal research' will foster such a change.

In the 1990s in qualitative sociology and social policy research, there was a turn towards biographical methods. Running parallel with the 1996-9 experience of Sostris as a practical research project using a particular biographic-narrative methodology (later to be called BNIM) was also the authors' experience over the same period of gathering together and getting published a volume with a broader remit covering a variety of biographical methodologies, entitled *The Turn to Biographical Methods in Social Science: comparative issues and examples* (Chamberlayne, Bornat and Wengraf, 2000). Its 'introduction' situates this biographical turn in general intellectual history but also in the area of policy and social research thinking and methodology.

Prue Chamberlayne, a significant force in this UK/anglophone turn towards biography, had been trained by Gabriele Rosenthal in one particular method – the Berlin *Quatext* biographical method. This rich mix of (i) two-subsession narrative interviewing as developed by Fritz Schütze and (ii) a twin-track future-blind interpretive methodology as developed by Rosenthal and Wolfram Fischer-Rosenthal in *Quatext* was used by Chamberlayne and Annette King in their *Cultures of Care: UK and the two Germanies* project (Chamberlayne and King, 2000). It was the proposal for the primary use of this method that was proposed and accepted for the Sostris project which – to our considerable but delighted surprise – the EU research commissioners accepted.[7]

To summarise Sostris's scope and range, it consisted of two phases: (i) individual biographies of people in six categories in the seven countries; (ii) in the seven countries the study of 'innovative social agencies' that were seen as using 'biographically-sensitive innovative practices. The key feature was that the almost (but not quite) exclusive method of this inquiry into social exclusion in risk society was to be by way of biographical-narrative interviews of a particular sort.

---

[7] The interpretive methodology of *Quatext* was derived from a number of sources (including the 'Grounded Theory' of Norman Glaser and especially Anselm Strauss, see Apitzsch and Inowlocki 2000 for details). Rosenthal decisively 'configured' the elements of the whole. The acceptance of the Sostris proposal for qualitative biographical research would not have occurred under Anglophone dominance in the UK.

Early on in the Sostris project, we referred to "the method" or to "Gabriele and Wolfram's method". We then needed a public label for it in discussion in the *Sostris Working Papers* and elsewhere, so it became first 'BIM' and then 'BNIM'. In the next section we provide an abbreviated account of BNIM, the focal biographical research method used by Sostris.

BNIM – future-blind twin track moves towards situated subjectivity

The training and coaching experience and the materials provided from Berlin became the basis of the first Anglophone full-length textbook presentation of BNIM (Wengraf, 2001). Current mutations of the method and philosophy of BNIM can be found in the constantly-updated free *BNIM: Short Guide and Detailed Manual* (2012). What follows can only be a very brief and partial condensation or reminder.

Preceding any attempt to do other things with the materials generated by the BNIM interview – for example, extracting themes from the narrative in the transcript-- the default purpose of the BNIM interpretation procedures is to achieve an understanding of the evolving 'dated situated subjectivity', a history of the case evolution (HCE) of the person as a 'situated subjectivity' making their changing way in a changing world over time. (Ideally, an example of an HCE would be provided, but reasons of space prohibit this. Details of examples and procedures can be found in Wengraf, 2012-). What we can do here is to indicate in close-up detail the methodological step immediately preceding the construction of such an account of the whole case.[8]

BNIM's twin-track prequel prior to synthetic whole-case sequel

In order to produce the BNIM history of the case-evolution, the researcher starts by working along two quite separate tracks and while doing so tries to avoid 'cross-contamination' between them. That completed, the researcher then in a case-account brings together the insights and provisional interpretations generated in the two previously-separated tracks. This twin-track approach is one of the key distinguishing features of BNIM. A sample illustration of the separate tracks is provided in Table 3.1. (Familiarity with the case presented is not required for following the illustration.)

---

[8] As in Sostris Part 2, and in the Bromley-by-Bow study, the 'case' can also be an organisation/ institution, studied largely but never entirely and often not predominantly through biographic narrative interviews with those involved.

The 'objective' side		The 'subjective' side	
Biographical Data Analysis Phases of the Lived Life		Subjectivity Data Analysis Phases of Mutating Subjectivity	Teller Flow Analysis of Interview Phases of Sub-session 1 only (plus)

• Until 9 - Security in large family
• 9-11 Change of school, of village, school again and then loss of mother
• 11-16 Housework at home for out-of-work father, bullying at school for status. Left school with no qualifications
• 16-24 Leftwing union militant in NUM and in his colliery. Secure work-community with activist mentor. Rugby and pubs and NUM travel. Starts relation with future wife
• 24-25 Showdown between NUM and Tory government; scabs divide the NUM nationally and locally. Miners defeated
• 25-29 After defeat of miners, moves to non-scab other pit, continues militancy till it is shortly to close.
• 30 'Industrial gypsy' as mobile crane operator in private sector. Starts to do 'O levels', has rugby accident, is ill and then made redundant. Short nervous crisis.
• 31-37 Career shift. Voluntary work with kids with learning disabilities, and then move into Social Work and climbing qualifications and status ladder. Thinking of going to university.
		• >16
		  Teacher taught me to challenge: "How do you know they really landed on the moon?"
		  I bullied my way to topic of pecking order in my school
		  No problem about not having a single qualification. Left school and father's house.
		• 16-24
		  Rugby, learnt the vital significance of solidarity underground, excitement of NUM-paid travel and meeting people. Unreflective ordinary racism.
		• 24-25
		  Sudden division of community and unexpected "I saw how naive I'd been". "Till then I thought, now I see". Pride in the "Magnificent Seven"
		• 25+
		  Perpetual anger at 'betrayal' and Thatcher's victory.
		• 31-37
		  New start. Struggle to overcome 'bitterness': I wouldn't wish…. I'll be professional… Do your bloody job… His wife rang me up and thanked me. Never got over mother's death. I might have been an SW earlier if… regret no qualifications.
		  I'm not challenging, my daughter doesn't challenge, the union doesn't challenge. **Lucky.**
			Sequence of the initial account
			I Mother's death (tormented and broken report with argumentation)
			  family, especially father leaving school without qualifications
			  mining, 'strong characters'
			  failure of strike: divisions of NUM
			II own life from 19-25 onwards: many fluent narratives and reports ("I could tell 200-300 stories")
			  Trips to America. Struggles with colliery manager. Accident
			  Mentor and his socialisation as a union militant
			III Death of the mines ⊗ Report, PINs, then argumentation-theorising about society and politics)
			IV Maturity + Luck
			  (report + much argumentation and evaluation)
			  Caring and Education - Report
			  Handling of post-strike disillusion, anger, against cynicism and for principle ("scab story"). Luck for self and wife; and fear for daughter [She doesn't challenge'] Sadness for community. "village was dead, quite dead"… crime/alcoholism. At work, 'starting to give up and feel defeated because I don't challenge'. Family: nice feeling at moment, [but] everyone walks a very tight rope'. I've gotta continue to develop….

Version A Cycle of disrupted security: first the family crisis; then re-security in the mines; then divided mining community and re-security in the second pit; then insecurity in private sector and semi-re-securisation in social work career.		1) Ordinary family till mother's death 2) Became 'housewife' looking after younger brother and home for alcoholic father. Bully at school and no interest in school work or qualifications 3) Ordinary miner until the 1984-5 miners strike 4) Reflexivity and end of naiveté after 1984-5 5) SW qualifications and overcoming the bitterness of the politically-divided ex-mining village community	Bildungsroman transition from the disaster years of 11-16 to naive militant 16-25 to realist for a post-mining professional new career (31-). Tortured argument around mother's death, fluent narrative around 16-25 before the strike; righteous argument about his and especially his daughter's future in job-insecure individualist Britain.

Table 3.1 Illustration of the twin tracks and three columns of the BNIM method
Source: Modified from Wengraf (2012).

1. The **first track** is that of the objective side: the living of the lived life (known as the BDA, biographic data analysis). A phase-model of the 'objective course' of that life (or life-period) is represented in the first column (column 1).
2. The **second track** is that of the subjective side: this involves two components, represented in the middle and the right-hand-side of the Table:
   i. a phase model of **successive states of subjectivity during the course of the life-period** (here I shall call this a Subjective Data Analysis, SDA) – column 2
   ii. a phase model of the **telling of the told story in the interview**, initially called rather misleadingly a thematic field analysis), now understood primarily as a Teller Flow Analysis, TFA – column 3

The researcher's biographical data analysis (BDA) leading to the construction of a model of the objective phases of the life-period being told about is summarised on the left hand side. The subjective data analysis (SDA) leading to the construction of a model of subjective phases of the life-period being told about is summarised in the middle. The TFA (the Teller Flow Analysis of the sequence of the improvised telling in the micro-period of the interview itself) is summarised on the right hand side.

The default question of BNIM interpretation concerns columns 1 and 2. Each column provides a different phase model, but one covering the same time/period (the life or part thereof).

> *How did a person who went through the **phases of the living of the lived life** like column 1 come to go through the **phases of their subjective life** like column 2?* (And the question can be reversed).

The third column relates to the phases of the BNIM interview (column 3)

> *How do we understand the **current phase of situated subjectivity** as revealed in the succeeding **phases of the BNIM interview** as summarised in column 3?*[9]

Critical Realism requires, as we have said, something like the attention to the 'factualities of the lived life' as expressed in column 1 so as to understand and situate and not be seduced by the 'present story perspective' that organises and structures the self-presentation in the phases of the interview itself (column 3), but in which traces of earlier and other perspectives (state of subjectivity/mind) can also be

---

[9] In the following diagram, there is not space to provide data from more than subsession 1

detected and are worked up separately (column 2). The twin-track biographical method of BNIM provides both material and procedure for such work.

Other features of BNIM interpretation

A key feature of individual and collective life as it is lived is the 'unknowability of the future'. Hegel said that life can only be understood looking backwards, but that it has to be lived looking forwards. We are constantly planning what to do next, knowing that we do not know what will happen next, and more or less anticipating that as well. The crisis of Western finance capitalism around 2010, the rise of China to be the contemporary equivalent of 'the workshop of the world' that Britain was in the late 19th century, computer technology, the impact of global warming, the death of species and the final stage in the exploitation and destruction of the planet's natural resources: all of these have had and will have repercussions for people, families, whole economies, particular regimes.

A Critical Psycho-Societal Realism requires realism about the action of 'agents' in such a situation of inevitable feverish acting and conjecturing (and desperately apathetic denial and agonised complacency) and de facto future-unknowing and future-blindness. Biographical method has to 'reconstruct' the future-blind nature of the evolved and mutating future-making subjectivity at a particular point in time, or over a glocal moment.

BNIM has several ways of attempting to avoid 'error' and gain richer texture in its understanding of individual action, in its case-reconstruction. I will mention three:

(i) the twin-track interpretation procedure already described;
(ii) the future-blind panel that kicks off and destabilises the researcher as they start on each track;
(iii) the profoundly historical nature of BNIM's interpretive procedures.

We reiterate that researchers try to avoid 'contamination' between work on the two separate tracks. How?

First, completely ignoring how these facts (or some of them) were used in the telling of the told story, the BNIM research panel considers the initial hard-data of the objective biographical chronology (BDC), the basis of BNIM's first interpretive track. Later on, the researcher continues to develop and eventually write-up a good enough provisional BDA (Biographic Data Analysis) of the pattern of the objective events of the person's life-period (column 1).

Then, on this basis, given that hard-fact chronology (BDC) and always-provisional 'objective history' (BDA), *and totally ignoring* it, there can then be a full exploration of the digitally-recorded known historical sequence of the way the teller told the story in the, say, 2-3 hour interview that was recorded (the TFA, Teller Flow Analysis (column 3).

Then, on the basis of all the subjective data available, *continuing to ignore the biographical data analysis,* the researcher constructs as far as they can a model of the different phases that the individual might be seen as having passed through over the life-period under inspection (the SDA, Subjective Data Analysis – column 2).

This is a form of triangulation: the senses of the 'dated situated subjectivity' (the patterns inferred) derived from the study of the objective data and from the study of the subjective data rarely coincide completely. To bring the results of the separate two tracks together, the researcher has then to work to answer the default BNIM question: *How did a person who lived their life like this (pattern inferred from BDA) come to tell their story like that (pattern inferred from SDA)?*

The answer to this question requires the researcher to produce a *History of the Case Evolution* (up to and including at least in principle the interview itself).

Having dealt with one feature of BNIM – the two tracks and delayed synthesis, the constant focus on reconstructing the 'lived experiencing' of the situated subjectivity moving through the moments of their life – let us now turn to another feature: the kick-start interpretive panels invariably deployed at the beginning of each of the two tracks.

Future-blind panel interpretation to replicate 'experiencing' of the experiencing subject

For BNIM in a way we think is required by the principles of Bhaskar's Critical Realism (and other traditions such as reflexive feminist research), the researcher is no less a fallible and persuasive 'agent' than is the subject. Each researcher is also a dated situated subjectivity – suffering from the illusions of the epoch and conditioned by their psycho-societal formation, and hence with their own hotspots and their blindspots. Consequently, a critical epistemology requires 'scientific procedures' designed to minimise the effects of this psycho-societal conditioning and positioning of each and every researcher.[10]

Not only does BNIM attempt to 'reconstruct' the (unknown) 'experiencing' of the biographical subject through two separate sub-procedures (the twin tracks), but it also starts off each of the two tracks by a kick-start panel in which

---

[10] The notion of 'positioning' as developed within say social psychology we think is given more historical and societal 'grip' by Bourdieu's notion of the 'historical field' of the macro-society in general and institutions (such as academic ones) in particular. Several BNIM studies have used Brourdieu's notions of 'habitus' and 'field'.

the interviewer-researcher is forcibly exposed to hypotheses they would never have dreamed of on their own. BNIM requires that the start of the interpretive process for each track take the form of a BNIM 'panel' considering the data particular to that panel.

In addition, these two track-specific 'kick-start' panels are run in a tightly-prescribed fashion. The four or five members of the panel proceed 'chunk-by-chunk'; they proceed future-blind not-knowing what chunks come next or later; for any given hypothesis put forward, they are encouraged to generate counter-hypotheses and tangential hypotheses; their primary type of hypothesis to generate about each chunk should be:

> *What was the interviewee likely to be experiencing at the moment (experiencing hypothesis) and, if that particular experiencing-hypothesis was right and they were experiencing something like that, then what might we predict about the future experiencing and action (these are called 'following hypotheses', risky hypotheses about what might follow later in the data series, and what future experiencing and action might then occur)?*

Those interested in the working of the BNIM panels and the tight prescription of the procedures to be followed within them can find further details in Wengraf (2001; 2012-). The operation of these panels on the series of data provided to them worked powerfully in the *Sostris* national teams and in and for the international meetings as a constraining and enabling structure or practice. It prevented centrifugal forces of the initial heterogeneity of the researchers before Sostris started and subsequent quite different conditions of academic work, traditions, and life-requirements from subverting the collective trans-national temporary practice that Sostris was. They fostered a powerful and disciplined imaginative realism about the lived experiencing of the subject of the research, as well as a particular style of 'writing up' (see Sostris *Working Papers*) which showed everybody the 'two track working' practice.

In and then after each kick-start panel, the researcher spends most of their time writing up the hypotheses and interpretations of people whose hypotheses about present experiencing and future action of the person interviewed are significantly different and very often completely opposed to those that the researcher thinks is obvious: an exciting and sometimes infuriating self-enriching experience!

If thinking is a social activity, then the individual researcher thinking on their own is both crucially important but also liable to be profoundly dangerous for the critical realist or simply scientific imagination. The kick-start panels of 4 or so people profoundly and irreversibly expand the 'imaginative universe' of the individual researcher. The key role in deciding which of seven different possible interpretations of a given data-chunk are unlikely to be true is played not by the unreliable debating quickness of an individual panel-member but by the later trickle down of later chunks of fact. Things the interviewee said next. Things that were done or happened later in the life. Things said in the interview; things done in the life.

The kick-start panels – if sufficiently heterogeneous and well-run – strengthen immeasurably the capacity of the individual for imaginative realism and for overcoming their inevitably transmitted initial hotspots and blindspots. They generate a powerful sense of the complex dynamics and contingencies within individual biographies. The panel is there primarily to generate hypotheses around experiencing and choices of life-options that no individual researcher on their own would ever think of.

Having sketched out very briefly a few of the characteristics of BNIM as a method available for use, and its capacity for triangulation and reducing individual impressionistic interpretation, let us turn to its use in the Sostris project at the end of the last century.

Sostris Phase One: the Sostris practice

We now deal very briefly with some features of what we may call 'Sostris practice' which may be of interest to those interested in the substantive field of cross-national biography-based research. We especially deal with Sostris Phase Two – the study of 'innovative social agencies' – and the follow-up research study (separately funded) of the 'Bromley-by-Bow Centre' (East London) which used both BNIM (again) but also other methods of observation and (to a lesser degree) documentation[11].

In the late 1990s, many 'cross-national studies' tended to take the form of studies by 'national teams' working with different concepts and methodologies in relative isolation from each other, but with a post-facto 'synthesis' by the lead researchers put together towards the end of the project as a common report came

---

[11] The more public presentation of the work of Sostris can be found in the volume *Biography and social exclusion in Europe: experiences and life journeys* (Chamberlayne, Rustin and Wengraf, eds. 2002); in particular, brief accounts of the project are in the introduction by Rustin and Chamberlayne (Rustin and Chamberlayne, 2002) and in Chamberlayne's 'Conclusions: social transitions and biographical work' (Chamberlayne, 2002). An earlier and more extended summary can be found in the *Final Report of the Sostris Project* (Chamberlayne and Rustin, 1999), where the method is termed 'socio-biography'. Both the edited volume (2002) and the Final Report draw on the rich stock of cross-national materials largely recorded in the nine *Sostris Working Papers*, of which seven are Case Study Materials for each category (within and across the societies under study).

to be needed. The work was presented as 'trans-national and integrated'; the practice was very largely 'intra-national and juxtaposed'.

Certain features were characteristic of the Sostris research programme: (i) initial common training by a highly skilled methodological team led by Roswitha Breckner who also moved between national teams over the period of the research to 'trouble-shoot'; (ii) national team production to prescribed formats of four-monthly category-specific international meetings and category Working Papers; (iii) BNIM's tight specification both of the two sub-session Schütze-type interviews and the twin-track interpretative structure using BNIM panels and conforming to BNIM procedural rules. There are others but these are perhaps the major ones.

The point being made here is that a very tight configuration of sequenced practices characterised the Sostris project, both at the level of national teams interviewing and interpreting cases, but also at the level of the macro-practices of the cross-national teams representing their cases to each other in the monthly meetings and representing them more generally in the category-specific *Sostris Working Papers*. This fostered a relatively high level of 'disciplined imagination' among the teams and a high degree of coherence in their mutual presentations and eventual publications.

Sostris Phase Two and the Bromley-by-Bow study

The EU contract with the Sostris group included a third-year study of 'innovative social agencies' (organisations) that Sostris came to consider as dealing in a biographically-sensitive way with those at risk of social exclusion. Such a concern for understanding and evaluating organisational strategies for supporting those at risk in a risk society was to prove very fruitful. It can be seen as an evolving experiment in a slow expansion of the scope of biographically-concerned research from the individual-at-risk to the organisational, the third of the four levels of the Froggett model (as discussed earlier). This experiment started an incomplete process of using a greater variety of research methods while maintaining a focus on the situated subjectivity of the individual-at-risk, an exploration that suggests directions for a productive psycho-societal critical realism not afraid of any method or combinations of method.

The seven national teams eventually identified some 13 experiments in 'innovative agencies', some successful and some not. These were described and the results theorised in firstly in *Sostris Working Paper no.8* (1999) and then in Wengraf's (2002) chapter 'Biographical work and agency innovation: relationships, reflexivity, and theory-in-use'.

At this point, our concern is exclusively with what can be learned from these researches about a critical realist psycho-societal method going beyond the study of the 'category sampling of individuals' method of Sostris Phase One to the 'organisational regime and culture sampling' concerns of Sostris Phase Two and the Dunhill Project, but continuing to be based on biographical research into situated subjectivities.

'Innovative social agencies'

None, we think, of the 14 national researchers who made up the Sostris team were organisational sociologists; their common culture was the training in BNIM provided at the start of Sostris Phase One. Phase Two required the description and evaluation of organisations. The method of these hasty explorations was summarised as follows:

> Although social agencies are not individuals, our methodology.... continued to be biographical-narrative in character... We wanted to experiment with their 'lived life/told story' methodology, adapting it to the understanding of an institution. National teams conducted biographic-narrative interviews with the individual founders and/or leading members of the institution and/or typical members of frontline staff and/or clients. They were asked to tell the history of how they came to be involved in the organisation (or set up the organisation) and what happened after that. Where they could, the national teams also collected self-presentational documents produced by the institution and engaged in some (very limited) observation (Wengraf, 2002: 248).

There were therefore three core data-collection methods involved in this experiment: (i) the well-tried and agreed BNIM interviews with different categories and generations within the organisation, (ii) some degree of institutional observation and (iii) some concern with official self-presentational documents in the public arena. A core method of the interpretation of the data was the distinction central to BNIM between the lived life and the told story, relatively objective facts and relatively subjective self-presentations. In Wengraf's 2002 summary of the results of Sostris Phase Two, he wrote as follows:

> We have indicated the varying ways in which the organisations see themselves as handling 'the whole person' or as being restricted to dealing with particular issues or aspects of activity (counselling

for the soul, meals-on-wheels and home helps for the body, or biographical reflexivity for the client's self). We have suggested that organisations with strong external relations *and* empowering internal relations *and* oriented to (pre) figurative work concerning relations and reflexivity for ' the whole person in their whole situation' are likely to have high leverage effects on improving the resources, strategies and 'states of mind' of the individual. However, we have also stressed that the adequacy of those organisations that do wish to deal with the whole person depends very much on the *particular theory-in-use* of 'whole persons' that their practice (whether they realise it or not) enacts.

Wengraf then cited Rustin (2001: 158-9) comparing institutions whose regime practice different 'theories-in-use' of the whole person in their whole situation:

Outright denial of the existence of the unconscious domain, within the behaviourist psychological tradition, [and perhaps implicitly within current rational-actor concepts of thinking? TW] characteristically generates interest-based and coercive models of organisation....[as compared to] institutions where inner states of mind (notably anxiety) are taken seriously and as matters for reflection rather than for onward projection or punitive reprisal (Rustin, 2001: 158-9; material in square brackets added).

Part of the conclusions that Wengraf came to was:

Our evidence suggests that only where there are the material and human resources for appropriate space and appropriate time for reflexive and relational work that fosters 'getting to be known as a (hi)storied person' can significant changes be made of a supportive and remedial kind (Wengraf, 2002: 262).

We hope we have suggested above the sort of psycho-societal thinking that started to emerge towards the end of the Sostris project, and the type of multi-method (though BNIM-based) mix (some commonsense observation, some looking at publicity documents, some use of secondary statistics, etc.) that was starting to be used in the understanding of successful and unsuccessful would-be supportive and remedial organisations.

Out of Phase Two: Bromley-by-Bow: emerging concept of a 'full spectrum' psycho-societal methodology

Two members of the Sostris group in the UK (the authors of this paper Chamberlayne and Wengraf) then were associated in a new bid for organisational research led by Lynn Froggett to be focused on one of the 13 organisations studied in Sostris Phase Two, namely the Bromley-by-Bow Centre (BBBC) in East London. The concern here was to explore the way in which the Centre worked with older people, though this required a broader understanding of the dynamics of the organisational culture and regime. The bid was successful and the three were joined by Stef Buckner who became a full-time participant observer for the three years working on the site of the Centre. The results of the Dunhill-funded research can be found in Froggett et al (2005) and again all that can be done in this place is to notice the direction of methodological development around the BNIM core and of psycho-societal thinking. From the *Final Report*, one can assemble the following account:

> Our methodology has evolved somewhat. Originally, our proposal centred on four methods of data collection: use of available statistics, interviews, observations of institutional activities, and participation in collaboration with people in the Centre.
>
> Over the three years, we became more aware of the value of informal participation in the life of the Centre and came to focus more upon understanding the use of art and artwork as a form of activity. We also developed a more organic co-researching, co-learning relationship to the Centre:
> - Observations of interpersonal and organisational processes through formal meetings and observation of the Centre's day-to-day activities and interactions
> - The participation in the Development Group process as a reflective experience of how people think about their work, how ideas emerge and how they get put into practice [*Participant Action Research, TW*]
> - Consideration of the ways in which themes relating to biographies and processes were encoded within the organisational myths and stories
>
> Our original strong focus on biographic narrative has been complemented – largely as a result of our learning from the Development Group – by a much greater attention to art. This has led to

finding parallels between 'syncretistic thinking' in the Centre and in our method of free associative synthesising during processes of interpretation. Our 'psychology of inner worlds' has become increasingly informed by psychodynamic concepts. Our 'sociology of outer worlds' in this study is primarily informed by an increasingly 'ethnographic eye' for the detail of what people do and how they relate in institutions, their routine practices and their unexpected crises. This is supplemented by analysis of existing information gathered in statistical studies of neighbourhood (Froggett et al., 2005: 28-46).

A considerable expansion can be seen from the original 'BNIM-plus' methodology of Sostris. The Dunhill BBBC study shows an equal prominence given to ethnographic observation and participatory action research, as well as simple 'wandering about and talking'. One could say that the core of this methodology was fivefold:
(i) interviews, including BNIM;
(ii) participatory action research and
(iii) participant and non-participant observation of public and private meetings and processes;
(iv) documentation including those of art-processes and art-events;
(v) internal and external statistics.[12]

We think that the earlier cited phrase sums up where we largely were at the close of this post-Sostris research:

> Our 'psychology of inner worlds' has become increasingly informed by psychodynamic concepts. Our 'sociology of outer worlds' in this study is primarily informed by an increasingly 'ethnographic eye'

---

[12] In private, Wengraf lamented that among the considerable skills of the research team we lacked those of an accountant and political economy expert. The capacity of the management to 'shield' the staff and the volunteers and the users of the Centre and us from knowledge of the hidden workings of its financial management and incentives-and-constraints only started to be at last fully appreciated (but still not understood) by us towards the end of the three years. It should be stressed in mitigation that our brief was to explore the ways the Centre worked with (older) people, not political-economic grounding of – nor mechanisms behind – such ways of working.

for the detail of what people do and how they relate in institutions, their routine practices and their unexpected crises.[13]

Such a broader set of used methods clearly required a set of complementary skills within a research team. Given the costs of training, it is unlikely that any one researcher could have the trained expertises required to carry out fully psycho-societal research.

Conclusions: towards a critical psycho-societal realism using biographical methods

Archer (2010) has argued strongly that a Critical Realist approach to understanding individual agency requires a methodology that gives access to the 'internal conversation' of the individual agent, to the 'deliberation' that the agent undertakes in all their 'contexts of action' as these unroll throughout the life journey of the agent. We would argue that such 'deliberations' are, in Bhaskar's words, the required "starting points" for a depth understanding, but that a 'deeper' psycho-societal approach is needed to 'understand' such expressed mentation. The Particular Incident Narratives (PINs) pursued by BNIM interviewing, it can be argued, provide a proxy for records of some 'internal conversations' recalled at a later date by the agent.

The interaction within BNIM interviews and the written outputs in terms of interview transcripts and interviewer field-notes also provide complex and difficult-to-decipher material about the multiple re-evaluations of such 'internal conversations' at-the-time and also subsequent overlayerings of interviewee perspectives after-the-time.

The first BNIM interpretive track provides a steady injunction to investigate the 'objective context' of the interviewee over time; the second provides an equally steady injunction to study the data about present but also past states of mutating subjectivity that the telling of the told story provides. The typical practice of BNIM panel-work and multiple interviewing of people from the same and different categories within similar or different sampling contexts does much to provide correction of the hotspots and blindspots of different individual

---

[13] From the notion of psycho-societal thinking and research put forward in this 2012 paper, our less-than-adequate concern for macro-sociology in 2003-5 can be seen in the reduction of the 'outer-world' to the observational face-to-face ethnography, and the failure already mentioned to explore the 'funding regime' of the organisation in context. We didn't get to Institutional Ethnography (Campbell and Gregor, 2002; Devault and McCoy, 2003) let alone glocal and organisational political economy. Our reference to 'statistics' – albeit only neighbourhood ones – shows our good intentions and weak macro-societal achievement. But there were funding and commissioning constraints on our inquiry as well, not just on the Centre. We did what we could.

researchers and even of different collective disciplines, national traditions, and glocal blindness. All these devices go to support a critical realism.

However, our experience with Sostris Phase Two and with the Bromley-by-Bow study that emerged from it has given us a strong bias towards the productivity of multi-method methodologies in which interviewing (and BNIM interviewing) plays one of the four core roles (interview, observation, documentation, participation). The BBBC study strongly suggested a 'full spectrum methodology' as resources for the 'best practice' for the research purposes of any particular research project. A multi-project team would need to consider what they need from a full spectrum of methods – from macro-societal sociology and political economy to intra-psychic psychology and interpersonal micro ethnography – all within a profoundly historical Critical Realist understanding of the psycho-societal and with a lot of participation and participant action research.[14]

This requires multi-disciplinary formations feeding into the perspectives and methodologies of any given psycho-societal research team, and the clear design of research sequences and deliverables to maintain the integrity, and focus, and on-the-job training, of the research project. It requires appropriate funding for such collectively-polymathic (or at least multi-mathic) research teams to do all that is necessary – especially in terms of cross-societal encounters – to ensure the full carrying out of the particular project – which, once concluded, provides the basis for enhanced psycho-societal research capacity among those who have been involved.[15]

In order for the area-disciplines of both the 'psychological' and the 'sociological' to have an area of research focus in which neither can claim a monopoly of omniscience, then the Dunhill study as well as more general considerations to me suggests the important area of most productive overlap as being that of the comparative study of 'agencies' (organisations).

At the organisational level identified by Froggett as one of the four levels or domains of inter-relation, both disciplines are still fruitful and self-conscious of their limits and of the virtues of other concepts and methodologies.

Psychology is no longer on its safest home ground of the intra-psychic and the immediately social. Sociology is no longer on its safest home ground of the

---

[14] For a recent BNIM-using multi-method approach to women's citizenship and women's movements, see Roseneil (2012) and Jolly and Roseneil (2012).

[15] This does not mean that *any* psycho-societal research project must have *all* the methods suggested here. Fitness and necessity for purpose is central. However, a psycho-societal approach does require sufficient expertise in (psychological) research disciplines focused on the 'inner world' of the intra-psychic (and intra-group, maybe) as well as in (sociological) research disciplines focused on the 'outer world' of the societal and institutional. Sophistication in the concepts and methods and products of both sorts of discipline are needed for psycho-societal research to command respect in the work it does. One-sided psychologisms and sociologisms (even juxtaposed) won't do it.

macro-societal and international. Psychology has not yet reached the point of absurdity of pronouncing abstractly and definitively on the psychology of the species or the dynamics of the whole society; Sociology has not yet reached its point of absurdity by pronouncing definitively and abstractly on the intra-psychic and the delicate movements of the interpersonal and inter-subjective. Hence in my view, the importance of the 'history of the organisation (and its external and internal regimes)' as at least one privileged 'observatory' for researching the psycho-societal at work.

There are already a panoply of methods and of research procedures that can forge initially-disparate teams into more unified psycho-societal research programmes, and critical realist research needs to avoid being limited to a one-sided affiliation to any one academic discipline – whether one of many psychologisms or one of many sociologisms. The Sostris and Bromley-by-Bow experiences – in both their strengths and their weaknesses – offer, I hope, some useful guides or at least material for reflection on how to proceed towards a research programme that might be called a fully Critical (and) Psycho-Societal Realism.

References

Apitzsch, U., and Inowlocki, L. (2000). "Biographical analysis: A 'German' School'?". in Chamberlayne, P., Bornat, J., and Wengraf, T. (eds.) *The Turn to Biographical Methods in Social Science: Comparative Issues and Examples*, London, Routledge.

Archer, M.S. (1995). *Realist Social Theory: The Morphogenetic Approach*, Cambridge, Cambridge University Press.

Archer, M.S. (2003). *Structure, Agency and the Internal Conversation*, Cambridge, Cambridge University Press.

Bhaskar, R. (1998). *The Possibility of Naturalism: A Philosophical Critique of the Contemporary Human Sciences*, 3rd edition, London, Routledge.

Burkitt, I. (2012). 'Emotional reflexivity: feeling, emotion and imagination in reflexive dialogues'. *Sociology*, vol. 45 (3).

Campbell, M and Gregor, F. (2002). *Mapping Social Relations: A Primer in Doing Institutional Ethnography*. Ontario, Garamond Press.

Cavalletto, G. (2007). *Crossing the Psycho-Social Divide: Freud, Weber, Adorno And Elias*. Hampshire, Ashgate Publishing.

Chamberlayne, P. (2002). 'Conclusions: social transitions and biographical work'. in Chamberlayne, P., Rustin, M., and Wengraf, T. (eds.) *Biography and social exclusion in Europe: experiences and life journeys*. Bristol: The Policy Press.

Chamberlayne, P., Bornat, J., and Wengraf, T. (eds.) (2000). *The Turn to Biographical Methods in Social Science: Comparative Issues and Examples*, London, Routledge.

Chamberlayne, P. and King, A. (2000). *Biographies of Carers in Britain and the Two Germanies*. London, Polity Press.

Chamberlayne P., and Rustin, M. (1999). *Final Report of the Sostris Project – from Biography to Social Policy*. London: Centre for Biography in Social Policy: University of East London.

Chamberlayne P., Rustin M., and Wengraf,T. (eds.) (2002). *Biography and Social Exclusion in Europe: Experiences and Life Journeys*. Bristol: The Policy Press.

DeVault, M., and McCoy, L. (2003). 'Institutional ethnography: using interviews to investigate ruling relations'. in J. Holstein and J. Gubrium (eds.) *Inside Interviewing: New Lenses, New Concerns*. Thousand Oaks: Sage Publications

Froggett, L. (2002). *Love, Hate and Welfare: Psychosocial Approaches to Policy and Practice*. Bristol, The Policy Press.

Froggett, L. and Wengraf, T. (2004). 'Interpreting interviews in the light of research team dynamics: study of Nila's biographic narrative', *International Journal of Critical Psychology* 10: 94-122.

Froggett, L., Chamberlayne, P., Buckner S., Wengraf, T. (2005). *Bromley by Bow Centre research and evaluation project: integrated practice – focus on older people. Project Report*. University of Central Lancashire.

Gramsci, A.(1971). *Selections from the Prison Notebooks*, Edited and translated by Quintin Hoare and Geoffrey Nowell Smith. London, Lawrence and Wishart.

Hoggett, P. (2008). 'What's in a hyphen? Reconstructing psychosocial studies'. in *Psychoanalysis, culture and society* Vol. 13, p. 379–384.

Hollway, W. (2004). 'Psycho-social methods'. Editorial, special issue of the *International Journal of Critical Psychology*, Vol.10.p.5-11.

Jolly, M. and Roseneil, S. (2012). 'Researching women's movements: an introduction to Femcit and Sisterhood and After', in *Women's Studies International Forum* 35, pp.125-8

Kuhn, T.S. (1962). *The Structure of Scientific Revolutions*. Chicago, University of Chicago Press.

Luxemburg, R. and Bukharin, N. (1972). *Imperialism and the Accumulation of Capital*, Edited with an introduction by Kenneth J. Tarbuck. Translated by Rudolf Wichmann, London, Allen Lane the Penguin Press.

Roseneil, S. (2012). 'Using biographical narrative and life story methods to research women's movements: FEMCIT', in *Women's Studies International Forum* 35, pp. 129-31.

Rustin, M., and Chamberlayne, P. (2002). 'Introduction'. in Chamberlayne, P., Rustin, M., and Wengraf, T. (eds.) *Biography and Social Exclusion in Europe: Experiences and Life Journeys*. Bristol, The Policy Press.

Sostris (1998-1999). *Sostris Working Papers* 1-9. London: Centre for Biography in Social Policy, University of East London, mostly available on-line from Centre for Narrative Research.

Wallerstein, I. (2004). *World-systems analysis: an introduction*. Duke University Press.

Wengraf, T. (2001). *Qualitative Research Interviewing: Biographic Narrative and Semi-Structured Methods*. London, Sage.

Wengraf, T. (2002). "Historicising the 'socio', theory, and the constant comparative method", in Chamberlayne, P., Rustin, M., and Wengraf, T. (eds.) *Biography and Social Exclusion in Europe: Experiences and Life Journeys*. Bristol, The Policy Press.

Wengraf, T. (2002). 'Biographical work and agency innovation: relationships, reflexivity, and theory-in-use'. in Chamberlayne, P., Rustin, M., and Wengraf, T. (eds.) *Biography and Social Exclusion in Europe: Experiences and Life Journeys*. Bristol, The Policy Press.

Wengraf, T. (2010). 'BNIM, agency and the psycho-societal'. Paper produced for the conference "Social agency. Theoretical and methodological challenges of the 21st century humanist sociology". Wrocław (unpublished manuscript), 24pp.

Wengraf, T. (2013). 'Krytyczny realizm i metoda psychospołeczna: badanie zmiennego sprawstwa za pomocą biograficzno-narracyjnej metody interpretacyjnej'. in: Mrozowicki, Adam, Nowaczyk Olga, Szlachcicowa, Irena (eds.) *Sprawstwo - teorie, metody, badania empiryczne w naukach społecznych*. Krakow: Zaklad Wydawniczy Nomos (forthcoming).

Wengraf, T. (2012-). *BNIM Short Guide and Detailed Manual*. Free electronic updated edition always available from tom@tomwengraf.com.

4. Biographical Costs of Transnational Mobility in the European Space

Antonella Spanò, Elisabetta Perone & Markieta Domecka

Introduction

There are some paradoxes connected with the processes of transnational mobility in Europe. On the one hand, they are actively promoted by the European bodies according to the logic of open European opportunity structure and, on the other hand, they lead to high biographical costs, which often may be underestimated. There are various types of biographical conditions leading to the decision of moving abroad; it could be the search for self-development and self-expression, transcending the ascribed gender roles, professional advancement, escaping financial difficulties or traumatic family situations, desire to live with a partner coming from a different country and many others. Seizing the opportunity to leave a problematic context of life may lead to biographical metamorphosis, where individuals encounter and explore something essentially new in their social world and their biographical identity (Schütze, 2008a: 23). Bringing the change, however, metamorphosis is also a potential limbo situation, where the old worldview and the feeling of self are lost and the new ones have not been developed yet. Having analysed over two hundred[1] of autobiographical narrative interviews with people living transnational lives and using now the illustration of three different cases, we want to show how crucial it is, while analysing European transnational mobility, to take into account the subjective processes of reflexivity and biographical work in order to understand what happens with individuals when they move in geographical, cultural and social space. The three cases by no means exhaust all the varieties of transnational life courses but they

---

[1] In the Euroidentities Project we have collected and analysed 230 autobiographical narrative interviews within the following sensitized groups: Transnational Workers, Educationally Mobile, Farmers, Civil Society Organizations, Cultural Contacts and Intimate Relationships. The elements of transnationalism were present in all these groups with the exception of Farmers. Working on this chapter we focused mainly on the 60 interviews conducted in UK and Italy. The three cases presented here are young women of Italian origin sharing the cultural background (including tightly prescribed gender roles and family obligations) but at the same time differing in terms of type and amount of possessed resources and dominant mode of reflexivity.

are emblematic and contrastive examples showing the role of qualitatively and quantitatively distinct resources for becoming active or inactive agents in the process of transnational mobility. The answer to the question of what people make out of the European opportunity structure should also contribute to the development of more comprehensive and better tailored European social policy.

Building on the tradition of critical realism (Archer, Bhaskar et al., 1998) we analyse transnational mobility in the European social space as the interplay of structural conditions, shaped among others by the European free movement policy, and actions stemming from intentions and biographical projects of human subjects. Mobility may be a factor enforcing or hindering the biographical process of becoming an active agent, which is directly connected with the dominant type of reflexivity practised. Following Archer, we understand reflexivity as an intrinsic property of human beings. It is the exercise of mental ability shared by all people to consider themselves in relation to their social contexts and vice versa (Archer, 2007: 4). It is "the mental activity which, in private, leads to self-knowledge: about what to do, what to think and what to say" (Archer, 2003: 26). It is reflexivity which makes active agents who are able to exercise some governance in their lives; who develop and define their ultimate concerns, elaborate projects and attempt to accomplish them in order to advance or protect what they care about most (Archer, 2007: 7). Reflexivity practiced through internal conversation does tasks for people that "could not be accomplished in any other way" (Archer, 2012: 14). On the grounds of biographical research this inner activity is referred to as biographical work – ongoing reconsidering of one's life, one's inner states and one's overall personal identity (cf. Schütze, 2008a: 6). It is this type of work which is done by autobiographical recollection and reflection about alternative interpretations of one's life course. These are self-critical attempts of understanding one's own misconceptions of oneself and self-erected impediments as well as the impediments imposed by others and by structural conditions. Biographical work also involves imagining future courses of action that support the overall biographical identity (Schütze, 2008a: 6). Biographical work, constituted by conversation with significant others and oneself, goes hand in hand with reflexivity and internal conversation as defined by Archer (2003; 2007).

Biographical costs of transnational mobility

Presenting the three cases below, we will demonstrate that the intensity of biographical work done in situations of transnationalisation is directly related to the biographical costs involved. The less biographical work is practised, the higher are the social, occupational and biographical costs of mobility. We may mention here emotional costs, like the suffering connected with separation, problems with adaptation and loosening of emotional bonds, as well as professional costs, where it is discovered that the opportunities at home country have been lost, and the prospects abroad are not as promising as they seemed to be. There is also the phenomenon of marginality (Park, 1928) involved, where belonging both to the place of origin and the place of residence becomes problematic, accompanied by the overall feeling of 'being a foreigner everywhere' and the process of becoming a stranger (Simmel, 1908), an eternal wanderer.

In the three scenarios of transnational mobility, which are by no means exhaustive, we will show how mobility becomes the main structuring principle of one's biography with the pendulum movement of leaving and coming back only to leave again. On the surface, there may be an appearance of the autonomous type of reflexivity as people make an effort to present themselves as self-directed individuals. In fact, however, their life is not developed to any design as they are mainly directed by their emotional needs they are not fully aware of. In such cases, the destination is not really important. Anywhere is good enough as long as it brings the illusion that by moving they change their lives, solve their problems and get a chance to be happier (cf. De Botton, 2002). We will also demonstrate how especially high are the biographical costs of mobility in the case of fractured reflexives (Archer, 2003), being completely unable to formulate any biographical projects and consistent scheme of action. Restraining themselves from taking decisions does not mean that people do not suffer the consequences of the decisions taken by others or the consequences of structural conditioning.

The desire to move abroad is often a part of an escaping strategy (Spanò et al., 2011). Individuals feel forced to leave certain family dynamics, where strictly prescribed gender roles, unequal treatment of siblings, addictions, health problems, conflicts leading to separation and divorce result in a trajectory of suffering. Feeling torn apart and trying to avoid taking sides in family conflicts, people leave. The decision to move abroad is potentially a biographical turning point and indeed, in many cases, it brings the conditions for biographical metamorphoses. It is thus surprising that this crucial decision may be experienced by some people as no change at all. This is Rita's case, presented below, who says that her life "is always the same"; devoid of plans, dreams and aspirations, no matter where she happens to live. This resembles the case of fractured reflexivity, as described by Archer (2003; 2007), where people are unable to conclude upon a certain course of action; they go around in circles, which only serves to augment their disorientation and distress. Fractured reflexives are passive agents in a sense that they are "people whose subjectivity makes no difference to the play of objective circumstances upon them" (Archer, 2003: 299). Their internal conversation performs no mediatory role and permits no intentional relationship between self and society (Archer, 2003: 300). Being 'passive' does not mean 'cease acting', which in a social world is hardly possible. It rather means deprivation of any interior control and exposition to the vicissitudes of the external environment (Archer, 2003: 301). The relationship between self and society is marked by disorientation. Fractured reflexives are disoriented about their concerns and about the ways to realise them. Thus, instead of leading to purposeful courses of action, their self-talk is primarily expressive. The main concentration is on the proximate and the short term. They develop an attitude of "taking things as they come".

The European opportunity structure has the potential of exerting a powerful influence on individuals, who actively interpret and make use of the possibilities provided. It has been observed (Spanò et al., 2011), however, that the possibility of developing a transnational life and the unfolding of an individual action scheme depends on previous experiences and their reflexive elaboration on the one hand, and on the other, on the set of resources, both material and immaterial, at one's disposal. The biographical outcome of mobility depends precisely on the combination of these elements.

Three scenarios of transnational mobility

1. Cinzia, a pendulum movement in search of belonging

Cinzia is a 29 year old woman from a middle class Neapolitan family with a brother slightly younger than her. Her biographical pathway is characterised by an evident trend towards transnational mobility that is in fact presented, right from the start of the interview, almost like an innate characteristic:

> "My desire to leave, to travel, to know new cultures, is something that anyway is really inside me."

Following her narrative it becomes clear that behind her desire for movement there is a difficult family history, which must have been a source of dissatisfaction/discomfort if not of actual suffering. Of course what has been crucial is the competition/jealousy with her brother, who is presented as a person in need of care, because of his fragile character:

> "He is… the opposite of me in these things let's say, he has never moved away from home, he has always you know been here at home, a much calmer person, in fact sometimes my mum says the character that my brother has precisely the character I should have because she says it's not possible that he… Perhaps now yes, now

he has grown up, now he works so also he you know he is grown up but some years ago he was anyway you know the shy one and she used to say, 'but is it possible that you have the character your sister is supposed to have?'."

We have to take into account that Cinzia's family history is also influenced by cultural models typical of the Southern Italian context, where the greater attention is given to male children, usually not only the object of a great investment – both in economic terms and in terms of expectations – but also greater 'care', especially on the part of the mother, because they are deemed little suited to carrying out the functions of daily life. Forced to cope with this unequal gender model Cinzia reacts by structuring her identity through just pointing upon the characteristics positively valued in her milieu. Risk, courage and independence, that usually represent the distinctive features of masculinity, become for Cinzia the test of her presence in the world, but above all, of her 'value' in the eyes of the family, the distinguishing mark which gives her visibility and recognition. Indeed, just coming of age and leaving secondary school, Cinzia decided to go to live for a period of time in London. From an emotional point of view, this decision can be seen as a 'challenge' to her parents. We can hypothesize that it wasn't permission to leave that Cinzia was expecting but an objection, which would have shown her the affection and attachment of her parents towards her. It is worth noting that Cinzia has never understood the big contradiction between the care shown from her parents when they prevented her from enrolling the art lyceum because of the too 'open' mentality of this school, and the extreme easiness with which they allowed her to leave.

> "OK, I'll do languages and in fact I do languages however, then at eighteen they let me leave, they accepted this thing, perhaps I don't know they thought that during the five years ((*smile*)) I might change my mind and on the other hand, I remember perfectly how I started the fifth year of senior school you know I was thinking a little about the best way to get away."

Cinzia's desire to leave was directly related to the disappointment with her family environment. She was a potential communicative reflexive but she lacked interlocutors in her native context. She longed for acceptance and belonging, and since that need could not be satisfied either at home or in her peer group, she wanted to search for it elsewhere. Her decision to leave was also a certain kind of test that Cinzia's parents failed. Their 'yes' has given rise to a feeling of abandonment which later has shaped the perverse mechanism of departure-return which characterizes Cinzia's life and that so far has not come to a stop.

Her tendency to leave, in fact, is clearly linked to the difficulty she has in finding a congruous position inside the family. Indeed, once returned home she started to work as an entertainer in holiday resorts: a new way she found to stay away from home. Cinzia's moving doesn't appear driven by professional reasons (to go away towards something) but by the need to leave (to go away from). The encounter with a young Dutch man at the tourist resort where she worked constitutes the opportunity to reinforce her 'coming and going strategy'; in fact, the decision to follow him to the Netherlands represents a new 'good reason' to go away, as she herself says:

> "And there I meet my reason for staying four years in Holland, because I spent four years in Holland ((*smile*)), in reality, OK, I met this boy and in the end I decided – I hadn't known him long – I said I'm leaving for Holland".

Though Cinzia attributes her desire to move to her sense of independence, analysing her autobiographical story more in-depth it appears evident that what is more decisive in the developing of her pathway is the need of 'belonging' to a community, if not of an actual 'adoption'. We can find traces of this not only in the events of Cinzia's life – marked by repeated departures and returns aiming at finding her place – but also in her narrative. Recalling the first time abroad, that is to say the period when she lived in London, she says, for example:

> "Abroad all the people who are not from that nation become your family. It is something really nice."

Her need to find a family becomes even clearer in the excerpt which describes her relationship with her Dutch boyfriend's family, which quickly became for her a substitute for her own family.

> "With the family with whom I stayed for three years I was treated better than a daughter because anyway he just had a brother so for them, for his mum and dad I was the daughter they'd never had, welcomed into the home immediately."

The prevalence of the emotional issues in the case of Cinzia is confirmed by the fact that, independently from having a good permanent job in a major airline company in the Netherlands, at a certain point she decides to return to Italy because of two events both occurred in the sphere of affects: the breakup of the sentimental relationship with the Dutch partner and the death of her father. Her return home, however, wouldn't last long. Once again Cinzia cannot find her place in the family; so, after a while, she chooses to work on cruise ships, therefore putting into action again a pattern based on distancing from home. Also at the end of this work experience she will faithfully reproduce the same pattern, firstly going back to live for a period in Holland, where she hopes in vain to reconstruct the past familial climate; and later moving for a short period to a small town in Ireland, where unfortunately again she cannot feel that sense of belonging to a group she aspired to. In the end, although at the time of the interview Cinzia would seem to be in a stable phase, considering that she has been living in Naples for one year working as a shipping agent with a permanent contract, there are clues of potential new journeys:

> "And so well who knows when the next experience will be? Because as I say it's something that I still have inside, a thing that maybe I've always done (…) this is a thing that I've always had inside me and then anyway it was confirmed by the fact that you start the first experiences, if you like it…. There's nothing you can do about it ((*smiling*))."

It is clear that at a certain point mobility became the structuring principle of Cinzia's biography. By creating a spatial distance, mobility represents for her the means to explain her painful sense of non-belonging to anywhere, as appears from her own words:

> "I realise every now and then that I have become a vagabond without destination ((*smile*)) (…) when you have experiences, especially such long ones, they are wonderful but horrible at the same time because you no longer feel at home anywhere; it's a continual wandering in the end ((smile))."

Cinzia's biography may be an example of impeded communicative reflexivity. Not being able to find caring interlocutors in her native context, she leaves only to come back again in hope to find acceptance and love. When it is not possible, she leaves once more, for a different place, where she finds for a while a type of family she had longed for. As soon as the new arrangement turns out to be too fragile to be maintained over time, she leaves yet again, searching for a way to satisfy her need to belong. The costs of her 'coming and going strategy' clearly appear at two different levels: the emotional-relational level and the professional level. Concerning the emotional sphere it is evident that leaving so young caused an emotional break, whose consequence is a hardening of relationships within the family: the relations both with mother and brother appear at the moment complicated, while the opportunity to get in touch with her father is irremediably lost because of his premature death. As for the professional aspect, the price that Cinzia pays is no less significant. Since her mobility has constantly been driven by a need to move away, Cinzia has not been interested in her professional growth: the outcome is the lack of a career with defined boundaries. Indeed, not only her current job (shipping agent) does not have any connection with her study of languages, but her whole work experience seems to be a sort of patchwork of experiences without any coherence.

2. Rita: mobility bringing no change[2]

Rita was born 40 years ago in a small town in Southern Italy. She comes from a family of the lower middle class, both her parents work as office workers in the public administration. Also in Rita's case we find a painful situation in the family at the origin of her history. Her parents work all the day, and during her childhood she spends a lot of time alone: in fact, her two sisters were born long after, being 8 and 11 years younger than her respectively. Her solitary wait for her mother's coming back from work, staying at a window overlooking the void, represents the vivid image of her deep sense of solitude:

> "There is something that often comes back to me, anyway the fact that I who was often at home, I mean I was almost always alone at home because my mum couldn't afford a baby sitter, my relatives didn't live near and she often left me alone and I was always in my room looking outside waiting for my mum [...] I clearly remember this standing in front of the window fantasizing, I mean really amazing imagination, you know? And looking outside without looking at the people because there were no buildings in front, at the time there was still a plot of land, and in distance there was a building so I would look at the road and wait for my mum."

The birth of her sisters on the one side marks the end of her loneliness but on the other signs the beginning of a new difficulty. Rita, in fact, too early finds herself charged with the responsibility of looking after them; she plays the role of a maternal substitute, so that the children call her "mummy". Her mother, meanwhile, has to take full care of the family ménage, without any valid support from her husband:

---

[2] Originally this case interpretation had been written by Pasquale Musella, member of the Italian team of Euroidentities Project, who participated in the joint analysis and co-presented the first version of the paper at the ESA Conference in Nuremberg in September 2010.

> "Then [my father was] very careful with money, I mean also because of this we had a life of sacrifices, because my mum had to pay for everything. I mean he worked and put money aside to buy a house, my mum had to pay the bills, buy books, clothes, I mean with one salary and three children, you know, you cannot... You can't treat yourself, give your children pocket money, in fact I never got pocket money neither did my sisters."

The relationships with her parents are not satisfying. Rita's father is in fact a strict man, worried about the judgment of other people; he is not only an authoritarian figure, always commanding and controlling everything, but also a frustrating person, inclined to prevent and block any desire of the children. Rita feels observed and judged by him continuously:

> "Yes and then anyway I mean... we didn't do much, we weren't... precisely because of my father, you see? Just think, my father never gave us... he never wanted us to have a bicycle, I mean the town I mean our house had a courtyard where we could play anyway and well I learned to ride a bicycle really late and one of my sisters can't even now precisely because my father forbade so many things."

In her present perspective it is her father who is the cause of her deep and persistent lack of self-esteem.

> "I am a person with zero self-esteem and I think that it already began at that time I mean also... in my opinion also my father had to do with it a little, this fear of making a mistake and then inevitably you make a mistake. I mean, I still remember... fifteen years ago more or less we were somewhere in the countryside doing something, I had to do something and he stood there looking at me and in my opinion he was looking to see if I made a mistake, I was so terrified I made a mistake."

As for her mother, Rita feels the weight of having had to replace her in the maternal role. Moreover, still now she reproaches her tendency to play the role of a victim; a tendency that Rita believes she has inherited from her:

> "In my mum there is a side that I don't particularly like and that I recognize also in me and perhaps it's precisely for this reason that I don't like, I mean this thing that... I mean this lack of... I

> don't know… for example your relatives do something to you and you rather than say openly I don't like it, she comes up with some 'witty' remarks saying "oh yes, I am always wrong" this is a thing which always really annoys me, I mean when she does it with me I really become a beast because… Are we talking about something in particular? Don't come out with an expression like "everything I say is wrong"! When I hear this kind of words I really get angry! Eh… and I'm a bit like this, I don't say that but when I'm a bit nervous I feel that the world hates me, that no-one wants me, that no-one loves me."

Finally, also Rita's relationships with the external world (teachers and classmates) are problematic: in particular, her living at home as an adult makes being and feeling part of the group of the peers difficult for her.

The difficult aspects of her childhood and adolescence, in particular those connected to the female gender role, seem to have fostered in Rita the need to build a different model of femininity. The way adopted in order to achieve her desire to be a kind of women distinct from her mother, has been leaving her small town of origin. After she finishes school, in fact, Rita begins a pattern of biographical action in order to distance herself from her town. During the years spent at the linguistic high school she began to love the study of foreign languages, so she decided to move to a big city, Naples, and to enrol at the university, where she specialised in Russian. Rita at that point, deciding to leave her natal context behind in search for a new model of life is an autonomous reflexive in making. The arrival in Naples represents therefore a flight towards a broadening of her horizons (a kind of 'escaping towards'). Her life as a student away from home is enhanced by an unprecedented freedom. Away from the narrow-minded mentality of her town, paternal authoritarianism, maternal victim attitude, and the responsibility of having to look after her sisters, Rita can finally become what she really feels to be, live her age, behaving like any other student. Among other things, the positive value of those years is accentuated by the fact that Rita experiences a completely new and different self-image, as her new friends seem to accept and appreciate her ideas and her way of being. These new significant others therefore represent an important mirror (just like Cooley's theory of the looking-glass self, 1902), as they send back a positive image of her:

> "I remember one of the first things is that I was at home with friends and they were people even apparently completely different from those I had mixed with up to that moment, there were people who played music, who loved punk, who smoked joints,

right? Erm... and they were people different from me anyway but I mean I didn't feel different from these people... Erm... the thing is that I liked those people, I considered them very interesting and I remember that one of my first thoughts that one day I expressed an opinion if I'm not mistaken it was actually on a piece of music but not simply I like it I don't like it, but a real opinion with reasons I like it because blah blah blah and clearly all messed up as I am, I'm an idiot, I'm saying God knows what, when I saw the reaction of these people who were listening to me and didn't make me feel stupid I said well then... what I think isn't all wrong! I mean, it was a comparison with another reality, with a reality completely different from that of my school friends at senior school or acquaintances in town."

Over the years, her strategy of escape towards a more open environment started to show the first signs of giving way. Rita in fact remains enrolled at university for many years, going on very slowly in her studies: she knows that her life in Naples as a student away from home could not last forever. It is in this phase of her life that Thomas, who represents an essential element for continuing the biographical action pattern started many years before, comes on to the scene. Very soon Thomas, a German artist who moved to Naples some years before, becomes the fulcrum of Rita's life. It is thanks to him that she finds a reason to stay some more years in Naples after graduation; it's through him that she discovers an artistic vein she had no idea about till they met. The potential to take the form of an autonomous or a reflexive somehow throughout the years becomes more difficult to realize. Rita does not ask herself what she really needs and wants in her life. She does not plan her career nor shows any other concerns. She starts going adrift becoming more and more dependent on her partner.

After spending another year in Naples they decide to move to Berlin, a city better suited to their ambitions in the artistic field, where they are still living in a multi-ethnic and Bohemian quarter. In Berlin Rita must start all over again. She is not able to make use of the languages she had learned over the years at school and university. She also has some problems to learn German. Under these conditions Rita's work situation – after five years spent in Berlin – is rather problematic. Her work in the artistic field makes little or nothing in financial terms, and she is forced to do occasional and poorly paid jobs. Moreover, the social capital accumulated in the past also reduces because her best friends live in Naples. In fact, Rita does not have any life projects other than those Thomas has for her. Indeed, she is quite dependent on him: she has not learnt good German, she does not earn enough, and furthermore she is not able to move autonomously in the artistic world:

> "He has always had this conviction that I am an artist I mean he believes in me, in my opinion I think he believes more in me than in himself, I mean he always says that I know perfectly what I want, I don't believe it though I mean for me to have him near to advise me on proportions, on the combination of colours, I mean when I work I never close a file because I work with photomontages so they are always digital data, I never close it, I never say this work is finished if first he hasn't said okay, okay."

We could even say that if apparently Thomas has been the one to carry out her project of moving from the periphery (her place of origin) to the centre (Berlin), in reality he represented for her a decisive reversal of her course, if not a real regression. In fact, the encounter with Thomas plunged her back into the condition of a daughter, this time of a supportive and caring father as she never had. Therefore, the transfer from Naples to Berlin turns out to be an involuntary turning back compared with the Neapolitan period.

Both Rita's initial aims to realize a more evolved gender model and to become an adult (in the sense of active agent) failed, mainly because of her dependence on her partner. But at the moment she does not appear ready to make an assessment of her life: she does not see the fragility of her condition of dependence on Thomas, her lack of self-esteem, the absence of a credible perspective of becoming part of the Berliner art world. In the interpretation she gives of her current situation she tends to brush over difficulties and to accept her condition of economic marginality in return for serenity that Berlin offers her:

> "In reality you know my life is almost... is always the same I mean, a life of... I mean I don't have expectations you see? I'm not one to go to the cinema every week, dancing, out every evening so with what little I earn, that's fine, it's the quality of life I like I mean I'm relaxed, there is no-one stressing you, you're not afraid to walk down the street alone."

The idea of returning to her home town or to Naples is not feasible since, in each case, Rita would have to deal with places which she strongly wanted to move away from. The trap she fell into is therefore a condition of paralysis, in the sense that she can neither go forward nor back. In Rita's case, as in Cinzia's one, we can see how mobility does not necessarily correspond to a deep metamorphosis of personal and social identity, and how it can actually feed further distortions in the biographical development, if negative elements such as the lack of self-esteem remain or are even reinforced in the new context. Moreover, Rita's case reveals that mobility may lead to a zeroing of both the skills obtained and the social networks built at home, especially if moving abroad is interpreted as a watershed, an element of radical discontinuity between the past and the present. We can also see how in the case of women, even with a high level of education, transition from more traditional towards more modern contexts does not necessarily equate to a journey of emancipation. Moving from an area of the periphery to the outskirts of the centre can give rise, as for Rita, to a condition of marginalisation where people can neither turn back nor manage to make room for themselves in the new society. The fact Rita has no more expectations, no plans or dreams, shows she has developed into a fractured reflexive.

3. Nevia: mobility as a condition for biographical metamorphosis

Nevia, a 29-year-old woman, comes from a social milieu very different from the ones of Rita and Cinzia. Born in a big city in the Centre-Northern part of Italy, she grew up in a privileged, upper-middle class family. Even in her case, however, there is a great fragility due to a difficult family situation. Nevia, in fact, has been a victim of the processes of deinstitutionalization of family, and above all of two people – her father and mother – who have separated not only as husband and wife, but also as parents, and for this reason, have subjected Nevia to all sorts of traumatic experiences.

Nevia's father is an unstable man who (being previously married with children) leaves his second family (Nevia, her mother and her younger sister) for another woman after only three years of marriage. Due to this fact Nevia has to pass through numerous experiences of abandonment and separation, as well as numerous moves. After the separation, in fact, the family firstly moves to another Northern town, where the paternal grandparents live, and later to a smaller town, which was the home of her maternal grandparents. Her father moves close to a big city in another region and only rarely comes to see his daughters. While the first two transfers were not particularly traumatic, as the family – even without her father – maintained its integrity ("I think it was still a happy moment of life", she says), the next move was absolutely traumatic: at the age of 11, without any explanation except that their mother was no longer capable of looking after the children, Nevia together with her sister has to move to their father's house.

> "I don't remember seeing him a lot and I don't know what he was doing but all of sudden one day he came and he kind of said, oh well, you know, -ehm- I talked to -eh- kind of the local NHS and -eh- we don't think that your mum can make it with you so you're coming to stay with me. OK ((*laughing*)). So basically one day, I don't know, my sister and I we leave and we go to live

with my dad, who for me at the time was kind of like a total -eh- foreign ((*laughing*))".

While Nevia coped with the separation from her father by strengthening her emotional tie with her mother, she responds to the confusion caused by the sudden separation from her by constructing an apparent situation of stability in her new pseudo-family (her father, new his partner and her daughter), and specially by becoming deeply attached to her father and hostile to her mother, even more when Nevia hears that she started to live with a new partner.

"So -eh- I wasn't happy with her, I was very jealous about my mum and I didn't like thinking that -ehm- she was living with another man... The whole thing I really didn't like, it was very, -ehm- if you like he was with my mum, which I didn't have a lot of contact and stuff."

In fact, the irresponsibility of her parents – who constantly accused each other without thinking of the consequences on the children – sets off in Nevia a pattern of 'emotional pendulum', which consists in turning to one of the two parents in response to an experience of abandonment or betrayal on the part of the other. When her father decides to move to the United States, Nevia is not prepared to lose her relative stability by going back to her mother, who, as she feels, had rejected her. Therefore, she decides to go with him, unlike her younger sister, who prefers to go back to live with her mum and her new partner. During the time spent in Texas, Nevia (who meanwhile discovered that she has insulin dependent diabetes) strengthens her attachment to her new family, and her step-sister, who is almost the same age and who finds herself facing the same problems with adaptation.

"So, I don't know, I think it was two years where basically -ehm- I was more a family type of person, I relied a lot on the family... I mean I get along with everybody, I did get along with -ehm- Elena as my, who was my dad's partner ((*laughing*)) -ehm- and then there was Sara, she was a year older than me, so I think we were very close at that time because we were going to the high school together and we had to face a lot of, you know, problems with the school".

Therefore two years later, back in Italy, the option of going back to her mum, who now has a family with her second husband, her sister Alessandra, and a new baby, is something that Nevia does not even consider. Now she feels she can fix her roots: she starts doing well at school and makes new friends. Moreover, Nevia encounters her 'super love' and his family, which in some way 'adopted' her.

> "And then finally in the fifth year it was okay... And, yeah, I met, I made good friends -ehm- even if it was just two years of basically high school in Italy at the end. I made good friends because they were all -ehm- it was very -ehm- close to where I live and so I met a lot of people who I had also met when I was doing my -ehm- middle school... Plus that year when I finished basically high school -ehm- I met this guy and ((*sighing*)) basically he was my super first love ((*laughing*))... If I had to look in the past and say, what was the best time of your life? I think university and the friends that I met there and going out with this guy, I think it was all very, very good, And I also got really, really close to -ehm- his family, he had -erm-, I think he had the perfect family, the one that I didn't think I had... really they were treating me like I was their daughter".

It is once again the father who threatens the equilibrium that Nevia has so painstakingly built. In fact he decides to divorce his new wife, who moves to another city: so, Nevia loses the woman who for years has been taking care of her, her daughter who had became a sister to her, and the little sister born of the remarriage of his father. Nevia tries with all her might to preserve her private life and to maintain the stability of her family, by taking up the role of a wife:

> "My dad was alone, so he was there, you know, imagine alone, super selfish person -ehm- big Italian man like he wouldn't be able to cook something, anything. So kind of, I was doing, I was kind of taking care of him because I felt a bit sorry and, you know, I was the lady in the house, which you might say that. So I mean he had somebody helping out with the cleaning and everything but I was cooking and, you know, doing shopping together and so I was spending a lot of time with him."

Just like a wife, she feels betrayed when her father begins to look for a new (Eastern European) partner on the Internet, when he begins to travel often to meet women 'selected' on the computer screen, and when he even brings some of them home, to 'try them out' in living together. Nevia feels done out of her role of 'lady of the house', and above all betrayed by her father, who puts the needs of his partner of the day before those of his daughter:

> "And, I don't know, I remember I was coming back in the evening from uni and I was going in the kitchen, you know, started to cook something because they were doing nothing. And, and I opened, you know, the cupboard in the kitchen and everything was like, you know, they fell over. Things had been moved around and I was like, (dad) did you move the stuff? Oh, you know, I think she did that because, you know, she wants to feel a bit at home… it was really frustrating because I wasn't doing anything, I wasn't doing anything bad. I was living in my own place but not feeling like I was in my own place and most of it my dad was not saying anything… he wouldn't say –eh- you should be nice to Nevia, he didn't care."

Once again Nevia reacts by re-activating the 'emotional pendulum': now the pole of attraction becomes her mother, whom she starts to visit very often during the weekends. But this time, made stronger by the security she acquired in the last years, she changes course, and rather than return to stay with her mother, she initiates a new path that will take her to choose her life and the place to live, not as a victim of others' decisions, but as the protagonist of her own choices. The first step is leaving on an Erasmus programme, a very relevant experience for the development of her biography. The nine months spent in France, in fact, prove to her that, rather than asking for love and inner security from outside, she is capable of building them up on her own:

> "For me it was really the first time, oh gosh I'm living away from home, not with my dad, and it was a very relaxing -eh- experience. I always stay with the same guy I was going out with in Milan and I managed to break through that year but it was, I was so happy and I really liked the school there and everything. So it was very good/."

The second step is, once returned in Italy, going to live on her own. Her new situation of personal stability resists when her father – who through Internet met a new girl and decided to marry her – tells her that he is going to work in the Far East for a number of years with his new (fourth) wife and even when her beloved boyfriend, after almost eight years of relationship, leaves her. This new abandonment represents a totally destructive event for Nevia, as she had found in him a male figure that was not only the antithesis but also a substitute of her father:

> "-Eh- he was (studying) psychologist… So it was the first time that I met a person that was really listening to me and -eh- I could really talk to him."

Nevertheless, she does not fall into the temptation of returning to live with her mother ("I didn't go back to live with my mum because it was always kind of a bit too late and, you know, I didn't need her, as she says") and continues her way towards autonomy by beginning to work. It is now that Nevia undertakes a moratorium period in which she experiences, perhaps for the first time, a lifestyle not driven by control (a disposition without doubt accentuated by her disease, which compels her to a measured and careful lifestyle):

> "And another friend of mine she'd been dumped as well basically the same time, so it was (better). I thought (??) because I was kind of, the way I would behave before and probably when you have a boyfriend you go out a bit less compared to friends that are single. And my God that year, you know, was crazy, I think I was going to work, going out after work for aperitif and then going out again, I was basically coming home at midnight, waking up at six to go to work".

After one year, Nevia takes the third step of her journey towards becoming, in Archer's terms, an autonomous reflexive. She decides to leave and this time moving is her own decision ("It wasn't often my true, true choice… So this time I really, I got rid of any influences on anything"). The destination is London, "a comfortable place to stay" and to start what she calls "a new era" of her life. Taking distance allows Nevia to look at her past with new eyes. Today she is able to assign to each his or her part of the responsibility for what happened, also to herself: unlike her sister, who refused to transfer to America, she fell victim to her father's lies about her mother.

Though the biographical work she did thanks to mobility allowed Nevia to – at least partially – reconcile with her past, she is now paying the price by being far from her loved ones, and with the regret which derives from this.

> "My sister basically she didn't listen to what my dad was saying and she kind of kept going with her own -eh- thought just not listening and not thinking… But at the time I was very, I was very close to him and not too close to my mum, so I thought, oh, you know, let's go…. and my sister she -ehm- she totally said, no. So it's fine because she was like the younger sister and she said, no, me I'm not going -eh- to the US with dad, I want to go back with mum… and that's when we basically started to -ehm- we had two different lives, two very different lives, because I basically went with my dad and she went with my mum."

In her present perspective everyone can be understood: her abandoning mother who now is none other than a woman who in a difficult period of depression found herself deprived of her children; the boyfriend who left her is seen now only as a boy she asked too much help without giving anything in return. The only person still to blame is her father, responsible for the loss of her mother's affection, for the break up with her boyfriend, since it has been the suffering caused by her father which brought her "to dump on him all the stress", and even for her diabetes, which she imputes to the big shock of being separated from her mum.

Now Nevia is ready to shift her emotional focus from her family of origin to the one she feels able to create. Malcolm, her new English partner with whom she began living, is the opposite of her father: stable, helpful, attentive to her needs; with him Nevia lives a symmetrical duality, and with him she shares her plans for the future, including the idea of leaving London, which for her "is like probably a beginning" and perhaps of getting back closer to her mother and her sister. For Nevia it is finally possible to come back.

> "Malcolm is learning Italian now so he's really... So that's a good start because, you know, it might be an option. I don't say no, I mean, I'd be super happy to go to Italy if there was a more decent job situation. That's the only thing that holds me from going back now but I'd be super happy to go back home, maybe this time near my mum. Why not? ((*Laughing*)) So, that's it."

Conclusions

Summing up the cases presentation we would like to state once more that the outcomes of transnational mobility depend on the possessed resources and the level of self-reflexivity, or in other terms, biographical work. The amount of different types of capital is crucial but if it is not accompanied by the ability to make use of them, it does not bring expected advantages. This scenario is clearly visible in the case of Rita, who lacking self-confidence and convinced by her partner about her artistic vain, is not able to make use of her previously attained cultural resources. In this case, the inability to use capital is also connected with low level of aspirations. The false assumptions about one's possibilities are equally dangerous when, as again in case of Rita, they are too low (much lower than the actual capabilities defined by resources) and when, encouraged by the discourse of unlimited opportunities, they are too high, ignoring the constraints imposed by social conditions. The case of Rita also shows that mobility does not necessarily correspond to a deep metamorphosis of personal and social identity development, and actually it can create the prerequisites to feed further distortions in the biographical work.

Mobility may become the main structuring principle in one's biography, as we saw in case of Cinzia. It is not anymore a means to achieve, to escape, or to discover, but it becomes an end in itself. People may move in space without any sense of direction, any ultimate purpose, trapped in a 'flight with no way out', disconnected from places and from other people, becoming "a vagabond without a destination". The price one pays for it is the loss of home. The ties with the family of origin become weaker, as one feels excluded from the shared problems, worries and joys building up family life; and the chance to start one's own family in the course of time becomes smaller. Settling down in one place for a longer period of time is problematic as the best known reality is the reality of moving. There are also professional costs paid as a result of transnational mobility. What is supposed to be an open opportunity structure in some cases turns out to be an occupational trap. Mobility promises occupational advancement, as in the European space supposedly it is possible to search for jobs in all labour markets and to construct freely one's career. However, the autonomous construction is possible only when people have many different types of resources at their disposal. Those who do not possess economic, cultural and social capital, are much more limited in their choices and instead of successful, highly specialised constructions, they build patchwork careers, consisting of different kinds of jobs, available at a certain time and place, which then do not form any coherent pattern and do not lead to any significant occupational advancement. The existing opportunity structure is not equally accessible to everybody. For those who do not possess significant resources or are not able to make use of them, European mobility brings a danger of a biographical and professional trap. As we could see in the cases of Cinzia and Rita, mobility not only did not level down the initial inequalities, but it multiplied them.

Transnational mobility may bring the conditions for biographical metamorphosis, leading to the development of autonomous or meta-reflexivity, as we saw in the case of Nevia, but also for biographical trap, as clearly visible in the Cinzia and Rita cases. Deciding to move people may, paradoxically, search for stability and continuity in their lives, acceptance and belonging, which they missed in their place of origin. There is some hope involved that the new environment will bring them what they need most: a new family and new purpose in life. It may turn out, however, that instead of a better and more fulfilling life, they find themselves blocked, unable to move forward or to go back. For the difficulties in one place, moving to another place seems to be a remedy, but it is only an apparent solution as soon it is discovered that moving, when not accompanied by biographical work, leads only to further marginality. We observe here that the

Matthew effect is as strong as ever, privileging those who initially have been well equipped in different kinds of material, symbolic and biographical resources.

As observed before (Spanò et al., 2012) "the process of integration does not distribute its beneficial effects in the same way to everyone. The traditional factors of inequality at the individual level (gender, level of education, social class) and the societal level (the different positions of countries in the 'hierarchy' existing between the Member States along the North-South geographical axis, and the temporal one, Old and New) still play a determining role". It is equally important to look at people's reflexivity in order to understand what kind of experience European mobility is for them. As the analysis of different cases of transnational mobility has demonstrated, except the usually taken into account types of resources, like economic, social and cultural capital, biographical work leading to higher self-awareness and facilitating the definition of one's ultimate concerns, is itself a resource of great value. As Archer rightly stated, "the imperative to be reflexive is becoming categorical for all" (Archer, 2012: 1). Therefore the outcomes of the process of mobility and transnationalisation in Europe directly depend on the efforts individuals put in reflexive elaboration concerning their previous experiences, their position in the world and the possible courses of action they can undertake in the changing context.

Biographical costs of mobility, though real, cannot be defined *apriori*, apart from the actual experience. The analysis of biographical conditions leading to mobility and the later costs this decision entails opens up a new perspective for the policy makers. Most of the social policies issued until now have addressed individuals on the move without taking into consideration the conditions leading to mobility and the difficult processes of adaptation and potential later homecoming. The promotion of European transnationalism has been so far one-sided, stressing the positive aspects of mobility and passing over possible risks and traps. As in all social processes, there is a darker side also in the case of transnational mobility, which should be stressed as well, allowing it to enter the public discourse and social awareness. Social policies should not be limited to the structural level only. Creating opportunities to move freely in Europe is a very important initiative but it needs to be accompanied by a reflection that individuals may profit more from the possibility to live and work abroad if their decisions stem from and are followed by biographical work. Following critical realists we recognize the fact that there are properties and powers particular to people which include reflexivity towards and creativity about any social context which they confront (Archer, 1998: 190). These reflexive powers should be supported in all possible ways in order to allow people to make the most of the structural opportunities provided.

References

Archer, M. S. (1995) *Realist social theory: the morphogenetic approach.* Cambridge, UK: Cambridge University Press.
Archer, M. S. (1998) 'Introduction: Realism in the Social Sciences', In: Archer, M. S, Bhaskar, R., Collier, A., Lawson, T. and Norrie, A., eds. (1998) *Critical Realism: Essential Readings*, London: Routledge, pp. 189-205.
Archer, M. S. (2003) *Structure, agency and the internal conversation.* Cambridge, UK: Cambridge University Press.
Archer, M.S. (2007). *Making Our Way Through the World: Human Reflexivity and Social Mobility.* Cambridge, UK: Cambridge University Press.
Archer, M.S. (2012). *The Reflexive Imperative in Late Modernity.* Cambridge, UK: Cambridge University Press.
Archer, M.S., Bhaskar, R., Collier, A., Lawson, T., and Norrie, A. (eds.) (1998). *Critical Realism: Essential Readings.* London and New York: Routledge.
De Botton, A. (2002). *The Art of Travel*, Penguin Books.
Cooley, C.N. (1902). *Human Nature and the Social Order.* New York: Charles Scribner's sons.
Park, R.E. (1928) 'Human migration and the marginal man'. *American Journal of Sociology*, Vol. 33 (6): 881-93.
Schütze, F. (2008a). 'Biography Analysis on the Empirical Base of the Autobiographical Narratives: How to Analyse Autobiographical Narrative Interviews'. *Part I, INVITE – Biographical Counselling in Rehabilitative Vocational Training. Further Educational Curriculum.* EU Leonardo da Vinci Programme. http://www.uni-magdeburg.de/zsm/projekt/biographical/1/B2.1.pdf (link valid on 27/07/2012).
Simmel, G. (1908). 'The Stranger'. in Levine, D.N. (ed.) (1971) *On Individuality and Social Forms: Selected Writings*, Chicago University Press, pp. 143-149.
Spanò, A., Nagel, U., Musella, P. and Perone, E. (2011). 'From Europe to Europeans and beyond: Meanings of Europe through people's biographical experience', *Przegląd Socjologiczny [Sociological Review]*, Vol. 60, No. 1, pp. 217-249.
Spanò, A., Musella, P., and Perone, E. (2012). 'Cross-Cultural Couples in the Old and New Europe: From Bi-Localism to Emotional Transnationalism'. in Miller, R. (ed.) *The Evolution of European Identities. Biographical Approaches*, Palgrave Macmillan, pp. 233-254.

5. Biographical Approach in the Study of Identities of Ethnic Minorities in Eastern Europe

Lyudmila Nurse

> *What kept alive the determination to remain "European" was history. And in the New Europe, history is geography*
>
> (John O'Sullivan, *The Spectator*, 2012)

The focus of this chapter is the application of principles of sociological realism to the analysis of biographical narratives in the Eastern European context, particularly in what could be described as an "emergent" region. The use of biographical methods allows us to understand how personal biographies of Eastern Europeans intersect with the larger historical changes of the region's borders and political and social institutions and helps us to contextualise the interpretation of the conjunctions between the emerging new societal structures and individual lives and narratives.

Realism's "open-endedness" as regards choice of research methods as is mentioned in Carter's chapter (Carter, this volume) could be turned into a strength through the use of the biographical study of a combination of unstructured and semi-structured modes. This combination of modes could achieve the optimal balance between the rigidity of structured interviews and the complexity of unstructured interviews, which sometimes lose a sense of time or any thematic constraints. In addition, this approach allows for the comparison of themes and profiles across a spectrum of actors. This is especially relevant in studies of ethnic minorities in the Eastern European context in the development of a "bottom-up" approach to the typology, based on ethnic self-identification, as compared to the formal classification and grouping.

This chapter is based on a study of individual and collective identities of ethnic minorities in Eastern Europe in an EC FP7 project.[1] Biographical study

---

[1] EC FP7 ENRI-EAST project: Interplay of European, National and Regional Identities project, a multi-disciplinary, mixed methods cross-national study of trans-boundary ethnic minority population was conducted in eight countries of Eastern Europe along the new borders of the EU (2008-2011), www.enri-east.net.

was one component of the ENRI-EAST project. Major historic and geopolitical changes in Europe after WWII (post-war border changes, the disintegration of the USSR, Czechoslovakia and the successive enlargements of the European Union to the East) emphasized the need to review the political, social and cultural status of Europe's ethnic minorities. Some of these minorities are virtual communities that were created after the break up of larger nations due to border or political changes and the emergence of new nationalisms in newly independent states (Laitin, 1998; Sik, 2000; Sik and Toth, 2003; Brubaker, 2006; Brubaker et al., 2006).

Though formally identified and recognised as ethnic minorities by the new nation states, the internal dynamics of ethnic minorities is very complex. Their current and future position is heavily dependent on the strength of the individual's self-identification. It is individuals who decide to be "absorbed" into or to "blend with" the majority culture of the "new" country of their residence, or to resist the cultural influences of the majority. Alternatively, they may leave the locality, despite being born and bred there, and move further afield. The emotional and practical dimensions of individual life strategies and choices, the "internal conversations" (Archer, 2003) and external deliberations regarding where they belong, as narrated by ethnic minority individuals, were analysed from both generational and gender perspectives. A special approach which has been developed in the ENRI-EAST project towards ethnic minorities in Eastern European countries contributes to a wider European political debate regarding the transfer of power to sub-national layers of government such as the UK, Spain and Belgium.

In the following parts of the chapter we look at the constraints of formal ethnic classifications and "grouping" (Brubaker, 2006) of ethnic minority populations in Eastern Europe focusing on the findings from an empirical study conducted in Vilnius, Lithuania. Then we demonstrate the development of a biographical approach to the empirical study of ethnic minorities in Eastern European countries in the ENRI-EAST project which is followed by an analysis of biographical narratives, which forms a case study of Vilnius minorities. The last part: "Identity management: biographical resources of ethnic minorities" contributes to the debate on the limitations of the categorization and "groupness" of the ethnic minorities suggesting that persons of ethnic minorities have to be treated as individuals, rather than as merely part of homogeneous minority populations, and indeed need to be framed as actors (Brubaker, 2006:8).

Biographical reflections[2] and ethnic self-identification

Among the main research questions which were specifically addressed in the ENRI-EAST project, which was primarily focused on ethnic minorities, were: What did it mean for ethnic minorities to belong to a nation or region, or to be European? What was specific about the regional, national and European self-identification of ethnic minorities, in the EU-non-EU borderlands? What are the practices, narratives and discourses concerning the compatibility and incompatibility of identities under the conditions of belonging to a minority in these countries? How are identities constructed in order to fulfil a possible need for differentiation between Europe, the nation and the region?

There are many issues regarding the definition of an ethnic minority population, including issues of minorities and citizenship, individual and minority groups (Wolff, 2008; Brubaker, 2006; Laitin, 1998; Mullerson, 1993). Such a detailed discussion is beyond the scope of this chapter, and therefore this chapter is concerned with the individual narratives of those who identify themselves by their ethnic origin.

The initial results from the quantitative ENRI-Values and Identities Survey (ENRI-VIS), which was conducted prior to the biographical study, provided us with a unique opportunity to see a first "snapshot" of the collective identities of

---

[2] METHODOLOGICAL NOTES: *Language:* The interviews were conducted in the language in which informants felt most comfortable to be interviewed. This did not exclude interviewing ethnic minority representatives in the official language of the country where they lived or any dialect they might choose. (For example, ethnic Russians in Lithuania had a preference for being interviewed in Lithuanian whereas as a rule (with some exceptions), the younger generation of informants chose the new official language of the country where the interview took place). Interviewers noted dialects and languages and any shifts during the interviews in their reports. Interviewees were allowed to "switch" between the languages, because each of the languages represents a particular layer in their identity and a certain stage in their life, which were of significance. *Selection of informants for biographical interviews:* The main objective of the study to decode the meaning system of ethnic identities self-identification across the ethnic minorities in eight Eastern European countries determined the principles for selecting informants from various generations, genders, ethnic minority background and proximity to the place which they call "home" (those who were born and bred there, moved in childhood with their parents, or other). Personal circumstances of the ethnic minority population played a crucial role in the mechanism of identity-making and self-identification. Therefore, by using a relatively large sample regarding nationality, ethnicity, location, gender and age group we aimed to ensure that it represented a diversity of opinions regarding subject-matter and provided insight into our research questions. Additionally, we considered covering some of the same localities as were used in the quantitative survey. Informants from the earlier quantitative survey (ENRI-VIS) and from the musical survey were also approached again, successfully for a second contact in Hungary. *Generations:* The informants in our study represented roughly three generations of ethnic minorities: the younger generation who were born and brought up in the post-communist era (16-22); the middle generation who experienced the transition from the post war and communist era and were affected by significant geopolitical, economic, social and cultural changes (35-60); the older generation who would have experienced the Second World War (65+). The selection is also split evenly between male and female informants.

the "grouped" minorities. However respondents were also selected on the basis of their self-identification, not on formal categorisation (ENRI-East reports). The findings of the survey enabled us to narrow down research questions for the biographical study. It became clear from the findings of the quantitative study that locality plays an important role in ethnic/national/ European self-identification of ethnic minorities. What was not at all clear is how its role changes as a result of major geopolitical border shifts in the Eastern European countries resulting in the evolution of newly independent states, discourses of new nationalisms and EU enlargement in the east of Europe. Historical and cultural aspects of this enlargement were "intertwined", and affected both the "biographies" of places and individuals in a very intimate way which required internal reflection, decision-making and action. And lastly, there is the question of where these changes would lead ethnic minorities in terms of their future, the whole range of their coping strategies and future existence. In this respect channels for forming the cultural identities of various generations, for example through language, music, literature, faith and the mass media, were issues which were significantly addressed in the biographical study.

The biographical study begins with more general descriptions of people's nationality and ethnic origins; the place of a "kin-nation" state in defining these national identities and how people feel about the "kin nations", leading to more specific issues related to gender and generational differences in people's relations to their ethnic origins. The description of the origin of ethnic minorities was one of the most difficult issues for the informants. In most cases people had never moved anywhere; it was the borders of the Eastern European countries which kept moving. People's own recollections of their place of origin were mainly connected to specific places and localities (e.g. Vilnius Poles; Latgallians). Each of the 153 interviews conducted was unique in the way the informants described the sequence of places and countries until they came to the description of the place they described as home. Most of the interviews in fact began with the questions: *How long have the informants been living there? What was their childhood or first memory about the place? How has it changed since that time?* This opening was followed by the informants' life stories, starting from their place of birth before continuing into themes defined by the ENRI-EAST experts. We had already emphasised the fact that it was important that informants were allowed to tell their own story, so the topics suggested to the interviewers were more of a check-list to explore various issues. However, as practical experience of conducting interviews showed, clarification or probes were required.

As mentioned at the beginning of this chapter, our methodology for the selection of the informants, based on people's self-identification, caused practical difficulties in identifying who to interview, due to the historic aspects of the ethnic minorities origin in Eastern European countries. This same factor later enabled us to appreciate that the process of self-identification naturally comprises elements of "internal conversations", cultural memories and external deliberations. It was not an uncommon situation for the informants to be in doubt about what their "real" ethnic identities were once the narration of their lives had begun. In many cases national identities and nationalities were confused. We continually had to come to terms with the issue of constantly changing nationalities. A person could be born and go to school in one state and then work and retire in another without leaving a location. The impact of these circumstances on ethnic self-identification has been explored.

The interviewees were offered a choice of language, which, with some exceptions, were official languages of the country of their residence. The use of different languages within the same life story created a challenge both when the interviews were conducted and when analysis was undertaken. Each significant segment of a life story was a language- related narrative with its intimate meaning and "internal conversations". The meaning of the words were time- and place-related and could have been difficult for outsiders to understand. Often people tended to speak the language that was, for decades, the main language of communication in public places.

We earlier emphasized the difference between ethnic origin/background and nationality, aware of the danger that informants might confuse questions of nationality and citizenship, the latter likely to be determined by the country where they lived. If the ethnic origin was not mentioned in the course of free narration, some prompts were used to "locate" the informant's ancestors. One such method was to ask about family background, particularly concerning the parents, grandparents and spousal family. Another method was to discuss their linguistic background. Language as a constituent part of national identity was anticipated by the team, (Bjorklund, 2006; Wright, 2000; Wolff, 2008) in considering it an important part of defining both individual and collective identity At this stage of the interview it was appropriate (however not in every circumstance) to ask informants to fill in the family tree chart, which was prepared by the field work teams.

Development of the Biographical Approach to the Study of Ethnic Minorities

There have been significant developments in applying narrative and biographical methods to identities studies within the framework of different disciplines: social psychology (Taylor, 2010); qualitative social science studies (Schütze, 1977; 1981; 1987; Miller, 2000; 2005; Fisher-Rosenthal, 1996; Roberts, 2002; Chamberlayne, Bornat and Wengraf, 2000; Chamberlayne, Bornat and Apitzsch,

2004; Semenova, 1998). However studies of ethnic minority populations have, with some notable exceptions such as Voronkov and Chicadze (1997; 2003) and a recent publication by Aarelaid-Tart and Bennich-Bjorkman (2012), largely failed to exploit the potential of the biographical approach.

The main advantage of using biographical methods in the study of the identities of ethnic minorities is the ability to examine ethnic identity as a process, progressing from childhood to adolescence and into later life. This process always includes the individual's own reflection on the geo-political changes that have taken place, providing a category of actor-centred research[3]. Since the object of the study is the individual and the events of his or her life, narration of that story is a continuation of identity development in the process of interviewing (Taylor, 2010: 35; Brubaker et al., 2006). Although the main method of data collection in the ENRI-EAST study was by biographical interview (an individual's life story in free style, in chronological order), we had to consider adding some elements of layered "structured" thematic-based dialogue with an individual for a certain period of time. Biographical interviews also accommodated conversation about other available "life course or personal documents" (Roberts, 2002; Semenova, 1998). These documents and concrete objects included photographs and portraits, newspaper cuttings, autobiographical publications, books, ethnic and national symbols (flags, coins, medals) that cast light on the individual's life course (Nurse, 2012).

A case study of Vilnius minorities: from one country to another without changing address

The analysis of the biographical interviews of some members of the Polish and Russian ethnic minorities in Vilnius[4] showed that that their sense of ethnic/national affiliations were affected by a unique combination of historical circumstances (global and local) and the individual's reflections and decision making. Thus despite Lithuania's close geographical proximity to Latvia and Estonia and shared Soviet experience, it remains a distinct case with regard to its eth-

---

[3] In the ENRI-EAST project the biographical material played two roles. Firstly, it produced accounts of individual biographies which were used as sources for analysis of the individuals' reflections on and definitions of their ethnic, regional and European identities. Secondly, it served as a tool for decoding meanings in the system of informants' self-identification and therefore complemented findings from other sources of information in the project such as the ENRI-EAST Values and Identities Survey quantitative survey.

[4] To demonstrate development of our method in the study of ethnic minorities, I have selected six biographical narratives from the ENRI-EAST study from Lithuania, out of 36 which were conducted. The interviewers were native Lithuanian speakers with a strong command of the Russian and Polish languages.

nic minorities and the dynamics between ethnic groups (Hroch, 2000; Johns, 2003:684; Lane, 2001, cited in Johns, 2003:684; Assmuth, 2012).

The history of the Lithuanian nation state has been significant for the whole of the Baltic States and the neighbouring countries of Russia, Belarus and Poland. (Hroch, 2000; Lakis, 1995; Kallonen, 2004; ENRI-EAST Minorities Reports [7, 8, 9], 2011). Lithuania made its mark in nation- building by being the first republic to declare independence from the Soviet Union in 1990. This was recognised by the then USSR a year later in 1991, only a few months before the USSR itself dissolved. Ethnic minority rights were duly recognised by the new Lithuanian state in 1992 and language rights in 1995, and compared to neighbouring Latvia and Estonia, Lithuania experienced a relatively calm transition period regarding its ethnic minorities until a new bill on the education of ethnic minorities in Lithuania was recently passed. (ENRI-EAST Minorities reports [7, 8, 9], 2011; PR dla Zagranicy, 2012).

Statistically Lithuania could be considered a relatively homogeneous country with ethnic minority populations comprising less than 17 % of its total population (ENRI-EAST Minorities reports [7, 8, 9], 2011; Kallonen, 2004). However it is the geo-political origin of the country's ethnic minorities and their sense of belonging to the place that matters. Significant differences within the ethnic minority populations are another issue which is beyond the reach of the statistical approach. This difference is related not only to the relative "age" of their ethnic minority in the place where they live, but also internal differences within the ethnic minority population (e.g. religious difference between Orthodox believers, Old Believers and non-believers as in the case of Russians and Belarusians). Old Believers are still remembered for being rebellious from the time when they were forced to flee from the persecution of the Russian Orthodox Church authorities; most of them fled to the Urals and Siberia, where they settled and founded villages. The rest fled to the Eastern European parts of the then Russian Empire, maintaining their religious beliefs and Russian identity. But even now to the Russian-speaking population in Lithuania and in some other Baltic countries of the later waves of immigration (Aarelaid-Tart and Bennich-Bjorkman, 2012) they are some sort of "other" Russians.

However the Poles are the largest ethnic minority group in Lithuania. Some of the interviewees in our study referred to the fact that their ancestors had lived in Vilnius since the 15th century, they belonged to *"šlekta"* [noblemen in the Lithuanian-Polish united country the Grand Duchy of Lithuania]. This historical fact emotionally connects them with their "imagined community" (Anderson, 1991) of Poles, and makes them surprised that modern day Lithuanians "tend" to forget the joint Lithuanian-Polish history and heritage of the past. One of the explanations which came up in many of the interviews was that a different version of history is taught in the Lithuanian and Polish schools. However the Polish minority's feeling of closeness and identification with the majority population has one significantly strong common institution in the form of the Roman Catholic Church, which was mentioned in almost every biographical account. The Polish minority interviewees also emphasized the fact that sharing Slavic roots with the Russians made it easier for them to understand the Russian language, which along with Belarusian "contributes" to Vilnius Polish dialect, so distinctively different from the "mainland" Polish.

Selected biographical narratives are from Lithuanian citizens who self-identified themselves as Russian or Polish and all of them were born in Vilnius. The biographical narratives were selected from two generations of Lithuanians from ethnic Russian and Polish minorities, 3 male and 3 female (a summary of the biographical cases used in the analysis is in Table 5.1).

Katarzyna[5], Artiom and Sergeij are secondary school students. They are the younger generation of Lithuanian from the ethnic minority population: ethnic Poles (Katarzyna, 17), ethnic Russians (Sergeij, 18) and mixed Russian origin (Artiom, 17) for whom the "new" Lithuania is their home country and the rest is history and cultural memories. Aldona (43), Roland (46) and Olga (47) were also born in Vilnius and for them Lithuania is also their home country, but their ethnic identity formation had started in the different – Soviet – past of that same home.

The style of the narrations includes many references to the events that took place in real time and that significantly influence a sense of belonging to the place of their birth – Vilnius.

Katarzyna, Artiom and Sergeij are from the younger generation of the Polish and Russian-speaking ethnic minorities in Vilnius. They all and also their respective parents were born in Vilnius, and can claim to be "truly" local. Their biographical accounts cast light on the recent changes in the ethnic minority populations in the new Lithuania and naturally their plans for the future. Artiom and Sergeij chose to give their interviews in Russian whereas Katarzyna spoke Lithuanian.

After agreeing to speaking Lithuanian to her Lithuanian speaking interviewer, Katarzyna immediately went on to talk about the Lithuanian language and how she, an ethnic Pole managed to learn it, by *"communicating with her friends in the neighbourhood"* and *"speaking as she could"*, which was not perfect, but helped her to learn to speak Lithuanian and Russian in addition to her native Polish, which was spoken in her family, by the age of four.

She also added that if she had been born in England, she would learn the English language naturally, just by being there and this is how she learnt Lithuanian. This linguistic "openness", is one of the skills ethnic minority informants

---

[5] All names are fictitious. The objective information which is used in the analysis is: respondents' age (year of birth), place of birth-Vilnius, and their citizenship; subjective information includes informants' self-identified ethnicity

THE STUDY OF IDENTITIES OF ETHNIC MINORITIES 123

Historic events time-line	Name	Born in	Age	Place of birth	Legal status	Language of interview	Ethnic origin, as initially identified by informant	Ethnic identity, as identified by informant at the end of interview
Independent Lithuania (1990-)	Katarzyna	1994	17	Vilnius	Lithuanian Citizen	Lithuanian	Polish	**Vilnius Pole**
	Artiom	1993	17	Vilnius	Lithuanian citizen	Lithuanian	Russian/Polish/Lithuanian	**Russian in Lithuania, citizen of the World**
	Sergeij	1992	18	Vilnius	Lithuanian citizen	Russian	Russian/Lithuanian	**Russian**
Lithuania under the Soviet rule (annexed in 1940-1990)	Aldona	1967	43	Vilnius	Lithuanian citizen	Lithuanian	Polish	**Pole from Vilnius**
	Roland	1964	46	Vilnius	Lithuanian citizen	Russian/started in Lithuanian	Polish	**Polish/citizen of Lithuania**
	Olga	1963	47	Vilnius	Lithuanian citizen	Lithuanian	Russian/Belarusian	**Russian/Lithuanian, could not decide**

Table 5.1 Summary of the biographical cases

referred to while their biographical narratives were evolving and which is one of the sub-conscious indicators of being truly "local" in a place like Vilnius. Without directly identifying her ethnic origin, Katarzyna describes her family origin in greater detail, by putting emphasis on her self-identification as being "local":

> "Local (laughing), because my grandparents were born here; they say that there is some family in Poland, but some distant family, some sort of cousins and so on; if I am not mistaken we have already the **third or the fourth generation (emphasis mine LN)** who were already born here [she means in Lithuania]. This is very different from a **real Pole**. So in this sense they do not speak proper Polish because of this. Me too, when I meet with Poles from Poland, it is very difficult for me to communicate…"

Eventually Katarzyna stops short of self-identifying herself as Polish by diverting her explanation to the differences between a Pole in Vilnius and a "real Pole", due to the fact that her family, though of Polish ethnic origin, has lived in Lithuania for four generations, but she believes they are different from Poles in Poland due to the language they speak. This description in one way or the other is shared by the other informants of Polish ethnic origin in our study, who subconsciously compared their identity with an identity of an "imagined community" of "real Poles". This comparison has become obvious to them due to opportunities to travel to Poland to visit relatives or to do joint projects and also to see more people from Poland in Vilnius.

Another young Lithuanian is Artiom. Artiom's ethnic origin is quite complicated by his own account. Despite the fact that he, like Katarzyna, has a local identity, his deliberation places additional emphasis on the fact that he was born in Lithuania, after it became independent from the USSR. In his biographical narrative he also adds another important dimension to the identity of his home place, the fact that not long ago Vilnius was part of Poland, which creates this aura of complexity in his ethnic self-identification. Artiom is by his own words from a *"Russian-speaking family...."* in which they all speak Russian, though he went to Lithuanian kindergarten and after that to a Russian-speaking school..., but then there is a twist in the narrative, which not only explains the term "Russian-speaking family", but the fact that the historic past of Vilnius is deeply intertwined with the sense of self-identification of its minority populations:

> "As much as I remember, my father, it may be said, is a Pole. Because in principle Vilnius was Poland earlier and my grandmother lived there at that time. That is why she may be considered to be a *Pole and Lithuanian as well* (emphasis mine LN). So my

father is a Pole. So it may be considered. My mother descended from Russia, the city of NNN, as much as I remember...>...<And my mother's sister... their family can be considered to be absolutely Russian in Lithuania..."

Artiom continues his observation by saying that as far as his ethnic background is concerned:

"... I am as if of mixed blood, I have Lithuanian blood, Polish blood and Russian blood. But on the whole we speak Russian... **And we consider ourselves to be rather Russians in Lithuania (emphasis mine LN).**

After thinking for a while, he adds:

"Well, of course, [if] I think a little. I'm considered to be a Russian-speaking inhabitant of Lithuania. I have a citizenship of Lithuania, I'm absolutely Lithuanian... Nothing hinders me from speaking Russian. I don't feel any particular discrimination or something of the kind...>...<I am considered to be just the Lithuanian who speaks Russian..."

Artiom's process of self-identification is a remarkable example of how historical and political changes affect people's ways of thinking about their identity. Without travelling far, his family's biography stretches across the constantly changing geo-political borders of Poland, USSR, Russia and Lithuania. What is significant in his story is that the language of communication in his multi-cultural family is Russian. It is also significant that he comes to the conclusion that he is "European" after all. His "Europeanness" is supported by the statement that he can converse in various European languages. He is clearly in a position to choose who he wants to be.

Sergeij, is another young Lithuanian from an ethnic minority, who was born after independence. He self-identifies himself as being a Russian in Lithuania, but on reflection into his ethnicity he believes that it is the language which he speaks, not family origin, which makes him who he is:

"...I mean, I will always be a Russian in Lithuania. If I go to Moscow I will always be a Lithuanian. It is very difficult to somehow identify yourself for some nationality. That's why, well, it is wanted that you can live and stay serene there where you are...>

> < Yes. I think it is in general. I am studying in a Russian school and basically it is very difficult to name somebody exactly [pure] Russian in a Russian school. Because when there was the USSR, lots of [people] from Belarus, from Ukraine were coming here. And my own one grandpa is from Russia and the other grandpa is from Belarus. One is from… I am half-Russian. This is maximum…"

So compared to Artiom's ethnic self-identification, Sergeij's is not by any means an easy one; he is sure that language was the defining marker of his ethnic identity, because it is the only way he can identify who he is.

Three young citizens of Lithuania represent different ways of looking at their ethnic identification, each of them reflecting upon Lithuania's historical paths: Vilnius Pole; half-Russian, one-fourth Polish and one-fourth Lithuanian and Russian-speaking Lithuanian (half-Polish and half-Russian). What they all share is a sense of being local, through the fact they were born in Lithuania and their families are also "rooted" in the country in one way or the other.

What seemed to be significant in the younger generation of the minority narratives are their references to their family ethnic origins, the locations they are from, the languages spoken at home, with peers, at school and the changes which have been continuously taking place since their childhoods. Their references to Europe and also proficiency in the English language are evidence of our Global culture and communication. This is the new dimension in the younger generation identification which stretches beyond the traditional identity of the place whether they live. We shall demonstrate later how these layers of identification work as biographical resources in life decisions. The younger generation's "horizons" have not been "reduced" (Archer, 2003:11) by geo-political or social situations and the concerns of the older generation of ethnic minorities.

Aldona, Roland and Olga are from the older generation of local Lithuanians. All three were born in Vilnius, which according to their narrations was a very different place from what it is now. The geo-political border of the place was delineated leading to a formal/external redefinition of their identities, though it also prompted adjustments to their sense of ethnic self-identification. What for the younger generation of Vilnius is history, for them is very much a part of their biographical experience.

Aldona (43) is a Lithuanian of Polish origin. She, like Roland, Polish (46) and Olga, Russian (47) was born in the 1960-s in the time of the USSR. Her relationship with her home city is deeply rooted in historical and cultural memories of the place. Significantly, she still lives on the same street in the Old Town, where she grew up. She gave her interview in Lithuanian. But her reflection upon the fact that until the age of seven (mid 1970-s) she had not heard anybody speaking Lithuanian in her neighbourhood is quite remarkable.

"...I was lucky because I was growing up in this environment where lots of nationalities were then, lots of cultures... There were lots of Jews, fewer Belarusians, there were few Russian families, anyway, there were Polish families..."

Aldona's Polish grandparents had been deported to Siberia after the Soviet annexation of Lithuania; when they returned, they were not allowed to live in Vilnius. Most of Aldona's extended Polish family live in Canada, USA. She remarked that her grandfather was brave to remain in Vilnius and later was deported to Siberia. This family's narrative affected Aldona's identity formation process.

Another of the older generation, Roland self-identified himself as Polish and therefore was interviewed as a member of the Polish ethnic minority in Vilnius, but after starting his interview in Lithuanian, he switched to the Russian language. He was born in the 1960-s to a Polish family, which originates from one of the districts near Vilnius. His parents moved to Vilnius at the end of the 1950-s. Like Aldona, he was also born and spent his childhood in the Old Town of Vilnius. He went to a Russian school in Vilnius and after finishing it at the beginning of the1980-s he had to serve in the Soviet Army. Military service for all men was compulsory by law throughout the USSR. He served in the army in Latvia. Though his grandparents and parents are of Polish origin, he emphasized that his grandparents had spoken the "simple Polish" language, a kind of mixture of Polish and Belarusian: *"...not the literate one... literate Polish" (Roland)*, whereas his parents spoke Russian at home. He himself ended up going to a Russian school and speaking Russian and Lithuanian most of the time: Russian at home and Lithuanian at work. He found it was easier for him to speak Russian, which was widely spoken in Vilnius during the Soviet period, whereas *"Polish was rarely spoken* (PAUSE). *The usual* [common] *language was Russian..."*

The third of this older generation is Olga. Olga is a Lithuanian of Russian origin and she is also a "truly local" person. She was born in Vilnius in 1963. Olga is from a mixed family. Her father is a local Russian and her mother moved to Lithuania from Belarus in the 1950s to work at a shoe factory. Olga's paternal ancestors are the Russian Old Believers who settled in Lithuania in the eighteenth century. She gave her interview in Lithuanian:

".... Relatives of my father came here maybe even 300 years ago, when they were escaping, it means, from the new faith, were escaping from Russia. Yes. And as far as I know, here, in Lithuania, are lots of Old Believers...><... Here are kind of districts where they were just living...><... Well, there are some nuances which are little bit different and a cross differs, and they make the sign of the cross little bit differently".

Though Olga's maternal family originates in Belarus, the language of communication in her parents' family and her own family is predominantly Russian. But at work and with her neighbours she communicates in Lithuanian. Ethnic self-identification is a difficult issue for Olga, she could not say whether she is Russian or Lithuanian:

> " It is so hard to say. I even ask this question to myself very often. You know, this a very difficult question for me. Here I ask myself. Those Russian folk songs, which were sung by relatives of my father, by sisters, brothers and other were very close and beautiful to me...>...< but when I start to think, it is very hard for me to attribute myself to one nation. You know, Lithuania is very precious to me, because I was born here, I grew up here."

These narratives demonstrate the difficulties faced by the older generation in determining their identities which had to be reassessed and repositioned due to the new geo-political situation in the new nation state. Ethnic self-identification of two generations of ethnic minorities in Vilnius, as our analysis demonstrated so far, starts from the description of ethnic minorities in terms of who they think they are: family origin, place of birth, language spoken, and types of school attended, and type of neighbourhood remembered which also includes references to the "other" (Madianou, 2004; Barth, 1969). The "other" in the biographical stories are not only the "Soviets", the Russians, Russian-speaking, Belarusians, the Poles, real or Vilnius Poles, but also Lithuanians, the titular nation, the majority population of Lithuania. Though the scope of this chapter does not allow me to cover this minority-majority relationship part of the biographical profile of the place, which was also not part of the overall project design, there are some very significant reflections of majority-minority population interactions, which played an important part in the process of identity formation of the ethnic minorities. The fact that most of the interviews with the Russian and Polish minority population were conducted by Lithuanian sociologists, native Lithuanian and fluent Russian and Polish speakers, created a symbolic dialogue with an "imagined community" of the majority population.

Aldona's childhood memories of the Old Town Vilnius population refer to the fact that there were many people of different nationalities in the neighbourhood, but no Lithuanians. At the same time Katarzyna refers to her childhood place as a very different place as far as the Lithuanian population is concerned as the Lithuanians are the largest population in the town now. Sergeij's account of his home place demonstrates that he loves the Old Town for its beauty, but his account of intolerance among the locals (i.e. Lithuanians) was a real problem for him. He also explained that somehow this intolerance was against young people, who were attacked by Skinheads for speaking Russian or Polish in public places.

There is also a big difference between Lithuanians from the capital city and the rest of the country. "The other" Lithuanians outside of the capital city are very different, according to our informants. Everyone speaks only Lithuanian outside of Vilnius and Lithuanians are not aware in the same way as Vilnius Lithuanians of the minority population.

Aldona reflects on her experience of her interactions with Lithuanians outside the capital city:

> "....It is different when, for example, I go to N..., Š..., P...,[cities and towns in Lithuania] where everyone speaks Lithuanian. My brother's wife came from NNN [a city in the North-West Lithuania]. When I first time went to visit her, I said we came from Vilnius, but they told us that we were Poles, as if we were from Poland. It was twenty years ago. There is a lack of information about Poles living here in Lithuania (LAUGHING)...."

The minority/majority relationship, as was referred to in the biographical interviews was mostly about languages spoken in public places, the convention of spelling names, multi-lingual signs and the language of worship. The language of worship was mostly an issue for the Lithuanians and the Polish minority.

Roland's reflections are mostly about the area where his Polish family is from, which he describes in greater detail. But the focus of his story is that only few people in that area speak Polish correctly, unless they finished Polish school, or have a higher education degree or indeed communicate with their relatives in Polish. He also mentions the fact that there is a discrepancy in the language standards in that district when public sector servants, town/village hall (Mayorie) clerks speak proper Polish as compared to the rest of population, which he describes as a mixture of Polish-Belarusian, which he personally does not like and therefore, he prefers to speak Lithuanian and Russian instead.

Since the time of independence, the Lithuanian language has been much more widely spoken in Vilnius, which for some informants, like Katarzyna, is an advantage whereas other informants believe that other languages must continue to be recognised and spoken, namely Russian and Polish. However Sergeij on the contrary believes that the majority population must continue using the Russian language which some speak anyway and some would be happy to learn, and Polish. He himself feels it is a pity that he cannot speak Polish, which could be of benefit to him in communicating with other Polish speakers in the community.

But for the older generation of Lithuanians learning Lithuanian or being part of the Lithuanian culture was not a guarantee that they would become more Lithuanian. Aldona's older brother went to Lithuanian school without any prior knowledge of Lithuanian and therefore it was difficult for him and he did not succeed. This affected Aldona's choice of school. After observing her brother's struggles with the Lithuanian language, she had to make her own decision which school to go to. She ruled out the Russian school, on the basis of it being Soviet and decided to go to a Polish school. This was an important decision to make for a young girl.

Olga for her part, as a music teacher and a singer, was immersed in Lithuanian traditional music and has mastered traditional instruments. She is very passionate about singing in Lithuanian and seemingly enjoys the fact that she is the one who continues local cultural traditions, but when it came to her ethnic identification, she has not been able to decide where she truly belongs.

Therefore it is clear that neither language alone, nor even a profound knowledge of Lithuanian culture, customs and traditions, as in the cases Aldona's brother and Olga, could turn a member of an ethnic minority into Lithuanian.

Neither has the conversion into "proper" Lithuanian been facilitated by implementing the Lithuanian convention of spelling people's surnames. The issue of transliteration of surnames to sound and look like Lithuanian has spiritual and practical implications, but was mostly mentioned by ethnic Poles in the interviews. The spiritual is related to the fact that as devoted Roman Catholics, Poles believe that the name given to them when they are Christened cannot be changed by any "bureaucrats". But significantly, this policy of name transliteration has also a practical implication, i.e. property ownership, which is described by Aldona:

> "...Yes. I could change the surname because I have an argument for that. But I don't see any reason. There's no difference for me. I am [the name of respondent], I know that I am a Pole, there's no difference whether I am [the surname of respondent] or Šnic, well [laughing], I don't see...Other thing, I can't imagine, if Poles start to change their second names, these people have a possession such as houses, land, they will need to change all documents. If someone feels better, let him change it. I don't have this problem..."

There are several dimensions so far reflected in the biographical narratives which ethnic minorities in Vilnius are constantly negotiating, of which language of communication is mentioned more often. Another one is faith.

According to the biographical accounts of Vilnius Poles of the younger and older generations, the Christian faith, therefore the Roman Catholic Church, is a strong factor in community cohesion in Vilnius; it brings ethnic Poles and Lithuanians closer to each other. But the same mass in the Roman Catholic Church could equally distance both communities. Katarzyna in her reflection on the similarity of local cultural, religious traditions indicates both and also provides a personal reason for this uneasy combination:

> "I believe that all these traditions, celebrations are similar because they go hand in hand with religion, so I am a Christian, so with Lithuanians it goes hand in hand. But that's it. For example, if one goes to church to pray so the Polish language is more personal. Sometime when you go to Lithuanian mass, so it feels a bit alien. Or more contrasting even. Something like watching television [LAUGHING]."

Aldona explains this difference more profoundly:

> "...There is a difference. I rarely attend Lithuanian Mass, because I don't know how to pray in Lithuanian (laughing)...><... I must go to church because there is no Sunday without church. When I was in Š... and N..., I went to church on Sunday where Lithuanian Mass was taking place. I was surprised, for example, in Polish Mass we begin with plea for our sins, after that is the Eucharistic liturgy, and in Lithuanian Mass they started with a prayer for the country (PAUSE). It was very interesting for me. And I started to think about it (LAUGHING) why was it so important. And I think that there is some kind of Lithuanian tendency to make church popular, **narodowa** (Polish)"

Whereas Roland, a committed Roman Catholic, prefers the Lithuanian liturgy to the Polish, and also mass in the Lithuanian language:

> " I am Catholic, I believe. I do not go [to the church] often, I mean only during festivals, perhaps I shall go more often, when I get retired.... I recently... better to go to ***kościół***[6] to the Lithuanian service, than to the Polish. Somehow, though I am Polish (PAUSE), [it is] more understandable than in Polish..... Somehow, the approach is clearer, it is difficult for me to understand it in Polish, if they speak it, then meanings, that ......, now, [Lithuanian] is much clearer for me..."

---

[6] Church (Polish)

One Roman Catholic Church, two languages, two different liturgical traditions create more of a divide at a personal level, but it is clearly an important bonding factor among the ethnic communities in Vilnius, bonding the ethnic Polish minority and the majority population (i.e. Lithuanians). Christian belief seems to be a characteristic feature of the ethnic Russians as well, though the Russian case is very different from the latter.

> Roland: "Normally Polish are Catholic, just like Lithuanians. Religion is the same. All of them are religious. I do not know anybody who is not religious. Russians are said to be not religious, but as far as I am aware of there are a lot of religious people among them. People who lived under the rule of the Soviet government were possibly not religious. It was communism, you know, another injunction was there, when it was said that there was not God."

Sergeij's family are Orthodox believers, he recollects that everybody in his family is an Orthodox believer, apart from his father and himself. He adds that both his grandmothers were very religious, so religious that to resist observing Orthodox traditions and festivals for him is quite a challenge. However he doesn't hide the fact that he is not a believer at all.

But for Olga, faith is something she described as a source of her strength, but it is the faith, not a Russian Orthodox Church she is referring to. There are differences regarding deeper "internal" faith and the sense of belonging to the place of residence within the ethnic Russian community in Lithuania: there are people who identify themselves as Orthodox Christians, Old Believers and those who do not connect themselves to the Christian belief, plus those who converted to the Roman Catholic faith due to family circumstances. Though the Russian minority in Lithuania represents different waves of immigration to the country from Russia and Soviet Union republics; it is also more mixed with other minorities (Poles and Belarusians) linguistically and also with the majority population.

The Russian-speaking population in the Baltic States in reality represent a variety of ethnic and religious backgrounds as compared to the relatively more "homogeneous" Polish minority. There are more people from the mixed ethnic origins among the ethnic Russians in Lithuania; there are people of Slavic (Belarusians, Ukrainians, Polish) and other origins among the self-confessed ethnic Russians: Tatars, Armenians.

The Polish community is also more "homogeneous" as far as their faith is concerned; most of them claim to be Roman Catholics, though the difference between the Catholics of Polish and Lithuanian origin remains fairly strong. But at the same time inter-marriages have depended on the church denominations.

There is a deeper symbolism in the individuals' relationships with God (sacred names, sacred places, sacred events); ethnic Russians in Lithuania do also mention that due to the differences between the Christian beliefs, even their graveyards are kept separately, though close.

Identity management: biographical resources of ethnic minorities

It is clear that despite some similarity in general life circumstances in Lithuania for ethnic Polish and Russian minorities regarding their position as minorities, these ethnic minorities have responded differently to the new reality since Lithuanian independence. We have looked at the different age groups and genders of ethnic Russians and ethnic Poles in terms of their life strategies.

There are several nuances in the biographical strategies which could be summarised into several general options. Several individuals give an energetic justification of belonging to the place of their birth, childhood and life memories through very positive (each have an individual reason for this) attachment to it and a strong sense of local identity. At the same time all six informants are very particular about the difference between being Lithuanian and a Lithuanian citizen. Roland: *"I am a Lithuanian citizen, errr. I would not say I am Lithuanian, because I am not Lithuanian, but rather a citizen..."*. Sergeij comments that he believes he would always remain "a Russian speaking person" in Lithuania, and a Lithuanian in Russia (though he has never even visited Russia). Artiom, as well, described himself as a Russian in Lithuania; Aldona is very clear about her identity as a Pole from Vilnius, but Olga cannot decide whether she is more Russian or Lithuanian. In each case there is deeply personal reason for people to self- identify themselves.

The process of choosing, negotiating and responding to challenges of the place, is a part of everyday life: new skills, new language and new situations. Principally, the justification of being "truly" local almost represents their "birthright" to the place, biographical plans reflect upon what the place derives from individuals from different cultures. Though it is not justifiable to draw conclusions about gender differences based on 6 selected cases, nevertheless, women from ethnic minorities chose to speak Lithuanian at the interviews and made more effort to use it in everyday life.

Vilnius is a multi-cultural location, and as a matter of fact has always been like this, according to our informants' accounts. Geographically it is located right at the crossroads between Russia and Western Europe. What has continued to change is the official language of the place, though a variety of languages had been always spoken there.

Aldona provides the most "encyclopaedic" knowledge of this issue, by giving the historical facts related to the role of Vilnius University (it was founded in 1579 and it is one of the oldest Universities in Eastern Europe) in the development of medical schools in Poland. Vilnius also was the birthplace to Adam Mickiewicz, a Polish poet, who is now being claimed as a part of the Lithuanian cultural heritage, etc.

Vilnius has become what it is through the constant cultural inter-changes of population and specific languages which our informants described as "local" and those which have distinctive differences from the mainstream Polish and Russian languages. Some of the informants claim that the language of their origin is the one which is always going to be a constituent part of their identity:

> Sergeij (17):"...And nevertheless this is the only one language which I know [he means Russian]. My language, which I have known from childhood. That's why I identify myself as a Russian; I mean, the culture that from infancy was transferred to me with the help of the language..."

> Aldona (43):"Local one, and simple, which is mostly used in the region of Vilnius. There are Byelorussian words in that language, ee, there are also lots of archaism in Polish language in the region of Vilnius. The language is correct in the city. For example, when we had the visitors from Poland, family or acquaintances, they were very surprised that we talk in Polish very correctly in Vilnius ..."

Such claims should be anticipated, as the status of language as a constitutive part of identity is underlined by Kymlicka (1998) who considers it not only part of subjective personal identity, but also intrinsic to the definition of a nation state because of its prominence in what he terms the "societal culture". Whilst definitions of the nation state are beyond the scope of this paper, connections between language and national and regional identity were clearly evident in the responses from the informants.

At the same time ethnic minority informants refer to a similarity between the Slavs- Poles and Russians, as regards the similarity of languages (Katarzyna) and also some national mentality similarities (Aldona), but at the same time recent historic memories of the Soviet era, despite the fact that the Russian culture and classical literature separates the Soviets and the Russians (Aldona) do not create an easy ground for natural cohesion between the communities. This does work better on the personal level, though both Russians and Poles in Vilnius have to make a choice of either language of communication or religion.

Aldona "… For example, we Poles from Lithuania, we are more close to Lithuanians, we are [much] more reserved than Poles in Poland. We are calmer, we grew up in such reserved environment of Lithuanians that we are also similar to them. We differ from Poles in Poland. For example, if Poles walk on the street, you will hear them a kilometre away. Russians are also the same, but we are not, we are more reserved. And Lithuanians must be coming from Scandinavia. They are more reserved, closed. For example, they don't talk openly [open their heart]. I have Lithuanian friends and we start to talk about our lives, work, boyfriends, right? Well, I say everything the way it s. And they too started to be more open, those who know me better. There's no habit to say what people think, to share these things with others. Lithuanians don't have this habit, they are more reserved…"

Adapting or adjusting to this new state of affairs is clearly easier for the younger generation of ethnic minorities. There is a sense of understanding in their narratives why things go this way. But individually they recognise this status quo for completely different reasons: Katarzyna is naturally multi-lingual and this multi-cultural city suits her, she speaks about how Vilnius has changed for the better: western fashions, etc. Sergeij's acceptance of the status quo is of an opposite nature, he is planning to leave. His plans are to join his mother and her boyfriend who immigrated to England some time ago, and where he has been visiting her for the last seven years. He plans to continue his education in England. Therefore he is much too excited about this new prospect to be very upset by the Skinheads or the fact that it could be useful for him to be able to learn Polish, since he was born and bred in a place where he could pick it up. He also has a dream about living for a while in Sweden, he "fell in love with Sweden" when he visited his aunt who immigrated there. His observation, that being of Russian/Belarusian ethnicity, but coming from a family from Vilnius would never make him neither proper Lithuanian, nor proper Russian, therefore he calls himself "a citizen of the world and there is nothing is strange about this". Artiom, is also "lost" when trying to identify his "Motherland" and concludes that his: "… Motherland" is rather the World, if I can put it this way. I even do not know…"

Conclusion and discussion

Among formal markers of ethnic identity, scholars refer to language, but also religion, race, customs, cultural values. But the main limitation of the top-bottom definition of ethnic identity is that it assumes similarities within certain ethnic groups and differences, "boundaries" (Barth) between the other. A process of ethnic self-identification in the biographical narrations of all six informants referred to several markers of ethnicity. There is clear evidence of this in the informants' narratives (references to the language practice, surnames convention, converting signs into one official language). Significantly, the process of re-adjustment of ethnic minority populations in Vilnius coincides with a similar process of new identity development for the titular nation of the new Lithuanian nation state, which is repositioning itself from the periphery to the centre stage.

The geo-political delineation of the borders of places in Eastern Europe which resulted in new external identities of new nationalisms (nationalities, spelling of surnames, changed names of places) evoked the most constant deliberations about self-identification among the ethnic minorities. One of the ethnic minority informants in our Vilnius case, Roland, strongly believes that his original ethnic identity is the most important, because he cannot be Lithuanian, but a citizen of Lithuania: *"I am Polish, but I shall say simply-I am a citizen of my country* [Lithuania]." He also remarks that people's nationality is not written in passports any more. This remark is about the Soviet practice of writing people's nationality (based on ethnic origin) in their passports, but his statement could also summarise the role of agency in the process of ethnic self-identification.

These findings arose from semi-structured biographical conversations and could not be ascertained from macro-level surveys or purely quantitative analysis. Nonetheless, the findings from the bottom-up approach can certainly be applied in a much larger context and analysed on a greater scale. For example, in agreement with this definition, the biographical interviews of some ethnic minorities resulted in sudden changes in the official use of languages in a very multi-cultural community. It also resulted in the introduction of policies to transliterate families' names, which according to the biographical accounts of the informants contradicts their religious beliefs and national traditions. The introduction of dual signs in the city, which has been a home to multi-national communities for several generations, could also contribute to the sense of cohesion. The informants referred to such practices in Western European countries, though some Eastern European countries, for example Hungary and Slovakia can also be given as examples of such policies.

The fact that there is fluidity in the conceptions of identity, which is then affected by further reflection during the biographical interview, is shown clearly in Table 5.1, which notes that each informant demonstrates changes in their conceptions of their own identities over the course of the interviews. This is not to say that the biographical method was shown to provide true or more accurate self-identification: it is possible that, if given more time to consider, the respondents would have instead affirmed their initial statements regarding their identities. Instead, the application of the biographical method in this case demonstrated the fluidity of subjective self-assessments of national identity. This fluidity was not due to a significant change in biographical context – such as location or time – but instead because of the process of introspection that is central to the biographical method.

This finding has important implications for research that supposes accurate self-assessment by respondents of their identities. This returns us to the consideration of the relevant agent for identifying an individual's identity. As anticipated, the research showed that identification based on citizenship, although fixed in a manner that self-identification is not, fails to account for the complexities present in many people's considerations of national identities of both themselves and others. The value of taking nationality as either an indicator for data analysis or sampling for qualitative analysis is therefore called into question.

However, the aforementioned fluidity notes the difficulties in attempting to substitute a legal status-based approach for one instead with an actor-centred research agenda premised on self-identification. This is particularly pertinent with regard to the use of survey data. Questions of national identity – be they absolute or scalar – can only be said to be representative at that moment in which the individual provides their answer. That moment is constituted not only of the biography of that individual who is being researched, but also by the deliberations that have taken place within a fixed biographical context. Findings, therefore, are affected by the methodological approach used, and hence cannot be considered objective.

What this study has provided, therefore, is a demonstration that the claim of there being an objective identity with regards to subjective – in this case, biographical – experience, cannot be substantiated. The notion of there being an objective and researchable experienced fixed identity ignores the fact that what is considered to be such an identity is subject not only to experience, but also to fluid reflection on that experience that is affected by, among other factors, the methodological approach taken (i.e. the types of questions asked) to probe that identity. Such identification could therefore only be considered objective if qualified by a full elaboration of the context – both biographical and cognitive – in which the (self-identification) takes place.

Acknowledgements

The author of this chapter would like to express her thanks to the Lithuanian Social Research Centre (LSRC) in Vilnius, which conducted the actual field work in Vilnius: Dr Kristina Šliavaitė, Dr Viktorija Zilinskaite, Dr Monika Frėijutė-Rakauskenė, Irena Šutinienė. The translation from Lithuanian and Polish into English was made by the LSRC. The author used her own version of translation from Russian into English. The author herself was among the interviewers on the Lithuanian team and also acted as a trainer of the Lithuanian team in developing the biographical interview technique and remained in close contact with the interviewers throughout the biographical field work.

References

Aarelaid-Tart, A and Bennich-Björkman, L. (eds.) (2012). *Baltic Biographies at Historical Crossroads,* London and New York: Routledge.
Anderson, B. (1991). *Imagined Communities*, rev.ed, London: Verso Books.
Archer, M. (2003). *Structure, Agency and the Internal Conversation,* Cambridge: Cambridge University Press.
Assmuth, L. (2012). 'Rural belonging'. In: Aarelaid-Tart, A and Bennich-Björkman, L. (eds.) *Baltic Biographies at Historic Crossroads,* London and New York: Routledge: pp.107-124.
Barth, F. (1969) 'Introduction'. in Barth, F. (ed.) *Ethnic Groups and Boundaries: The Social Organisation of Cultural Difference,* Boston: Little, Brown.
Björklund, F. (2006). 'The East European "ethnic nation"-Myth or reality?'. *European Journal of Political Research*, 45:93-121.
Brubaker, R. (1996). *Nationalism Reframed: Nationhood and the National Question in the New Europe,* Cambridge: University Press.
Brubaker, R. (2006). *Ethnicity Without Groups*, Cambridge, Massachusetts, and London, England: Harvard University Press.
Brubaker, R., Feischmidt, M., Fox, J., and Grancea, L. (2006). *Nationalist Politics and Everyday Ethnicity in a Transylvanian Town,* Princeton and Oxford: Princeton University Press.
Chamberlayne P., Bornat J., Wengraf T. (2000). *The Turn to Biographical Methods in Social Science. Comparative Issues and Examples.* London and New York: Routledge.
Corbin, J., Strauss, A. (2008). *Basics of Qualitative Research. Techniques and Procedures for Developing Grounded Theory,* 3rd ed., Sage Publications. Inc
ENRI-EAST, Series of Project Research Reports, Institute for Advances Studies, Vienna, 2011:
- Report No 7:The Belarusian Minority in Lithuania, No7 (Authors: Matulionis, A., Beresnivičiūtė, V., Leončicas, T., Šliavaitė, K., Heinrich, H-G, Alekseeva, O);
- Report No8: The Polish Minority in Lithuania, No8 (Authors: Matulionis, A., Beresnivičiūtė, V., Leončicas, T., Frėijutė-Rakauskenė, M., Šliavaitė, K., Šutinienė, I., Žilinskaite, V., Heinrich, H-G, Alekseeva, O);
- Report No9: The Russian Minority in Lithuania, No9 (Authors: Matulionis, A., Beresnivičiūtė, V., Leončicas, T., Frėijutė-Rakauskenė, M., Šliaviatė, K., Heinrich, H-G, Alekseeva, O);

Fleming, M (2010). 'The ethno-religious ambitions of the Roman Catholic Church and the ascendancy of communism in post-war Poland (1945-50)'. *Nations and Nationalism*, 16(4): 637-656.
Humphrey, W., Miller, R., Zdravomyslova, E. (eds.) (2003). *Biographical Research in Eastern Europe.* Ashgate.

Hughes, J. (2005). "'Exit'in deeply divided societies: Regimes of discrimination in Estonia and Latvia and the potential for Russophone migration". *Journal of Common Market Studies*, 43:739-762.
Johns, M. (2003) "'Do as I say, not as I do': The European Union, Eastern Europe and minority rights", *East European Politics and Societies* 2003 17:682-699.
Kallonen, M. (2004). 'Minority protection and linguistic rights in Lithuania'. *Noves SL. Revista de Sociolinguistica*. (http://www6.gencat.cat/llengcat/noves/hm04tardor/docs/kallonen.pdf: accessed 16 August 2012).
Kymlicka, W. and Opalski, M. (eds.) (2001). *Can Western Pluralism Be Exported? Western Political Theory and Ethnic relations in Eastern Europe*, Oxford: Oxford University Press.
Lakis, J. (1995). 'Ethnic minorities in the postcommunist transformation of Lithuania'. *International Sociology,* June 1995 vol.10 no2, 173-184
Lawler, S. (2008). *Identity. Sociological Perspectives*, Cambridge: Polity Press.
Lewins A. and Silver C. (2007). *Using Software in Qualitative Research. A Step-by Step Guide*, Sage Publications Ltd.
Lijphart, A. (1995). *Multiethnic Democracy*. In Lipset, S. (ed.) *The Encyclopedia of Democracy,* vol.III, pp. 853-65.
Miller, R. (2005). *Biographical Research Methods*. Volumes I-IV. London: Sage.
Mullerson, R. (1993). 'Minorities in Eastern Europe and the Former USSR: Problems, Tendencies and Protection'. in: *The Modern Law Review Limited (MLR)* 56:6, November Blackwell Publishers.
Nurse, L, (2012). *ENRI-EAST Biographical Study. ENRI-EAST Reports. Vienna.*
Nurse, L., and Sik, E. (2011). 'Identity and music. Identity of place and cultural identities of generations' in: *Cultures and/of globalization,* Cambridge: Cambridge Scholars Publishing.
Nurse, L. (2011). *Music in the identities of ethnic Slovaks in Hungary.* Slovak journal of Political sciences, Volume 11, No 3, pp 249-266, Trnava: The Institute of Social Sciences, University of SS Cyril and Methodius.
Nurse, L. (Rapporteur) (2002). *'Youth Policy in Lithuania'*. Strasbourg: Council of Europe. (with P. Breen, M-E. Shionnemann, A. Azzopardi, J-C.Lagree, P. Lauritzen).
Nurse, L. (2000) *'Youth Policy in Romania National Youth Policy'*. Evaluation report by the international Group of Experts, Strasbourg: Council of Europe. (with J-M Pais, M. Dubois).
O'Sullivan, J. (2012). 'Boarding the sinking ship'. The Spectator, 12 May, 2012, pp. 20-21.
PR Dla Zagranicy (2012). 'Polish minority takes to the streets of Vilnius', Polskie Radio Dla Zagranicy 17.03.2012 18:30; http://thenews.pl//1/10/Artykul/93594.
Riessman, C.K. (1993). *Narrative Analysis. Qualitative Research Methods Series 30.* A Sage University paper.
Rodriguez, J and Fortier, T, (2007). *Cultural Memory. Resistance, Faith and Identity,* Austin: University of Texas Press.
Roberts, B. (2002). *Biographical Research*. Buckingham: Open University Press.
Sik, E. (2000). 'Diaspora: Tentative observations and applicability in Hungary'. In: Kiss, I. and McGovern, C. (eds.) *New Diasporas in Hungary, Russia and Ukraine.*, Open Society/COLPI, Budapest, pp. 20-41.

Sik, E., and Tóth, J. (2003). 'Joining an EU identity: Integration of Hungary and the Hungarians'. in: Spohn, W. and Triandafyllidou, A. (eds.) *Europeanisation, National Identities and Migration*, London: Routledge, pp. 223-244.

Semenova, V.V. (1998). *Qualitative methods: Introduction into Humanist Sociology.* Moscow: Dobrosvet. [Семенова, В.В. (1998). Качественные методы: введение в гуманистическую социологию. Институт социологии РАН, Москва, Добросвет], (in Russian).

Semenova V., and Foteeva, E. (1996). 'Introduction'. in: Bertaux, D. Foteeva, E., and Semenova, V. (eds.) *People's Fates: Russia XX Century. Family Biographies through Sociological Research.* Moscow: Institute of Sociology, Russian Academy of Sciences. [Семенова В., Фотеева Е.(Ответственные редакторы) (1996) Судьбы людей: Россия XX век. Биографии семей как объект социологического исследования. Институт социологии РАН, Москва]. (in Russian).

Taylor, S. (2010). *Narratives of Identity and Place*, London and New York: Routledge.

Woodward, K. (ed.) (1997). *Identity and Difference,* Sage Publications in association with The Open University, Milton Keynes.

Wolff, S. (2008). *Ethnic Minorities in Europe: The Basic Facts*. Centre for International Crisis Management and conflict Resolution. University of Nottingham. (www.stefanwolff.com/files/min-eu.pdf: accessed 6/8/2012).

Wright, S. (2000). *Community and Communication. The Role of Language in Nation State Building and European Integration.* Clevedon, Buffalo, Toronto, Sydney: Multilingual Matters Ltd.

6. Social Dialogue as a European Social Field: Setting up a "Critical Realist" Explanatory Framework of the Practices of the European Works Councils in Multinationals in Europe

Valeria Pulignano & Norbert Kluge

Introduction

In this chapter we refer to the broadly shared concept in social science of employee involvement as the basis for the creation of a socially-controlled market economy. In doing so we use a broadly realist framework in probing the social-economic phenomenon of employee involvement through interviews with the various participants involved (Edwards, 2005; Fleetwood, 2011). The concept of employee involvement is common to many different discipline areas in social science. Despite using the same terminology, the meaning and form that employee involvement takes varies considerably depending on the discipline. On the one hand, it could relate to trade union representation through joint consultative committee and collective bargaining, to worker cooperatives or to legislation designed to provide channels for employee representatives to engage in some forms of joint decision making with employers. On the other hand, and at a different level, it could encompass myriad mechanisms that employers introduce in order to provide information to their staff or to offer them the chance to engage in joint problem-solving groups or use their skills/discretion at work via job enrichment programmes (Wilkinson et al., 2010). However, in both cases the degree of involvement indicates the extent to which workers – or their representatives – are able to influence management decisions. This can range from merely being provided with information, through two-way communication, consultation, co-determination and control (Marchington, 2005). Whilst representative (indirect) forms of employees' involvement and collective bargaining emerge from the industrial relations and law literatures, no representative (direct) employees' engagement are more likely to have their roots in human resource management where the focus tends to be on the role of workers as individuals and their relationship with line managers (Wilkinson and Fay, 2011).

At the core of the concept of employees' involvement is the heavily academically disputed question of the relationship between economic and social integration at the European level. Economic integration is usually understood as the integration of product markets, which derives from the Single Market program launched by the 1987 Single European Act, then further developed in the project for Economic and Monetary Union (EMU) under the Maastricht Treaty. However, social integration at the European level is often broadly associated with the creation of supranational structures and institutions for the regulation of labour markets and employment relations in the European Union more generally (Platzer, 1998). Specifically, it can be argued that at the core of the discussion on social integration is some form of democratic legitimization, whereby the consent of employees is secured through their involvement in the process of employment regulation (Coates, 1980).

A range of legislative measures (i.e. directives) aimed at producing regulatory effects with regard to employment currently exist at the European level. Amongst these measures we specifically refer to the ones introducing representative structures for statutory employee involvement at both the national and cross-national level in Europe. The term "statutory forms of representative employee involvement" is often used to refer to measures containing regulations relating to information for employees, consultation and even participation in company boardrooms where applicable. We feel this term is crucial to explain one of the driving forces for strengthening the socially-controlled market economy in Europe (what is termed the "social dimension" of the European Union) because of its rooting in developed workplaces. However, against the background of formal legislation and macro-institutional structures at the EU level, which is evidently important, the article discusses how far concrete practices for employee representatives' involvement emerging at the transnational company level can contribute to Europeanization of social dialogue, and industrial relations more generally, and therefore to the creation of a Social Europe. Concretely it attempts to shift attention away from the macro political structures (*per se*), such as institutional arrangements and regulatory initiatives at the European level, to the micro effectiveness (*in se*) of the practices developed at transnational level with regard to employees' involvement. Is there any Europeanization of social dialogue through the transnational representative structures for employees' involvement at the European company level, such as the European Works Councils (EWCs)? How do the social actors operate within these transnational structures? To what extent is there a space for Europeanization of industrial relations? Specifically, this means to examine the practices of EWCs within individual companies and evaluate their effects for the future of

Social Europe. It also means to assess the extent to which Europeanization of industrial relations, in particular collective bargaining, can be developed at the European level (i.e. European Framework Agreements, or EFAs), within the context of these practices.

The chapter is structured as follows. After the introduction, the first part introduces the analytical framework. It discusses the concept of Europeanization and employee involvement and examines the rather contradictory view of relevant literature with regard to the current initiatives of employees' involvement in Europe. The second part introduces the methodology and the research design. It presents the empirical evidence about EU legislation on employees' involvement (current institutional arrangements) and the actual operations of EWCs in sixty selected multinational companies in different sectors in Europe. In particular, the development of different EWCs practices, the conditions supporting this development and their contribution to Europeanization are examined and assessed. We also discuss a link with the realist biography perspective as a promising venue for the follow-up research.

Europeanization and the controversy around workers' involvement

The construction and diffusion of European institutions and policies, and their domestic adaptation that followed the creation of the European Union, and in particular the process of European economic integration, gave rise to the widespread popularity and use of the term 'Europeanization' in academic circles after the late 1990s. This contributed to the generation of discussions concerning its meaning (for a summary, see Graziano and Vink, 2007). For example, Featherstone and Radaelli (2003) acknowledged the complexity of the ontology of Europeanization as well as its dynamic and asymmetrical character. Accordingly, the term Europeanization is applied within four broad categories: as an historical process; as a matter of cultural diffusion; as a process of institutional adaptation; and as the adaptation of policy and policy processes. This typology of Europeanization seems to highlight that the term can be used to assess the effectiveness of European-level policies at the domestic level, as well as to understand how new European opportunities and constraints affect national policies. The consequence may be the beginning of the harmonization of national policies and their convergence into a particular socio-economic model. Similarly, Marginson and Sisson (2004) argue that the term Europeanization refers to a tendency "in which there is discernible movement with common policies leading to common outcomes achieved by common processes" (Marginson and Sisson, 2004: 8). Specifically, by looking at the aspects of employment regulation, both authors conceptualize Europeanization as the process of setting an integrated framework for the regulation of employment relationships within the European area. Accordingly, Europeanization naturally follows the process of European economic integration. This is because the establishment of an integrated common market for products and services sets industrial and employment relations systems in competition with each other. The result is an intensification of regime competition at both macro and micro (workplace) levels, when capacities must be improved and costs reduced in order to respond to changing market conditions. As Jacobi (1998) argues, in these circumstances industrial relations must be Europeanized. Hence, Europeanization denotes the social process for the creation of European-level macro-level institutions for industrial and employment relations in labour market regulation that are in charge of imposing comparability and regulating competition. Institutional arrangements establishing European transnational and national systems for providing information to employees, consultation, and involvement (or participation to management decision making process) are considered central to the European regulatory process mentioned above, and therefore constitute an important element of the social process of European integration (Hall, 1992). In particular, the statutory character of workers' involvement is part of today's European social and economic life. Like the European legal environment for businesses and investors, it requires appropriate regulation, including corporate law and financial market regulation. This is also conducive to more successful corporate governance, which promotes the identification of workers with their company.

Following this stream of research, until now EU studies have produced a great deal of research on European macro-level institutions and organizations. As a consequence, various formal and informal rules of this field are well known and EU institutional policy and political fields have been deeply investigated. The problem is that ultimately we know very much about the functioning of macro-level institutions and their effects on national policy but this knowledge is very little compensated about a correspondent understanding about the people working in or around EU institutions in terms of social backgrounds. Although, cross-national developments have recently appeared involving national as well as local social participants and/or European and national organizations of capital and labour, few studies have actually provided sociological data on the *people* (*'social agents'*) who contribute to the development of a social process of Europeanization. Nevertheless, cooperation and coordination practices, developed by local and national actors across different levels, are seen strongly contributing to the Europeanization of industrial relations and labour market regulation more generally (Marginson, 2006).

Therefore, we think that this gap must be filled in for two reasons. Firstly, studying actors as social agents would improve existing theories on European integration, by shedding light on the social foundations of what happens at the micro level and how this affects the macro- institutional level of EU. In other words, it means to understand the conditions favouring or inhibiting the capacity to articulate between a 'bottom-up' and a 'top-down' approach in European studies. Secondly, conceptualizing EU institutions as a social field (Bourdieu and Wacquant, 1992; Fligstein 2001); may be fruitful in several respects, such as reassessing Europeanization and EU institutionalization as a social process. Consistent with this, elsewhere we have argued that there is not a "one-size fits all" model for Europeanization of industrial relations (Pulignano and Kluge, 2007). Kluge (2004) talks about an "unfinished puzzle", consisting of minimum standards, procedures, and institutional settings for labour relations practices which are not intended to substitute for, or alter, national systems and models. Our point for consideration here is how this set of regulative measures becomes activated by its practical application in companies and workplaces. Thus, our aim is to understand social phenomena as the product of an encounter between, on the one hand, individual and collective dispositions to act (*habitus,* cf. Bourdieu and Wacquant, 1992), and on the other hand, so-called relational contexts, which may be analyzed under various forms in organizations, institutions and field.

As some sociology has underlined concerning the history of modern states (such as for example Norbert Elias and Michel Foucault), there has been a direct link between the making of political power at the centre and the shaping of everyday life at the periphery. This is very important especially when we focus on the social actors exposed to European policy. There is a fairly developed, dynamic network of practices, which contributes constantly and continuously to the 'social making' of the process of social dialogue within Europe. This is more evident at the transnational level due to the fact that Europe has mainly – although not only – dealt with the transnational level in order to create structures for employee representatives' involvement within the 'transnational space' of multinational firms in order to respond to economic internationalization. Thereby, we claim that the "multi-level system of governance", as the model of European industrial relations referred to by Marginson and Sisson (2004), needs to be put on a more solid foundation. Concretely, this means carefully capturing the practices of the social actors as workers' involvement and management, together with the interplaying collective bargaining and trade union representation. The examination of these practices is crucial if we want to effectively assess the Europeanization of social dialogue as the process of local social adaptation originated by the EU, by looking at how far progress has effectively occurred on the employee side of workers' involvement at the transnational level, and how this has impacted on the development of an effective European industrial relations agenda.

By proposing a study centred on the social agents who operate in EU institutions of social dialogue at the transnational company level, such as the European Works Councils (EWCs), we consider EU institutions as a social field (Bourdieu and Wacquant, 1992) or as socio-economic phenomena (cf. Fleetwood, 2011). Without denying the importance of European or national institutions for Europeanization, we follow recent post-determinist neo-institutionalism approach in social science which focuses on a more Weberian view of these institutions. This means to stress not only the functions performed by the latter, but their distinct 'logics' and the different sets of values that govern them (Deeg and Jackson, 2007). In accordance, Streeck and Thelen (2005) have sought to develop a conceptual framework where institutions are conceived as 'resources' which can be used by the social actors in order to pursue their own goals on one hand, or are seen as 'constraints' which can impede the achievement of these goals on the other hand. Thereby, social actors are conceptualized as active 'agents' in society, and thereby capable to use different institutional national and supra-national systems as potential resources for action.

This approach is very much in line with a critical realist perspective, particularly Archer's (1995; 2003) realist social theory. Edwards (2005) puts forward an argument for why a critical realist perspective is promising for industrial relations research and Fleetwood (2011) develops a practical example of using a critical realist perspective for labour market related phenomena. In this perspective, social actors use institutional learning as a signal for proper societal self-organization and self-reflexivity. We consider this conceptual framework as relevant to explain the empirical outcomes (i.e. EWCs practices) of our study while using the Europeanization frame to assess the gradual process of transformation occurred in EU with regard to social dialogue, and industrial relations more generally. This is a crucial part of the hypothesis of this chapter, that is that setting up a new institution or legislation at the European supra-national level for the involvement of the employees is not automatically synonymous of an effective Europeanization. Rather, the action of the social actors operating within these European institutions needs to be examined to explain and to assess the degree of active configurations for workers' involvement within a European context.

Several structural factors have been identified in the legal and social spheres as concretely affecting the creation of a space for the involvement of employee representatives in Europe (Cressey, 2009). Firstly, there is the problem of fragmentation (Gold, 2010), which often focuses on the match between EU legislation and the cross-national diversity of industrial relations systems. These systems differ widely across the EU member states and once in place they generally seem to be strong and averse to change. In Europe, different national systems are characterized by diverse institutions governing the representation of interests and workers' involvement[1]. Despite the strategies the EU has historically developed to deal with the problem of fragmentation, it remains unclear and quite debatable to what extent the responses offered to tackle the issue provide a coherent way of encouraging the creation of a stable transnational space, where genuine employees' engagement can be encouraged in the light of attention to differences in the industrial relations systems across member states. A second, related area of analysis concerns the uniform compliance and/or enforcement of transposed measures. Several studies have highlighted the variation in compliance regimes across the EU (Gold and Matthews, 1996; Falker et al., 2005). An extension of this approach to the involvement of employee representatives would require an analysis of the procedures available to them to claim rights in cases of non-compliance, the effectiveness of enforcement agencies, and the possible sanctions that could be imposed in each member state. Third, a large volume of research has highlighted that the nature of employee involvement in Europe, within and across the different institutional structures, is complex and varied. It depends very much on a variety of company structures, sectoral differentiation, traditions, and trade union ideology (Hall and Marginson, 2005; Pulignano, 2007). Likewise, Keller and Werner (2010) points out the fragmentation of participation arrangements within a European Company (SE) as a result of sector-based and power relations factors within a Special Negotiation Body (SNB).

In summary, two arguments (or explanations) underpin the view emerging from relevant literature of the problematic nature of creating a European space for employee involvement. Radical critics argue that there is no such thing as Europeanization with regard to employee involvement. An illustration of this can first be found in the well-known analysis Streeck (1997) put forward with regard to EWCs being an extension of national systems of involvement. According, EWCs are heavily influenced by a company's home country. For example, with regard to a German multinational company, co-determination rights within German company law will apply only to the company's German workforce, even if the majority of its workforce is outside Germany, and the EWC will co-exist alongside the central works council, which is likely to be better resourced and closer to the management. Alternatively, some others argue that although the transposition of EU legislation on employee involvement into national settings, and its interpretation in line with domestic institutions and legal frameworks, has always raised issues of equivalence, the process of widening the EU has reinforced trends towards even greater fragmentation and flexibility. On the other side, it can also be argued that European enlargement has had far-reaching

---

[1] Traditionally we distinguish between: systems with strong legal foundations (as in Germany); systems where trade unions are social partners (as in the Nordic countries); systems based on voluntary agreements and company-based power structures (as UK); and systems governed by politics and the state (as in France and other southern European countries) (Gold, 2010)

implications for arrangements of employee involvement in Europe. Crucially, European enlargement has brought into the analysis the weak and non-homogeneous institutional and structural arrangements for employee involvement that exist within those countries whose systems of workplace representation often do not conform to the norm of coordinated arrangements typical of Western economies (Marginson, 2006). Alarmed by such a prospect, the necessity for EU-level intervention to establish and entrench the core institutional architecture of industrial relations in the new member states has been underlined. At the core of the argument is the fact that relying on internal dynamics within these societies will not suffice In sum, the arguments so far examined depart from a rather vertical, 'top-down' perspective while assessing Europeanization of social dialogue. They examine current EU initiatives regarding the forms and structures of transnational representation and employee involvement, and the impact of these initiatives on the existing variety of domestic institutional structures and cultures. Conversely, as we argue in this chapter, although European-macro institutional processes and dynamics are certainly crucial in influencing local behavior, the interface between EU intervention and employee involvement lies in the interplay between the company level, the industry, and more generally the EU levels of action. In other words, the interaction between 'top-down' and 'bottom-up' developments as above argued is important in contributing to an emergent process of Europeanization. It is obvious that a strong institutional foundation at the European level regarding the representation of employees' interests and their involvement has the capacity to influence the general direction of Europeanization. On the other hand, it can also be argued that good workplace policy concerning workers' involvement can also give corporate actors an outline and a sense of direction. This is because at the end of the day, it is ultimately the employers and employees who are in the position of whether or not to put concepts into practice. This compromises an important research task: namely to cast light on the various practices and specific modes of interplay between the different social policy actors and levels of action. Specifically, as we will demonstrate in the following sections, it means focusing on the existing local practices adopted at the workplace in respect of existing transnational structures for employee involvement, bargaining, and representation issues more generally.

Methodology and research design

The empirical fieldwork was conducted in the second half of the decade 2000-2010. Specifically, a series of company-based case studies were developed in 2006-2007 and updated in 2008. The aims of the research were as follows. To compare the use by the social actors – in particular the workers – of the statutory representative forms of employee involvement at the European level, such as EWCs, in each multinational company selected for investigation. This was done by examining the EWCs' practices at the company level. Further, we comparatively assess whether these practices reflect a particular behavior by the local actors (i.e. management, employees and trade unions) to use existing supra-national institutional structures for employee representation as a resource capable to foster the development of a new framework supporting cross-national workers' involvement at the European company level, and therefore favoring the so-called Europeanization of industrial relations more generally.

Keeping this in mind, we compared the practices of EWCs in sixty multinational companies with headquarters in five different countries (Germany, Belgium, France, Hungary, and the United Kingdom) and across different sectors (metalworking, chemical, food, public and private services, and transport). We chose a comparative, case-oriented research method because of its capacity to go beyond descriptive statistical measures and towards an in-depth understanding of the processes, individual motivations, and behaviors underlying certain social phenomena. As Mahoney and Goertz (2006) argue, in this method of research the aim is an in-depth understanding of a context or searches for the "causes of effects". This is very much in line with Maxwell's argument in accordance to which "context and causal processes are central to realist approaches to social science" (Maxwell, 2012: 40-45). In this respect, in-depth narrative-based case studies are the best way to analyze the processes characterizing the delivery of particular outcomes (practices) with regard to EWCs, as well as to underline the conditions fostering or hindering such outcomes at the company level. This is crucial to assess the degree to which the existing EU structures for the involvement of the employee representatives at the transnational company level contribute to the process of Europeanization of industrial relations more generally.

Moreover, a case-oriented research approach based on small-N cases is the most appropriate to combine with the use of a comparative method. This is because the research aims at searching for internal explanations; that is, not only to identify the conditions or variables explaining the development (or not) of certain practices with regard to the functioning of an EWC, but also to look at the extent to which the local social actors played an important role in guiding the development of these practices, i.e. to identify the "motives" behind such practices. Following Ferejohn (2004), we are looking for the "reasons for an action". Accordingly, an action is explained internally as an outcome of a deliberate process in which an "agent" is assumed to act for a reason.

The focus of the research is on the multinational company level, which is therefore the level where we need to maximize variety. However, the importance of the sector level in shaping local practices is also very much highlighted in the study of industrial relations (Marginson et al., 2003). Therefore, we have not kept the sector constant. Moreover, the selection of the countries is driven by conceptual reasons. We selected the countries where we could maximize institutional cross-national diversity. Although Germany and Belgium are usually classified as 'coordinated market economies', Germany has recently been through a process of reduced coordination, as an effect of institutional changes occurring in the political situation (for example, see Streeck, 2009). Whereas the United Kingdom remains a 'liberal market economy', France is categorized as a 'mixed economy', and therefore different to the Central and Eastern Europe to which Hungary belongs. Institutional diversity is relevant here, due to the need to assess the extent to which the functioning of a EWC is a reflection of national institutional settings alone. Each implementation of the EWC 1994/45 Directive roots back deeply into the relevant national environment of legal provisions, as they are all the result of subsequent transposition into national law.

The interviews used for the research (between 10 and 15 in each case study, for an average duration of one hour per interview) included a variety of participants: national and European-level representatives of employers and trade unions, local managers, local trade union representatives, and employee representatives. We used semi-structured but open-ended interviews to allow unanticipated issues to be examined, revising this iteratively during the course of the research to reflect new findings, but retaining a core set of questions. While we recognize that our interviews were not explicitly biographical in nature, we did endeavor to understand the role the individual subjectivities of the informants in mediating the forms and outcomes of employee involvement in companies studied.

All the interviews were recorded and transcribed. In the next section we will present the empirical evidence. It consists of two main parts. The first part presents the current EU legislation on employee involvement. Next, the actual operations of the European structure for the involvement of employee representatives at the European company level are examined and assessed in the light of the action undertaken by the social actors (employees and management) operating within these European institutions for the representation of workers' interests.

The involvement of employee representatives at the European level: current institutional arrangements and actual operations

Current institutional arrangements

A series of EC-driven macro-institutional initiatives involving statutory employee involvement was first launched from 1970 onwards. These initiatives mainly took the form of directives and they sought to set out comprehensive employment standards throughout Europe (Ahlering and Deakin, 2005).

As is typical of the results of bargaining for the interests of the different parties concerned (in this case mainly the social partners), each EU regulation in the field of information for workers' representatives and consultation represents a political compromise. It is also important to point out the controversial internal debates within the various parties in advance of reaching a compromise. For example, what makes things more difficult than for many other European issues is that the rules and provisions for employee involvement are deeply rooted in national legislation and cultural settings and experiences. Therefore, up to now the importance and extent of becoming involved in company decision making and control has been fundamentally contested internally within the affiliations of European trade unions as well as within the employers' federations themselves.

The prominent forerunners of recent EU directives on employee involvement were: the first draft proposal on a European Company Statute (1970); the Fifth Directive (1972); and what is termed the Vredeling Directive (1980). All these initiatives were later adopted in directives and enriched by other measures. There are currently some 15 directives that govern employee representatives' participation, in one form or another, across the member states of the EU (Gold, 2010). The most notable are the Directive on European Works Councils (EWCs); the Information and Consultation of Employees Directive (ICE); the European Company Statute (ECS) Directive; and the Recast 2009 EWC Directive. The others cover the extension of the rights for employees' participation in specific cases, such as: collective redundancies within companies; health and safety issues; and the restructuring of companies including the transfer of undertakings, cross-border mergers, and take-over bids. From the last group, we specifically mention what is termed the Tenth Directive, dealing with cross-border mergers of limited liability companies. The aim of this directive, which came into effect in December 2007, was to make corporate mergers across European borders substantially easier. With regard to safeguarding existing participation rights in the situation of a merger, a solution was decided on which in most cases refers to the mechanisms of the European Company Statute (ECS) Directive.

EU legislation for employee involvement at both transnational and national level was required because "no common minimum rules applied to European companies for timely and appropriate information and consultation" (Quintin, 2003: 5). By setting minimum standards, the law lessens competition between firms with regard to information, consultation, and participation arrangements. It creates a baseline standard which contributes to a single or universalist regulatory environment (Streeck, 1995). As a result, many of these minimum standards take effect as social rights (Patmore, 2010). Nevertheless, whereas transnational structures for the representation and involvement of employees are conceived as the most appropriate instrument for labour to respond to the process of economic internationalization, the rationale of setting up national-level rights of information for employees, consultation, and participation is consistent with the process of domestic adaptation to European regional integration more generally.

The distinction between the two rationales guiding the EU intervention on transnational and national statutory arrangements for workers' involvement is reflected in both the origins and the evolution of the different European directives dealing with both national and cross-border level representation issues. The origins of the European Company Statute (ECS) Directive can be traced back to 1959. The ECS was a proposal for a voluntary system of board-level representation with an accompanying EWC for companies that chose to register at the community level (Schwimbersky and Gold, 2009). The ECS model borrowed from the German system of co-determination. Following the Single European Act (1986), the proposal was revised and finally adopted in 2001, together with a directive on the involvement of employees (termed the Fifth Directive, 2001/86/EC). As opposed to the ECS proposal, the Fifth Directive was intended to harmonize systems of corporate governance within countries, among companies with 500 or more employees. Debates among the member states, employers' organizations, and trade unions ranged from the workforce size threshold (companies with 500 employees) through the means of selection of the employee representatives, to the principle of board-level representation. As a consequence, the Fifth Directive was not adopted.

In order to achieve further progress in this particular field of EU legislation, the information and consultation provisions available to workers within multinationals were separated from the issue of employee involvement. This mirrors the Vredeling Directive, which was originally proposed by the EU Commission for Social Affairs. The starting argument was the acknowledgment that in multinationals, managerial decision making often took place in locations that were outside the scope of national legislation regarding workers' involvement, thus weakening the effect of such national legislation. At the end of the process of negotiation, which took almost a year, in September 1994 the EWC directive (94/45/EC) was ratified. The EWC directive requires that all companies which employ more than 1,000 people, of whom at least 150 are employed in each of two member states, are legally obliged to establish a forum, or procedures for informing and consulting with their employees across Europe.

The Directive 2002/14/EC on the national rights for information and consultation to be given to employees was drafted in fairly broad terms, and therefore allowed member states considerable flexibility regarding the practical arrangements for the implementation of its provisions (Carley and Hall, 2009). The large range of flexibility options allowed by the directive firstly contributed to cooling down the climate of tensions between national governments, employers' organizations, and trade unions with regard to the introduction of binding rules concerning workers' involvement. Secondly, it contributed to undermining the legislative effects of the ICE regulations while widening the gap between different legal texts across the member states in Europe. Comparisons of legal texts have culminated in demands for the revision of those aspects of the directive (e.g. the definition of information and consultation, the timeliness of information and consultation, the definition of establishments and undertakings, and provisions governing confidentiality) which are perceived as not functioning well (Gold, 2010). In addition, the directive does not prescribe works councils and there is a complex triggering procedure before a mechanism becomes mandatory. Further, although the directive's scope is to modernize production systems in Europe while strengthening the voice of employees in the face of increasing restructuring and decentralization of industrial relations, other far less institutionalized procedures are possible within companies (Gumbrell-McCornick and Hyman, 2010).

Actual operations of EWCs: articulating social interests, in a multi-national governance system

In this section we will assess the extent to which the above presented macro-institutional European structures for employee representation have been able to stimulate the creation of an effective space for social dialogue in Europe, and therefore whether they represent a stimulator for the Europeanization of industrial relations. In particular, we concentrate on the EWCs structures for employee representation at the European company level. Against general expectations, we illustrate that different EWCs experiences have contributed differently – in both less and more positive ways – to construct a European collective voice as a crucial aspect for the Europeanization of industrial relations. The heterogeneity of these experiences shed light on the diversity of EWCs practices developed by corporate social actors – management and employees – within the multi-national European governance system. Therefore, they illustrate the capacity local social policy actors have to use and influence EU legislation and macro-institutions by identifying their roles and functions within them.

The study classifies the actual operations or practices of EWCs in each multinational company, and examines the conditions supporting these practices. They have helped to develop to a different extent a proactive and joint agenda between management and employees, and therefore they have contributed differently to fill in the institutional framework for European social dialogue while enhancing the social agenda at the EU level. This is illustrated, for example, by the different role played by the European industry federations at the European level to negotiate framework agreements (European Frameworks Agreements, or EFAs) at the EU level. In so doing, the empirical findings do not contribute to deny the value of the academic argument concerning the problematic functioning of transnational employee representation structures in Europe. Rather, they claim that it is not possible to objectively and unequivocally evaluate complex transnational institutions for worker involvement with a simple judgment of 'successful' or 'unsuccessful' solely based on an attempt to quantify (to measure) the impact of a relatively weak EU regulatory setting with regard to information provided to employees and their involvement in management decision making.

A more systematic analysis of the experiences characterizing the existing transnational institutions for statutory workers involvement is needed. This requires assessing the extent of Europeanization by firstly examining the different practices developed at the workplace by the social actors under the EU regulatory framework, and secondly identifying the diverse conditions sustaining the functioning of these practices. In other words, this means to embed workplace-level practices by local social actors into existing European macro institutional structures for employee involvement, and evaluating them by referring to the reasons and beliefs of the social actors and evaluate them as causal explanations. It recalls the tradition of viewing industrial relations institutions (including European-level institutions for the regulation of employment and labour markets) as the outcomes of struggles and compromises between different societal interest groups (Sisson, 1987).

First of all, let us keep in mind some important statistical facts that illustrate the probable direct impact of European directives covering statutory employee involvement: more and more workers have come under the umbrella of a transnational interest representation body. This means more and more representatives (12,000 -14,000 delegates, according to a recent ETUI estimate, cf. Jagodzinski and Paz, 2010) at the European cross-border level have had to deal for the first time with topics of transnational importance, such as internationalization, regime competition, and cross-border restructuring.

By taking a bottom-up perspective one can ask if the Euro-pessimistic interpretations are fully justified or if the glass may look more full than it is usually expected. Specifically, this means questioning for example, whether EWCs have the potential for dynamic development and positive transformation, especially when seen from the position where company developments become visible, rather than from a higher perspective. It has to be recognized that every case is unique and that each agreement on employee involvement stipulated at the company level represents the result of a political compromise reached through negotiations between management and the body representing employees. Although this framework sets clear limits on the possibilities for comparing and generalizing experiences of negotiations and their results, it also clearly illustrates that all relationships around the representation of interests are based on agreements that are locally negotiated in accordance with differing social interests, power relations, and the underlying particularities of a company. These factors concur to make labour relations "tailor-made". A 1998 study by the Hans-Bockler Foundation and the Bertelsmann Foundation (*Co-determination and new corporate cultures,* 1998) about the adaptation of a comparable, very formalistic and legalistic model of interest representation and co-determination at Post-fordist workplaces, such as in Germany, underlined the heterogeneity of practices developed locally by the social actors (management and employee representatives) under the umbrella of the national law on co-determination. Specifically the study found that despite conforming to national legislation on co-determination, practices of labour relations varied very much in accordance to the requirements of the company and the workplace environment. Hence a similar logic may help here to explain the resort to local practices and the importance of local experiences while assessing the effects of Europeanization with regard to employee involvement and industrial relations more generally.

Previous studies on EWCs in multinationals by the European Foundation for the Improvement of Living and Working Conditions reported on the diversity of practices in the EWCs concerned, but the survey was not able to identify a single example where an EWC had became a truly European-level representative body. We think that the reasons for this shortcoming in relation to identifying effective EWC practices are only partly due to a weak legal basis. As our findings highlight, other conditions can be identified as underlying the effective use of EWCs.

In the light of data from the sixty company cases, we differentiate between three basic types of EWC practices: EWCs driven by regime competition; EWCs based on commonalities and the joint interests of management and employees; and pro-active EWCs based on strong trade unions. This classification is based on a grassroots evaluation conducted in the second half of 2000 of the functioning and dynamics typical of EWCs (for more details see Voss, Kluge et al., 2010). It is discussed in the sections below.

EWCs driven by regime competition

The type of EWC based on regime competition is strongly characterized by growing internationalization and a threat to national labour regimes of relocation. Growth in internal competition between production sites of the same company as well as dramatically accelerated processes of cross-border restructuring and de-localization have significantly increased the pressure on employment and interest representation. Competition between production sites has therefore become an everyday phenomenon with regular media coverage. Competition for new investment projects is even more intense. The pressure being exerted by employers on employees is increasing and exceeds even the realistic threat of relocation. This leads to interest conflicts between different employee groups, which often appears in the form of distrust exhibited towards new member state members of EWCs. This type of EWC practice is strongly determined by growing internationalization, relocation and regime competition among national labour regimes, and it is therefore, clearly overstretched as an institution for the representation of cross-border interests and the transnational coordination of labour interests. In reality, this type of EWC practice mirrors its characterization as a vehicle for the international competition of labour regimes (Hancké, 2000). Among the features characterizing this type of EWC we note: difficult relations between management and employee representatives and trade unions; minimalist or even obstructive behavior on the part of management towards the EWC; difficulties in defining common cross-border interests within the EWC; the absence of any trade union strategy or agenda for EWC policy, resulting in generally passive behavior by both management and union representatives in the context of restructuring or other issues; and the lack of, or very weak, integration into relevant national industrial relations systems.

This regime competition type of EWC can be described as being 'in the shadows' with regard to its position and role within overall company-wide institutions and structures for interest representation, social dialogue, and employee involvement. Experiences of EWCs in the studied multinational companies, such as Siemens, Electrolux, and Bosch, for example, illustrate this type of EWC, which results from a whole bundle of difficult framework conditions. Specifically, several conditions concur to undermine the dynamic functioning of this form of EWC: very high diversity in company structures in terms of corporate divisions composition of the workforce, and local labour relations(e.g. see Siemens); a decentralized corporate HR culture with highly decentralized autonomy and labour relations under the control of local management; a high degree of internationalization of production and corporate functions; and the EWCs' structure and practice being predominated by headquarters (e.g. the cases of Siemens and Bosch, with a strong German group works council with strong institutions, representation interests, and co-determination in the home country).

Empirical data illustrate that confronted by growing internationalization and restructuring, the EWCs at both Siemens and Bosch found it very difficult to take on a proactive role independent of the interests of national representation. Indeed, it appeared that the right to information and consultation was only partly used, which followed the rather minimalistic management strategy regarding information and consultation in terms of both substance and timing. The minimalist management strategy concerning Europe-wide representation of interests and social dialogue is also illustrated by the fact that both Bosch and Siemens' central headquarters did not pay much attention to the labour relations situation and the corporate culture in their subsidiaries in Central and Eastern Europe. In particular, in 2008 when Siemens announced the closure of the Siemens SKV plant in Prague as the result of a worldwide restructuring plan, no information and consultation was provided by management to the employee representatives in the European countries. On the contrary, only the German economic committee of the local works council received some generalized data about the EU and detailed facts about the German sites that were to be affected by restructuring. It is argued that the strong control of German representatives over the Siemens EWC (known as the Siemens Employee Committee, or SEC) constrained the development of transnational mutual trust and employees' cohesion in the face of the challenge of cross-border restructuring in Siemens. Thereby it discouraged the conclusion of a framework agreement at the European level by the European Metalworkers' Federation (EMF) aimed at negotiating collective redundancies following restructuring (Pulignano et al., 2012).

EWCs based on commonalities and joint interests

The EWC practice based on joint and common social interests is typical of those EWCs characterized by a search for commonalities in interest representation to define joint ideas and strategies at the EU level. Examples of this EWCs practices are the German Telekom, the Belgian KBC Bank, the French Sanofi-Aventis group, and the Hungarian MOL. In contrast to the first type of EWC, these examples established EWC structures comparatively late. For example, Telekom and MOL established their EWCs in 2004 and although the EWC at KBC bank was formed in 1996, it was mainly related to the development of group-wide interest representation and coordination structures within various undertakings in Belgium.

One significant common feature of this type of EWC practice relates to the fact the EWC as the most important instrument for both the employees and the management enabling them to cope with the rather new experience of internationalization. In this context EWC has to be seen not only for employees in establishing company-wide structures of employee communication, information and exchange of experience, but also from management's point of view, since all the above mentioned companies have been confronted with the difficult task of having to integrate rather than divide parts and investments, acquisitions and mergers, as well as uniting very diverse management cultures under one roof. Similarly, Sanofi-Aventis (established in 2005 through the merger of the French Sanofi-Synthelabo and French-German Aventis) is an example of a corporate culture characterized by growing internal diversity and the task of integrating very diverse parts into a common corporate identity. An interesting feature of this type of EWC is the fact that management has used it as an instrument for supporting the creation of a corporate identity and achieving consensus. Very illustrative of this are the Belgian KBC and the German Telekom cases, where the respective management, confronted with the task of implementing a corporate identity through massive re-branding processes, tried to use European institutions such as the EWCs, to help integrate their foreign subsidies into the parent company. An apparent difference concerning the practices of this group of EWCs as compared to the first group is that practices and agenda development are driven by an exchange of experiences by local participants with regard to labour relations, corporate culture, and the societal effects of the consolidation of new acquisitions. For example, in some of the companies we investigated, European occupational pension schemes (e.g. in KBC) or a common agenda of European harmonization in social policy at the company level (e.g. in MOL) have been created. Strong trade union structures (e.g. Telekom and MOL), established employee involvement rights at the supervisory board in the field of private financial services (e.g. KBC), and the highly dispersed structure of local service branches and a high proportion of sales representatives (in the insurance field), have helped the development of the practices of this type of EWC.

Proactive EWCs

Finally, the last type is the pro-active EWCs: those strongly involved in company development, in particular in the context of transnational restructuring. We refer mostly to those French (e.g. Danone, PSA Peugeot-Citroen, Renault, and Total), German (e.g. Deutsche Bank), and US (e.g. GM and Ford) multinationals, where European (and sometimes international) framework agreements were negotiated after the mid-1990s. Key features include strong trade union involvement, EWC practices integrated into national structures and organizations of interest representation, and efforts to support national participation.

It can be argued that in the cases of pro-active EWCs, employee representatives and trade unions used the EWC as a tool to promote closer social relationships between EWC members and employees in the diverse geographical contexts where the multinationals' subsidiaries were localized. The best known experiences in this context are the GM and Ford EWC cases. They clearly illustrate that although working under different labour relations situations (more conflict-oriented in GM than in Ford) the EWCs played a crucial role in shaping the hearts and minds of the workers and local unions by developing many commonalities in their interpretation of the situation of restructuring. These commonalities soon became principles or norms to be followed by all those involved locally (i.e. employees, local unions, and company management) everywhere.

In particular, both cases suggest that the institution of the EWC provided the resources that were used by local unions within the framing strategy to build up cross-border worker coordination and articulate with the EU level. At both Ford and GM, the EWC became the platform for treating international competition as a grievance. In so doing the EWC agreed with the EMF that national union strategies could not solve the international problems created by international capital, and this resulted in a general statement that they used to point out the need for local trade unions and workers to cooperate across borders. Accordingly, the EWC sustained the strategy developed by the EMF by creating a shared perception and understanding of problems, interests, and strategies across European borders. The result was the negotiation of diverse European framework agreements between 2000 and 2010 in order to socially handle collective redundancies as the result of the various companies' restructuring plans (Pulignano, 2010).

Discussion and further research

Table 6.1 presents a summary of the type and content of the EWC practices supported by local participants at the company level. Empirical findings show that pro-active EWCs and EWCs with commonalities and joint interests are more responsive to a process of Europeanisation because they are in general better prepared to cope with challenges, both at group and workplace level, than are EWCs driven by regime competition. There is a clear correlation between early and effective EWC involvement and pro-active EWC practices at headquarters level. In terms of effective social dialogue at the multinational company level it is possible to identify certain factors contributing to the development of good EWC practices. Among these factors, a European collective identity (Knudsen et al., 2007) seems crucial. This is an important challenge facing EWCs. In fact, current studies demonstrate that very few EWCs have been able to develop a common sense of purpose that stretches beyond national borders. Kotthoff (2006) refers to this as the 'day-to-day Europeanization' of employee representatives' work. Therefore, one of the most important preconditions for creating cross-border reflections is intensified communication. It is no surprise that the increase of the number of possible meetings was one of the major demands of the Recast 2009 EWC directive.

Typology of EWCs practices	Content of the EWCs practices
EWCs driven by regime competition	Minimalist and obstructive behavior by management; no common interests among EWC representatives; no strategy or agenda for EWC policy; very weak integration of EWC employee representatives in the respective national industrial relations systems.
EWCs based on commonalities and joint interests	Commonalities in European interest representation to define joint ideas and strategies at the EU level; management use of EWC as an instrument supporting the creation of a corporate identity and achieving consensus.
Proactive EWCs	Strong trade union involvement in EWC; EWC practice integrated in national structures and organizations of interest representation and obligatory workers involvement (OWI), as well as efforts to support national participation.

Table 6.1 Summary of the type and content of EWCs practices
Source: Own elaboration based on Voss, Kluge et al (2010)

Given the relevance of shared collective identities for the emergence of good EWCs practices, a follow up research should be more explicitly focused on the question of the barriers and opportunities for the emergence of a European collective identity among employee representatives. The tradition of biographical research on European identities (see Wengraf and Spanò, Domecka and Perone in this volume and Miller, 2012) can be very helpful in this respect and provide useful inspirations. Inspired by an emergent body of biographical research on employee representatives in Europe (Gold, Kluge and Conchon, 2010; Moore, 2011; Mrozowicki, Pulignano and Van Hootegem, 2010), the follow up biographical study could analyze how organisational and institutional factors are reflected by employee representatives and mediated by their biographical experiences leading to various types of strategies at the EWCs level. In this way, it could help to explore more precisely the mechanisms behind the development of three types of the EWCs practices and explain the emergence of agential and innovative responses by social actors to the existing institutional and organisational arrangements.

Conclusion

This chapter has illustrated that the interplay between the European-macro (vertical) level and the cross-national (horizontal) level is crucial in explaining the extent to which community-level norms can contribute to the deployment of a transnational space for the promotion of social dialogue in Europe. Specifically, this means questioning whether European law (i.e. directives) in the field of employee involvement at the transnational level alone can be considered an incommensurable and unique driver for Europeanization of industrial relations more generally. The analysis developed in the chapter illustrates that this is a striking point, since it initially depends greatly on how positively employee representatives, their trade unions, and management in different organizational and national contexts view the results of negotiations and how they use (act-upon) institutional structures by using them as resources (or constraints) while making sense of European law and structures. It is more and more in the mindsets of interest representatives that cross-border operations have become a feature of everyday life, wherever they are located.

European directives and macro-institutions are useful but an insufficient tool for Europeanization. Legal norms and structures need to be complemented with practices that inform everyday life and the interests of different social groups. The European initiatives create an institutional framework, which by definition risks remaining an 'empty shell' unless it is filled in by real practices.

In our assessment of the effects of Europeanization in relation to representative forms of statutory workers' involvement at the transnational level, we have discussed the extent to which real practices fill in the European legal framework, as well as examining some conditions facilitating the development of these practices. Specifically, in the day-to-day life of modern global corporate organizations, the transition to more cooperative-dependent forms of work organization, the delegation of decision-making responsibility to individual employees, and the use of benchmarking as a management tool to increase competitive performance by cross-nationally comparing practices and policies have been addressed. These frequently mean that institutions, both the ones originally existing at the national level and those imported because of the EU, appear too formalistic, unwieldy, and sometimes practically irrelevant.

Large multinational corporations have become decentralized operationally, but centralized strategically (Whittington and Mayer, 1994). Therefore a balance needs to be constantly ensured between heteronomy and autonomy, that is central regulation from above (i.e. the parent company) and local responsibility at the bottom (i.e. the subsidiary company) so that local managers are encouraged alone and/or in bargaining with employee representatives and trade unions to find their own paths to continuous improvement. This is always a process of 'institutional learning by doing' or also power relations in order to fit in and further develop rules for employee involvement into requirements for new forms of plant and company organization demanded by the market. In view of this, in the chapter we have shown how important is to discover actors' reasoning and circumstances (or conditions supporting these reasons) in the specific context of social dialogue at the European company-level to explain the nature of the outcomes in terms of the functioning and practices of the EWCs. The empirical qualitative research has been conducted by using a realist analytical framework through semi-structured, open-ended interviews which provided rich data, detailed and varied enough to lead to a revealing picture of what was going on and of the processes involved. The use of biographical interviews would have probably enhanced the understanding of these processes because it would have increased the possibility to highlight also those processes not directly observable, but which can often be inferred from present behaviors.

References

Ahlering, B. and Deakin, S. (2005). 'Labour Regulation, Corporate Governance and Legal Origin: A Case of Institutional Complementarity', *Working Paper* no. 72/2006, University of Cambridge.

Archer, M.S. (1995). *Realist Social Theory: The Morphogenetic Approach*. Cambridge, UK: Cambridge University Press.

Archer, M.S. (2003). *Structure, Agency and the Internal Conversation*. Cambridge, UK: Cambridge University Press.

Bourdieu, P. and Wacquant, L. (1992). *An Inivitation to Reflexive Sociology*. Cambridge: Polity Press.

Carley, M. and Hall, M. (2009). *The Impact of the Information and Consultation Directive on Industrial Relations, European Industrial Relations Observatory*, available at: http://www.eurofound.europa.eu/eiro/studies/tn0710029s/tn0710029s.htm.

Coates, D. (1980). *Labour in Power?* London: Longman.

Co-determination and New Corporate Cultures. Survey and Perspectives (1998). Bertelsmann Foundation and Hans-Böckler-Foundation, Gütersloh: Verlag Bertelsmann Stiftung, available at: http://www.bertelsmann-stiftung.de/cps/rde/xbcr/SID-59775685-1D890BD4/bst/ReportAbschluss.pdf

Cressey, P. (2009). 'Obligatory workers involvement (OWI)'. in M. Gold (ed.) *Employment Policy in the European Union. Origins, Themes and Prospects*. Basingstoke: Palgrave.

Deeg, R. and Jackson, G. (2007). 'Towards a More Dynamic Theory of Capitalist Variety'. *Socio-Economic Review, 5: 149-179.*

Edwards, P. (2005). 'The challenging but promising future of industrial relations: developing theory and method in context-sensitive research'. *Industrial Relations Journal*, 36(4): 264-282.

Falker, G., Hartlapp M., Leiber S., and Treib O. (2005). *Complying with Europe. EU Harmonisation and Soft Law in the Member States*, Cambridge: Cambridge University Press.

Featherstone, K., and Radaelli, C.M. (eds.) (2003). *The Politics of Europeanization*. Oxford: Oxford University Press.

Fleetwood, S. (2011). 'Sketching a socio-economic model of labour markets'. *Cambridge Journal of Economics*, 35: 15-38.

Fligstein, N. (2001). 'Social skill and the theory of fields'. *Sociological Theory*, 19(2): 105-125.

Ferejohn, J. (2004). 'External and internal explanations'. in Shapiro, R., Smith, M., and Masoud, T.E. (eds.) *Problems and Methods in the Study of Politics*. Cambridge: Cambridge University Press.

Graziano, P. and Vink, P.M. (eds.) (2007). *Europeanization. New Research Agendas* London: Palgrave MacMillan.

Gold, M. (2010). 'Obligatory workers involvement (OWI) at the European Union Level: was it Worth the Wait? The Concept of "Functional Equivalence" Revisited'. unpublished paper.

Gold, M. and Matthews, D. (1996). 'The implications of the evolution of European integration for UK labour markets'. *Research Series* no. 73, London: Department for Education and Employment.

Gold, M., Kluge, N., and Conchon, A. (2010). '*In the Union and on the Board': Experiences of Board-Level Employee Representatives across Europe*. Brussels: ETUI.

Gumbrell-McCormick, R. and Hyman, R. (2010). 'Works Councils: The European Model of Industrial Democracy?'. in Wilkinson, A., Gollan, P., Marchington, M., and Lewin, D. (eds.), *The Oxford Handbook of Participation in Organizations*. Oxford: Oxford University Press, pp. 287-314.

Jacoby W. (1998). 'The Dilemmas of Diffusion: Social Embeddedness and the Problems of Institutional Change in Eastern Germany'. *Politics & Society*, 25(8):34-65.

Jagodzinski, R. (2009). 'Recast directive on European works councils: Cosmetic surgery or substantial progress?'. *Industrial Relations Journal*, 40(6), 534-545.

Jagodzinski, R. and Pas, I. (2010). *ETUI EWC database*.

Kelller B. and Wener F. (2010). 'Negotiated employee involvement in the Societas Europaea – a new mode to harmonisation and convergence or to heterogeneity and fragmentation?'. paper presented at the *9th Congress of European Industrial Relations Association*, University of Copenhagen.

Kluge, N. (2004). 'Workers' Involvement in Europe – A Still Unfinished Jigsaw'. in Jorgensen, H., Baerentse, M., Monks, J. (eds.) *European Trade Union Yearbook 2003/2004*. Brussels: ETUI. pp. 115-36.

Kotthoff, H. (2006). *Lehrjahre des Europäischen Betriebsrats. Zehn Jahre transnationale Arbeitnehmervertretung*. Berlin: Edition sigma.

Knudsen, H., Whittal, M., and Huijgen, F. (eds.) (2007). *European Works Councils and the Problem of European Identity*. London: Routledge.

Hall, M. (1992). 'Legislating for employee participation: A case study of the European Works Councils Directive'. *Warwick Papers in Industrial Relations*, No. 39.

Hall M., and Marginson P. (2005). 'Trojan horses or paper tigers? Assessing the significance of European Works Councils. Participation and democracy at work'. in Harley, B., Hyman, J., and Thompson, P. (eds.) *Participation at Work*. Basingstoke: Palgrave Macmillam: pp 204-221.

Hancké B. (2000). 'European Works Councils and Industrial Restructuring in the European Motor Industry'. *European Journal of Industrial Relations*, 6(1): 33-57.

Mahoney, J., and Goertz, G. (2006). 'A tale of two cultures: contrasting quantitative and qualitative research'. *Political Analysis*, 14 (3), 227-249.

Marchington, M. (2005). 'Employee Involvement: Patterns and Explanations'. in Harley, B., and Thompson, P. (eds.) *Participation and Democracy at Work*. London: Palgrave.

Marginson, P. (2006). 'Between Europeanisation and regime competition: Labour market regulation following EU enlargement'. *Warwick Papers in Industrial Relations*, 79, February.

Marginson, P., Sisson, K., and Arrowsmith, J. (2003). 'Between decentralization and Europeanization: sectoral bargaining in four countries and two sectors'. *European Journal of Industrial Relations*, 9(2): 163-87.

Marginson, P., and Sisson, K. (2004). *European Integration and Industrial Relations*. Basingstoke: Palgrave-Mac-Milan

Maxwell, J.A. (2012). *A Realist Approach for Qualitative Research*. London: Sage.

Miller, R. (ed.) (2012). *The Evolution of European Identities: Biographical Approaches*. Basingstoke: Palgrave Macmillan.

Moore, S. (2011). *New Trade Union Activism: Class Consciousness or Social Identity*. Basingstoke: Palgrave Macmillan.

Mrozowicki, A., Pulignano, V., Van Hootegem, G. (2010). 'Worker agency and trade union renewal: the case of Poland'. *Work, Employment and Society* 24 (2): 240-257.

Patmore, G. (2010). 'A Legal Perspective on Obligatory workers involvement (OWI)'. in Wilkinson, A., Gollan, P., Marchington, M., and Lewin, D. (eds.) *The Oxford Handbook of Participation in Organizations*. Oxford: Oxford University Press.

Pulignano, V. (2010). 'European integration and transnational employment regulations: the company-level experience of EFAs in the metal sector in Europe'. *European Labour Law Journal*, 1 (1), 81-88.

Pulignano V. (2007). 'Co-ordinating across borders: the role of European industry federations within EWCs'. in Knudsen H., Whittal, M., and Huijgen F. (eds.) *European Works Councils and the Problem of European Identity*. Routledge: London.

Pulignano, V. and Kluge, N. (2007). 'Employee involvement in restructuring: Are we able to determine the price?'. *Transfer*, 13(2), 225-240.

Pulignano, V., da Costa, I., Rehdfeldt, U., and Telljohann, V. (2011). 'Local actors and trans-national structures. Explaining trends in multinational company-level negotiation in Europe'. in Fairbrother, P., Hennebert, M.A., and Levesque, C. (eds.) *Transnational Union Action: New Capabilities for Building Labour Institutions*. London: Routledge (Forthcoming)

Quintin, O. (2003). 'High performance workplaces: Information and consultation rights for UK workers conference'. presented at a conference organized by the TUC January 2003, London.

Schwimbersky, S. and Gold, M. (2009). 'New beginning or false dawn? The evolution and nature of the European Company Statute'. in Gold, M., Nikolopoulos, A., and Kluge, N. (eds.) *The European Company Statute*, Oxford: Peter Lang.

Streeck, W. (2009). *Re-Forming Capitalism. Institutional Change in the German Political Economy*. Oxford: Oxford University Press.

Streeck, W. (1997). 'Neither European Nor Works Councils: A Reply to Paul Knutzen'. *Economic and Industrial Democracy*, 18(2), 325-337.

Streeck, W. (1995). 'Neo-Voluntarism: A New European Social Policy Regime?'. *European Law Journal*, 1, 31–59.

Streeck, W., and Thelen, K. (2005), *Beyond Continuity. Institutional Change in Advanced Political Economy*. Oxford: Oxford University Press.

Voss, E., Kluge, N., Kollewe, K., and Wilke, P. (2010). 'Behind the curtains – the relevance of European works councils for industrial relations in an enlarged Europe'.

in Struck O. (ed.) *Industrial Relations and Social Standards in an Internationalised Economy*. Munchen: Rainer Hampp Verlag.

Waddington, J. (2010). *European Works Councils. A Transnational Industrial Relations Institution in the Making*. Routledge: London.

Whittington, R., and Mayer, M. (1994). *'Beyond or behind the M-form? Organisational structures in contemporary Europe'*. Paper prepared for the *Strategic Management Society Conference*, Jouy-en-Josa, September.

Wilkinson, A., and Fay, C. (2011). 'New Times for Employee Voice?'. *Human Resource Management*, 50(1): 65-74.

Wilkinson, A., Gollan P., Marchington, M., Lewis, P. (2010). 'Conceptualizing Employee Participation in Organizations'. in Wilkinson, A., Gollan P., Marchington, M., and Lewin, D. (eds.), *The Oxford Handbook of Participation in Organizations*. Oxford: Oxford University Press.

7. Biographies and the Drafting of EU Environmental Policy in an Anthropological Framework

Tatiana Bajuk Senčar & Jeffrey David Turk

Introduction

In this chapter we discuss our experiences using biographical interviews during field research linked to a recently completed research project, the Anthropology of European Integration. This interdisciplinary project that drew on the overlapping concerns of critical realism and anthropology was focused on an analysis of the "integration experiences" of the first generation of Slovene EU officials, or Eurocrats, working in the institutions associated with the European Union in Brussels. We focus on a small yet strategic group of Slovenian "national Eurocrats" with whom we conducted interviews in Brussels from 2008 to 2010. By national Eurocrats we are referring to those Slovenes who are stationed in or travel frequently to Brussels as representatives of Slovenia as an EU member state. We decided to include national Eurocrats into our pool of interlocutors for numerous reasons; one of them being that our project coincided with Slovenia's Presidency of the Council of the European Union. Thus among the first generation of Eurocrats that were the focus of our research we included those employed at the Slovene Permanent Representation of the European Union and – albeit to a smaller degree – those Slovene civil servants who travelled from Ljubljana to Brussels.

In our research we were guided by previous ethnological research (Geuijen, Hart, Princen and Yesilkagit 2008; Thedvall 2006) who argued the significance of analyzing the role of national Eurocrats based in the EU institutions – as opposed to permanent EU officials – involved in the daily operation of the European Union.

Our discussion of biographical interviews will also include an assessment of the extent to which such interviews aided us in exploring the level of integration of Slovenia as an EU member state in the context of the negotiation of the Climate-Energy legislative package that was passed by the European Union.

Slovenia presided over the Council of the European Union during a crucial point of this negotiation process, and its level of integration into the European Union an important issue that could at that time have far-reaching consequences. In this light we can pose our research question in the following terms:

What are the lived processes involved in the integration of Slovenia as a new member state into one particular policy area (environmental) and to what extent has Slovenia, as a new member state, become integrated into European Union (EU) political processes not only at the formal level, but also at the level of the real social world of policy formulation, negotiation and implementation?

As a practical note, the reason this study is interesting in this general book on realist biography is that it is an example of a very small handful of people that we researchers had the opportunity to interview in an area that happened to be a juncture of two major historical currents: the first was the major historical enlargement of the European Union integrating several post-socialist countries, of which Slovenia was the first to take on the symbolically important rotating presidency of the Council of the EU. The second was the emergence of awareness of the coming crisis of global climate change in which the European Union was positioning itself as a major global actor – and the Climate-Energy legislative package, which happened to be negotiated intensively during the Slovenian Presidency, was an enormously important milestone in that positioning. The career paths of the Slovenes involved in this story just happened to get caught up in that historical juncture. (Indeed all of our interviewees happened to move on to new posts soon after the end of the Presidency.) Why this becomes interesting for this volume is not to understand the careers of particular individuals, EU environmental policy negotiation in general, a case of EU enlargement, small member state presidencies or other general processes. This is an ethnographic study of one particular small group of people in one interesting unique historical juncture as an example where realist biography is useful as a methodological tool.

The chapter has the following structure: After this introductory section we give a thorough accounting of the background and relevance of our research in the context of the context of climate policy negotiations under the Slovenian Presidency of the Council of the European Union; the roles of national Eurocrats in the European institutions; and assessing the accession of the newer EU member states. We then provide a justification for and an overview of the BNIM method used as a guideline for our data collection and analysis. This is followed by a brief presentation of the data collected. We then provide a brief summary of our analysis of the interviews in light of our research question. Finally we summarise our tentative results, give an assessment of their validity and provide some concluding remarks. While this is a quite narrowly focused study for the general reader of this book, the main purpose of this chapter is an example of realist biography in practice. In this vein, the extended section on the assessment of validity is intended as something to be considered by researchers interested in realist biography.

Background and relevance

In order place our biographical research into context we must have some understanding of the historical and institutional context in which our actors lived. We therefore discuss the general framework of environmental policy negotiation at the European Union, especially around the time that Slovenia held the rotating Presidency of the Council of the European Union; the role of national Eurocrats in the EU institutions; and issues of the accession of new member states.

The Climate-Energy legislative package and the Slovenian Presidency

The sui generis nature of the institutions of the European Union (EU) and their unique processes of policy making and implementation are receiving increasing attention, particularly in light of the latest two enlargements nearly doubling the number of member states and bringing in an enormous diversity of historical backgrounds (Best, Christiansen, and Settembri, 2008; Christiansen, Jørgensen, and Wiener, 2001; Christiansen and Larsson, 2007; Shore, 2000; Stevens and Stevens, 2001; Thedvall, 2006). The EU has actively promoted itself as the driving force behind global regulations to manage human impacts on the environment, particularly in terms of climate change and the global loss of biodiversity (Harris, 2007; Oberthür and Roche Kelly, 2008; Vogler and Stephan, 2007). Within this area, there is interest developing on the exact nature of the decision-making processes at the level of the Council of the European Union (hereafter Council) working groups (Costa, 2009; Vogler, 2008). The Climate Change sub group of the Council Working Group on International Environmental Issues (WPIEI/CC) forms the central policy-making nexus in this area for the EU. It is made up of climate experts from the Member States along with officials from Directorate General – Environment of the Commission who meet regularly in Brussels as well as at the UNFCCC COPs and elsewhere (Vogler, 2008: 4). The group drafts climate change conclusions for the Committee of Permanent Representatives of the Member States (COREPER), which then presents them to the Council (Vogler, 2008: 4). The complex system of negotiation places a heavy strain on the rotating presidency, and the smaller Member States tend to rely more on the permanent Council Secretariat for support (Vogler, 2008: 3). Leadership in EU policy thus depends on the rotating presidency with the support of the WPIEI/CC and the Council Secretariat. Furthermore, because of the political nature of this working group of nominally technical specialists, they have been able to push forward an ambitious climate change agenda to maintain the global leadership of the EU in this area (Costa, 2009). However there is some conflicting evidence that downplays the decision-making power of the lower level officials in the Working Groups or COREPER; and instead the 'ministers have a rather firm grip on Council negotiations in environmental policy' (Häge, 2008: 549). We hope to shed some light on this process.

One of the worries in this policy area is the effect of the most recent EU enlargements, bringing the number of member states from fifteen to the current twenty-seven. The twelve newest member states may not only have different environmental priorities that might impact on European policy, but the sheer difficulty of reaching agreement through the complex negotiations at the European level could easily hamper the leadership position of the EU. Thus Knill and Liefferink perhaps express widely shared worries:

> 'The consequences of enlargement in terms of increased stress on the institutions and increased diversity are being felt in each and every policy area of the EU. Also in the environmental field it will make decision-making and implementation more complex. For the overall level of environmental protection this can hardly be expected to work out positively.' (Knill and Liefferink, 2007: 221)

Slovenia is interesting as the first of the new member states from the 2004 enlargement to take up the rotating presidency of the Council of the European Union. Thus it has rapidly gone through the enlargement process to full integration as the country responsible for chairing the Council committees exercising the highest political authority in the EU for the January to June semester of 2008. However since Slovenia is one of the smaller member states, there is only limited information available on the social integration of Slovene officials in the Brussels institutions (Bajuk Senčar, 2009, Bajuk Senčar and Turk, 2011). This paper is intended as a further contribution.

National Eurocrats

Doubts concerning EU expansion and its effects on the daily operation of the EU can be understood to hinge on the level of integration of new EU member states into EU decision-making processes. We considered that Slaughter's (2004) disaggregated model of the state comprised of numerous multi-level networks of governance seemed to overlap well with the ways in which EU member state participate in the daily operation of the EU institutions. Member states have the opportunity and responsibility to participate at numerous levels within the EU institutions through individuals who operate as state representatives either in the form of national politicians (heads of government, ministers), national Eurocrats, or experts cast in a variety of roles – from the advisory to the technocratic. Thus while the state apparatus may develop its particular position on the numerous policy issues drafted, debated and negotiated at the level of the EU institutions, these positions are advocated and negotiated on behalf of the nation state by numerous social actors cum national Eurocrats at numerous levels of the EU institutional hierarchy. To understand Slovenia's integration into the "real-world" of EU policy formulation requires a focus on this particular group of social actors, trying to move towards a grounded understanding of integration that goes beyond formal integration associated with full membership. We suggest that Slovenia's integration into policy work on the Climate-Energy package both before and during the Presidency was in effect enacted by a specific group of national Eurocrats who were involved in day to day policy practice.

For the purposes of this analysis, we concentrate on the involvement of Slovene officials in the international environmental policy area of the EU. The major institutions involved in this area are DG Environment of the Commission and the Environment Council, which is one of the nine Council configurations defined by the Seville European Council in 2002 (Council of the European Union, 2002: 23). The latter is overseen by COREPER I, which covers the more technical economic, social and environmental issues, while COREPER II covers the remaining areas, which normally involve political, financial and foreign policy concerns.

The Environment Council is further split into two subgroups: the Working Party on the Environment (WPE) and the Working Party on International Environmental Issues (WPIEI). The WPE deals with internal EU legislation, while the WPIEI deals with external EU environmental policy. The WPE is thus subject to codecision with the European Parliament, while the latter need only deal with the Council, the Commission and the appropriate external actors depending on the specific Multilateral Environmental Agreement (MEA) in question. In the case of climate change, the Council has not authorized the Commission to negotiate on behalf of the member states (Creitaru, 2008: 95; Van Schaik and Egenhofer, 2005: 2). Therefore, the Council Presidency is the main representative of the EU, although it acts together with the succeeding Presidency and the Commission as a 'troika' under a strict mandate from the Environment Council of Ministers (Van Schaik and Egenhofer, 2005: 2). Another institutional feature that comes into play is the General Secretariat of the Council, which provides a permanent team of experts that the Member States may draw upon during their respective presidencies, at their own discretion.

The formal lines of authority during the Slovenian Presidency were as follows: The prime minister as head of government formally presides over the Council during the presidency. The Permanent Representative in Brussels is formally under the Minister of Foreign Affairs. The Deputy Permanent Representative heads COREPER I, which has competence over environmental issues. However, the environment section also works in close cooperation with the Ministry of the Environment and Spatial Planning in Ljubljana.

Our decision to focus on individual social actors and the networks in which they operate is especially pertinent in this particular analytical context given the fact that these national Eurocrats literally embody the connection that a new member state – which is in the initial phases of building up its networks of EU cadres – has with the EU. By focusing on this "pioneer" generation of Brussels-based national Eurocrats, we do not intend to downplay the role of the remaining actors within the civil service in the capital that aid in compiling and negotiating Slovenia's position on issues that are then negotiated in Brussels. Instead we wish to emphasize the unique position of this first generation of national Eurocrats and their significance as actors in Slovenia's integration into the operation of the EU, particularly during Slovenia's presidency of the EU. Our research goal was to remain as close as possible to the everyday experiences of particular social actors and the processes through observation and narrative, which would enable us to study local causality and the processes involved (cf. Maxwell, 2012). We believed that such an approach would provide us with the basis for a more grounded assessment of Slovenia's integration into the daily world of policy making in the EU.

Assessing Integration

From an anthropological point of view, integration is a complex phenomenon to study as it exemplifies a number of the identifying characteristics of our globalized world. We have dealt with the issue of integration elsewhere in detail (Bajuk Senčar and Turk, 2011) but will here touch only upon those issues most relevant to national Eurocrats. In addition to the complexity of integration as a social phenomenon, integration represents an epistemological challenge for the researcher. One must keep in mind the fact that given that there is an entire subfield of research dedicated to EU research and that EU integration discourses – both academic and other – are numerous, socially powerful and have a particular, often teleological, narrative structure. However, EU integration as an anthropological object of study is understood as a social process that numerous social groups participate in defining and maintaining. Integration in these terms is neither perceived to be neutral nor pre-determined.

It is necessary to leave analytical room in one's approach to integration research to account for the range of activities and understandings of integration as well as for the exercise of power involved in the maintenance of hegemonic depictions of integration as being neutral and self-evident processes. Failure to critically approach integration as a social phenomenon multiply defined may in fact ultimately result in integration research shifting away from the reality of integration processes to only an image of integration, albeit a politically or academically powerful one. Failure to do so can result in either the negation of agency or the presumption of essentialism, or both.

In the case of the negation of agency, integration becomes a universal, one-size-fits-all process, and that the persons experiencing integration play a passive role. This is particularly counterproductive in the case of national Eurocrats who are also often seen two-dimensionally, solely as national agents instead of more complex, active and mobile social actors. Viewing national Eurocrats solely as national agents can limit one's focus to the "nationalization" of the EU institutions and reinforces the opposition between nation and EU.

The presumption of cultural essentialism – that cultures are homogenous entities composed of shared values and codes of conduct – makes itself felt when processes of integration are considered simply a definitive movement from one culture to another – a shift of allegiances, in essence. EU integration specialist Gerard Delanty (2000) refers to what he terms the "myth of cultural cohesion" – i.e., that integration occurs when one becomes a member through assuming a different set of shared values and codes of conduct through socialization.

We suggest that concepts of integration based on essentialist views of culture do not accord with the reality of cultural life and ground-level experiences of integration. Instead, an understanding of culture as diverse and based on contiguity as argued by Joseph Maxwell (2012) would be a more useful basis for integration, particularly in the case of national Eurocrats. According to Maxwell, social and political theorists have generally assumed that diversity or difference is an inherent source of conflict and that commonalities are the basis for communities and societies (Maxwell 2012:51). The traditional understanding of culture as a set of shared values and beliefs is also based on the same presumptions, ones that replicate a strong opposition between similarity and difference in the context of solidarity. However, Maxwell argues for the existence of community solidarity based on the notion of contiguity, meaning adjacent or coterminous in time and space. Instead he suggests that incorporating the dimension of contiguity into concepts of community solidarity would also aid in recontextualizing the totalizing opposition between similarity and ultimately in the de-problematization of difference or diversity in within communities or cultures.

Contiguity in Maxwell's terms does not refer simply to social actors being in the same place at the same time (in addition, they need not be face-to-face but can be at a distance) but refers to a dimension of social relationships that concerns the way that people behave towards each other as opposed to the way they see each other as being alike. Thus "contiguity-based solidarity...derives from the ways in which people *interact*, and thereby come to know and care about one another" (Maxwell 2012:54; emphasis his). Contiguity-based solidarity, or a sense of identification within a particular group or culture, is not necessarily dependent solely on a sense of similarity but on the basis of lived experience, association, contact. Social actors may be different or complementary to each other in a particular group but still feel a sense of association, belonging and solidarity with one another.

Contiguity-based solidarity is much more relevant as a basis for understanding integration in the case of institutions in general and EU institutions in particular, where roles are not so much similar as they are complementary to each other. The overall success or effectiveness of the institution depends on the efficiency with which persons excel in their tasks and fulfill their role. The EU institutions are inherently diverse; one uses this term to refer to a conglomerate of institutions characterized by their distinct character as well as role in the everyday operation of the EU itself (i.e. Commission vs. Council vs. Parliament). They are also multinational in nature. For example, the Council committees are composed of representatives (i.e. national Eurocrats) from each member state – the work of national Eurocrats, who are also of course in close ties with the national representations and their national colleagues – is done primarily with persons of different nationalities.

Contiguity is especially appropriate to the specific role of national Eurocrats, whose position within the EU institutions differs from that of permanent Eurocrats in important ways. National Eurocrats are in essence national civil servants whose relation to the EU institutions is defined primarily by the role they are accorded by their national administration as national representatives. They are not employed by the EU institutions nor are they EU officials, but their role as national Eurocrats requires that they have a grounded knowledge of the EU institutions, their politics and modes of operation in order to be effective in their tasks. This is even more so the case when a member state presides over the EU and their role is expanded from representing their nation's interests to leading their committees and playing an active role in drafting EU policy.

Methodological overview

Having presented the historical/institutional context of our study as well as the theoretical issues involved, we now turn our attention to the interviews and their analysis. We briefly review the use of biographical interviews and give an overview of BNIM-style interviewing, the interviews done and the ethnographic methods that we used in our research.

Why biographical interviews?

Biographical narratives are useful tools for exploring the phenomenon of integration because they provide us with narratives that are grounded in experiences within the EU institutions. Furthermore, they aid us in preventing the imposition of epistemological limits and the elaboration of pre-determined scenarios that could range from the "nationalization" of the EU operations to the "shifting of allegiances" on the part of the national Eurocrats to the EU. Biographical narratives provide us with data concerning the processes by which certain forms of knowledge were acquired and sensibilities were formed – knowledge and sensibilities that are then also acted out in practice.

We collected biographical narratives using an open-narrative interview technique based in large part on the BNIM method (Biographical-narrative-interpretative method; refer to the chapter by Wengraf and Chamberlayne in this volume). Open-narrative interviews are characterized by the fact that they allow or require the interviewee to give their own form and sequence to their response to an initial, carefully worded question posed by the interviewer. This initial question requires the interviewee to improvise a coherent narrative on a broad subject – the subject of their life, a task that requires him or her to quickly make a selection of significant events to string together according to a logic that they employ to structure their narrative. This method provides a strict methodology of open-narrative questioning for the interviewer that allows the interviewees to structure their own narrative as freely as possible free of interventions on the part of the interviewer, who may pose additional questions only after the interviewee has completed his or her response to the initial question.

Summary of collected data

Within the framework of our more extensive research on the first generation of Slovene Eurocrats, we have collected approximately 50 life histories of Eurocrats across the EU institutions existing in Brussels, with different employment statuses and varied positions or grades. We made a conscious decision to include within this sample a strong percentage of national Eurocrats who were based in Brussels, worked in conjunction with the EU institutions, but represented Slovenia as a member state. For this particulary chapter we focus on our subset of Slovenes that participated in the Council Working Group on the Environment during the Slovenian Presidency of the Council of the European Union. For the purposes of our research we were able to interview essentially all the (handful of) main figures who specialized on environmental policy and worked with the Council Secretariat at different levels (from committee to COREPER I). We keep their names and narratives anonymous.

Analytical tools

Analysis of the collected interviews undergoes a series of stages. The first stage includes the compilation of the interviewee's profile and identifying the networks identified by our interviewees during the course of their narratives so as to map out their social positioning.

We then turned to analyze text of the biographical narrative. We employed ethnographic description and narrative analysis of interview transcriptions, focusing on analyzing the narrated life story in light of the actual (reconstructed) career trajectory, the biography's narrative structure, the processes and interactions that interviewees recounted in their European stories, and existing constructions of solidarity or integration. To gauge integration we focused on narrated processes of interaction and engagement with environmental policy structure, looking at interviews individually for data on the range and scope of participation. In adopting a predominately realist approach we do not look at processes as ontologically objective, so we study how they are acted out through the narratives of those involved. Our questions are also posed accordingly:

- Do the participants narrate stories indicative of effective integration in terms of their own personal agency in utilizing the structures of the institutions?

- In what terms do participants narrate relationships with networks in Slovenia and networks at the EU institutions?

The first question concerns what sort of processes of interaction and engagement we could identify in interviews as participants narrated their initial experiences in the EU as well as their preparations for and during Slovenia's presidency. We looked for stories in which participants narrated trajectories of experience accumulation, of preparation, and of the EU presidency itself. The second question concerned researching the ways in which interviewees saw their role as national Eurocrats, how and to what extent it evolved over time. In particular we were interested in the ways they narrated their roles both in the national civil service and in the EU as national representatives. Here we wanted to study the ways in which they developed the skills necessary to carry out a multidimensional, some would even argue inherently contradictory role. Our research of their narrated experiences also extended to gauging the extent to which these same narratives could provide a basis for assessing the role that such officials played between networks in Slovenia and networks at the EU institutions. Through exploring these processes we could probe the main theoretical focus of the study as stated in the introduction and to which we return in the conclusions. As realists (cf. Maxwell, 2012), we did not mechanically follow any particular methodological recipe, but combined different approaches appropriately in constructing our account. The validity of the final account is thus held more important than strict methodological orthodoxy, so we return to this important issue in depth at the end.

Summary of Analysis

Our informants were able to narrate quite well their introduction into the EU policy world. They related a range of socialization narratives that reflected the range of experience they had with EU affairs before assuming their position in Brussels or the particular nature of their assignment. In analyzing and comparing the collected narratives we could compile a set of stages of socialization understood in terms of the accumulation of experience, perspective and skills as well as the level of activity on the part of the working group member. While not all interlocutors would begin at the beginning of this trajectory, one of our interlocutors was quite frank about his experiences. He related in detail his first working group meeting assignment in Brussels to a working group meeting when he had theoretical knowledge but virtually no practical experience. He explained how he negotiated this first visit, from finding the right room to figuring out the seating order at the table and the speaking rules at the meeting itself. Some interviewees related the course of their experience with a particular working group, which could be quite lengthy. Some had been assigned to their working group from the moment when Slovenia as an accession state was allowed to have observers in meetings, learning from the interactions of their colleagues concerning the rules of engagement of working groups. By 2004, the status of the representatives assigned to working groups became active and were accorded full status, including voting rights.

In addition to relating the accumulation of what the speaker considered to be necessary experience and skills, these socialization narratives also addressed team-building and the accumulation of expertise in EU-specific negotiating skills, specifically those characteristic of the committee/working group format. The frequency of meetings and the nature of decision-making among working groups vary. There are, for example, working groups that meet only a few times a year and that can be covered by national civil servants from the capital. Other working groups meet at least weekly, if not more often, and are covered by Brussels-based Eurocrats. One of our interlocutors had meetings approximately four times a week. Team- building is strong among persons who meet so often and whose interactions unfold on both personal and professional levels.

Yet team-building does not necessarily guarantee active integration, as our narrators consistently made a distinction between active and passive working group members, those who were active in their working groups and those who were not, those who were not making themselves heard and who were simply rubber-stamping decisions made by the majority. New member state national Eurocrats were mostly considered to be "the quiet ones". Our interlocutors did not consider this to be simply the result of a lack of experience on the part of the working group member in question, but also due to the instructions that they receive from their capitals and the national interests involved. One of our interlocutors, for example, explained to us that the policy of their ministry at the beginning was to keep abreast of and report developments of the working group to the ministry – a position that he did not necessarily share but did not have the authority to modify. Others related how the main task for them at this time was observing interactions among their colleagues, learning what one termed "the Brussels way of thinking": how to articulate interests, represent them and attain them within a working group format. This also includes defining the role of the member state and its interests vis-à-vis the working group. Their narratives shifted when relating their activities one year into their assignment, at which point they were informed that Slovenia would be the first member state to preside over the Council. Their narratives of this period register a shift in their status from simply learning to be active working group member to preparing to chair these very same working groups. One of our interlocutors explained that just when he felt like he was really beginning to understand how things operate with the EU institutions and was working comfortably as a working group member things began to change dramatically.

One should also keep in mind that these persons were involved in setting up the first Slovenian presidency team, a task that represented a new stage in socialization for them both as working group members and as civil servants. We found that the preparations for the presidency, while important in and of themselves, played a pivotal role in the "Brussels" formation of our interlocutors, as their activities and interactions both with their colleagues and superiors in Slovenia as well as with their EU colleagues took on a new dimension. Their stories include accounts of intense preparation and assistance both from the Council Secretariat in Brussels, from the capital as well as from other member state teams for a role that significantly surpassed that of a working group member. This included an increase in tasks and duties, including research as to how other member states set up their teams within their permanent representations and drafting the working group schedule of meetings for the presidency together with the capital and coordinating with the Council Secretariat as to the dossiers and legislative packages which would be negotiated during these meetings. One of our interlocutors mentioned that the tables together with the reviews, assessments, and forecasts began to be drafted the very first week after they were informed of the date of Slovenia's presidency. These additional duties implied working with a new range of colleagues across the EU institutions (but particularly within the Council Secretariat), with Eurocrats from older member states, and with a broader range of officials from the Slovenian civil service. Eurocrats were accorded a broader realm of authority and narrated their development of a different, perhaps broader, perspective on the operation of their working group within the broader EU framework as well as the context of the EU's legislative process. In addition, our speakers relate the accumulation of professional connections and a lived intensity that distinguished them from other new member state colleagues as well as from their colleagues preparing for the Presidency from their own home ministry with whom they were in constant contact. One of our speakers defined the distinction between those who chair working groups and those who form the team with which they are in contact in their home ministry: "We have nothing to talk about." While we do not believe this comment was disparaging in nature, it does reflect the extent of the path travelled by this particular group of national Eurocrats in a few short years.

In addition to collecting narrative data on experiences of socialization, we focused on collecting and analyzing narrative material on the experiences of national Eurocrats during the period of the Slovenian Presidency. Our interlocutors regardless of their position were hard pressed to structure their experiences of such an intense period such as the Presidency into a coherent narrative, as their work days were often much longer than the traditional 8 or even 10 hour work day. We thus employed the interview technique of posing a carefully worded question concerning a speaker's experience with a particular legislative act or dossier of his or her choice. This was intended to elicit narratives in which a person could employ the legislative act as a common thread around which they could compose a story about their life experiences at that time in a manner that they would deem coherent and complete.

We were able to collect rich narrative material concerning the particular legislative acts for which each person in the presidency team was responsible. While the content of the narratives and the projects they were bringing to fruition are important, our analysis of these stories focused more on the way that our interlocutors structured and related these stories, how they placed themselves in the process, and the terms they employed to describe and evaluate their own activities in relation to these particular legislative acts.

What is relevant to point out here is that the life-span of dossiers, legislative acts and packages far transcends any six-month presidency period, and that a presidency team "inherits" the vast majority of the issues and dossiers with which it will grapple during its six months at the helm of the Council. A presidency team works in conjunction with the Council Secretariat to draft the calendar of its term and it is up to the presiding country to decide which dossiers will be accorded priority and to what stage they commit themselves to bring a certain dossier. It is then up to the presidency team to fulfill the responsibilities that it sets out for itself during those six months. Thus the span of a six-month presidency does not in any way extend to encompass the entire life span of a dossier or legislative act, as the life span includes stages in all the main EU institutions.

Of course the Slovenian Presidency was no different in this regard. In addition, Slovenia took on the last part of a presidency trio together with Portugal and Germany; Slovenia also had the responsibility of realizing the goals set together with its two trio partners. The role of Slovenia was to maintain the schedule on all existing dossiers and legislative packages while effectively resolving any unforeseen problems that could crop up along the way. Thus although the official priority area of the Climate-Energy package from the programme of the Slovenian Presidency cited above should carry some weight, it was not solely a Slovene goal, but one formulated in conjunction with the Council Secretariat, the German-Portuguese-Slovenian Presidency trio and other stakeholders outside of Slovenia. An important, "external" factor that also influenced the priority accorded to the Climate-Energy package during the Slovenian Presidency was the fact that the Copenhagen Climate Summit was to be held in 2009. The European Union wanted to develop a common position for Copenhagen, and thus this summit operated as deadline for all actors involved in drafting and negotiating all steps of this policy process.

Our aim in sketching out the relationship between national Eurocrats and the policy packages they were working on during the presidency is to properly contextualize the dossiers or legislative acts as social constructions of fields or contiguity whose form and purpose are defined by varied sets of Eurocrats in all three major EU institutions, national experts, and MEPs. In addition, we wish to point out the complex positioning of the national Eurocrats whose role during the presidency accords them a great deal of room for maneuver as well as a potentially great responsibility as coordinators of policy formation at certain stages and for a very limited time period. We believe that it is the sense of placement, leverage and initiative of national Eurocrats that define their roles – and possible impact – during the presidency.

Earlier, we mentioned evidence collected concerning national Eurocrats' acquisition of a broader perspective on the operation of the EU institutions and their legislative process. A more detailed and grounded sense of perspective, placement and responsibility can be understood as a process that was at least – if not before – set in motion with the preparation of the presidency schedule for each and every working group and the legislative acts. This allowed for prediction on the part of the presidency team of the legislative acts or dossiers that could be expected to come to the working group docket during Slovenia's six month presidency. This required not only a sense of the construction of legislative time but also a sense for the other legislative actors with whom a national Eurocrat working as a working group chair was coordinating in the legislative process, directly or indirectly. For example, one of our informants, when talking about the dossier on waste disposal and processing, began her story with the Austrian presidency, which took place in the first half of 2006. Her work in relation to this dossier included her interactions many months before the presidency with Commission officials from DG Environment and as well as with a key MEP from the Parliamentary Committee on Environment, Public Health and Food Safety, who was going to head negotiations in parliament on this dossier immediately after the Slovenian Presidency.

While like many Eurocrats our interlocutors identified strongly with the projects they were working on, we also found that they strongly identified with their role in the legislative process, that is, with their responsibility to prepare the dossier during a limited period of time in order to "pass it on" to the EU body responsible for the next stage in the legislative process. While one could argue that this is simply the way that they narrated the specificity of their placement as working group chairs, we would argue that the strong personal identification with dossiers is not a necessary result of this and speaks not only to a sense of identification with their role and responsibility but also to a sense of integration with the placement of a presidency within the broader EU legislative process.

For example, one of our informants chose to narrate his personal involvement in a precursor legislative act to the main Climate-Energy package: the directive on including aviation emissions within the Emissions Trading System of the European Union. While this may not have seemed to the outsider to be of such importance in comparison to the main legislative package (also negotiated during the Slovenian Presidency, but not completed until the French Presidency), negotiations of this precursor directive were completed with a breakthrough compromise brokered under his mandate at the end of the Slovenian Presidency, which made his own involvement so much more important from his personal perspective. This allowed him to focus on and take personal satisfaction for a major piece of European legislation where he felt his own involvement to have been instrumental if not crucial.

Our assessment of a strong identification with the dossiers and with the legislative process is based on our analysis concerning the ways in which our interviewees related their activities in relation to particular dossiers, their reasons for their actions, and the range of activities and/or strategies they employed to enable the legislative process to continue as planned. We found that our interviewees narrated the use of a wide range of strategies and activities in their efforts to complete their tasks. We found that the narratives corroborated interviewees' assessments that national Eurocrats worked well as a team, coordinating their work as dossiers went through different phases of policy negotiation. They were also able to work productively with MESP officials, including with the Minister of the Environment, who took an active interest in and aided negotiations concerning mercury legislation, which is also an important issue for Slovenia. However, we found little evidence of continual and close cooperation with MESP on issues that fell within the domain of working groups chaired by national Eurocrats based in Brussels.

Our interviewees also narrated stories about being incorporated into, brokering and even initiating numerous informal interactions "behind the scenes" to help keep the legislative process on track. The stories that our informants related to us suggest that the assumption of their roles during the period included having accesses to a broad range of social actors both inside and outside the EU institutional framework – including other Eurocrats, lobbyists and interest groups. At the most basic level chairing working groups implied a temporary shift in relationship with remaining working group members, as the chair is a broker and negotiation leader at both the formal and informal level. They become the person to contact, the person to call, the person to work with during those six months. However these interactions transcended the interactions among working group colleagues. They exchanged information, addressed particular interests, and drafted and coordinated actions with a range of social actors in order to resolve all issues that needed to be addressed for the consensus on a legislative act to be politically viable and successful.

Tentative results

The central research question we set out to answer was:

> 'What are the lived processes involved in the integration of Slovenia as a new member state into one particular policy area (environmental) and to what extent has Slovenia, as a new member state, become integrated into European Union (EU) political processes not only at the formal level, but also at the level of the real social world of policy formulation, negotiation and implementation?'

During the course of our research we were able to collect biographical interviews of of the key Slovene officials involved at the permanent representation of Slovenia to the European institutions in Brussels presiding over intense negotiations in one of the key policy areas of the European Union at the time – the Climate-Energy legislative package. We found that our interlocutors in their extensive narrations of their experiences before and during the presidency sketched out their activities as well as what we could term spheres of contiguity. Analysing the ways in which they defined themselves in these spheres of contiguity aided us in our assessment of the development of a sense of solidarity understood not in terms of shift in allegiance but in the identification with a particular role within the EU legislative process and the development of relationships with networks of EU policy actors across the EU institutions.

On the basis of our analyses we find that Slovene negotiators have become quite integrated into the political processes. They produced narratives of highly involved and active negotiators under intense conditions and were fully aware of the importance of their work and the pressure they were under to perform. They also discussed the crucial training, support and cooperation they received from their counterparts in an important policy area with broad political support not only on the part of other EU institutions but also across the remaining member states. This is quite important since, as noted above, the Council environmental working group (presided by Slovenia during the time of our study) was the key nexus for the drafting of EU environmental policy. While speculative, we suggest that the level of support and cooperation experienced might help explain why these Slovene participants do not seem to have had the feared negative impact on EU environmental policy negotiation. So while the European Union as a whole had a less than stellar performance in Copenhagen, this was not due to bureaucratic logjams during the Slovenian Presidency since a major part of the Climate-Energy legislative package was indeed negotiated during that period.

Assessment of validity and threats to it

As part of our commitment to realist social science we evaluate how the given data collected and analysis performed might have produced an inaccurate account of the phenomenon studied. For consistency and in order to help establish standards in this area, we roughly follow the three general and overlapping types of validity that Maxwell (2012, Chapter 8) identifies: descriptive, interpretive and theoretical. For our purposes, we distinguish (more or less in line with Maxwell):

- Descriptive validity: sufficiency and accuracy of the raw factual evidence collected for the purpose of probing the phenomenon studied;

- Interpretive validity: accuracy in our own interpretations of the meanings intended by the participants in the phenomenon;

- Theoretical validity: the appropriateness of the abstractions and theoretical categories and their interrelations employed in constructing and evaluating an account of the phenomenon.

Maxwell (2012: 144) also suggests framing validity in terms of plausible alternatives to our results and conclusions, which we also find appropriate. We deal with these issues below.

Descriptive validity

In evaluating descriptive validity we carefully consider whether or not the evidence used is sufficiently complete and trustworthy so as not to lead to a distorted account of the phenomenon. What evidence might be missing that could contradict our account?

In answer, we have interviewed all of the key participants involved from the Slovene permanent representation, so we can claim that there is little loss of validity due to coverage. On the other hand, we did not interview their counterparts from the other member states and institutions. We are therefore open to selection biases that would naturally tend to inflate the importance of the Slovene officials due to narrator bias and the tendency of people to be more aware of the impacts of their own agency than that of others. However, given that during the time of the Slovenian Presidency the Slovene officials were naturally in a privileged position vis-à-vis their interlocutors, we are more interested in the subjective vantage points of the Slovenes than their negotiating counterparts. While we would most likely gain by inputs from these counterparts, it is still the narrated experiences of the Slovene officials that we are after, especially since all of our interviewees, discussed one-on-one discussions with negotiating partners (rapporteurs from the European Parliament, for instance) that were key to brokering key compromises in the negotiation process. They made efforts to meet them personally.

We acknowledge that other parties may also act strategically behind the backs of the Slovene officials. However, since the principal arenas for negotiation are moderated through the officials of the presidency, the effects of such strategic acting would still have to be channelled through the presidency officials. The reason this issue is important is that if our interlocutors were to be isolated from the actual locus of principle negotiations, then it would severely compromise our assesment of their active engagement. (Of course they are nevertheless embedded in networks of negotiations which may well bypass them in part, but our concern is with the main course of negotiations while our Slovene negotiators formally presided.)

Concerning narrative bias, our narrators talked about range of dossiers, some of which succeeded, some of which did not. They were able to assess where things broke down and where their responsibility lay. This is key in assessing their perspective as evidence of their integration – understood as their effective action as coordinators and their perspective provides evidence of their identification with their role and responsibility as chairs (realistically defined) within the legislative process. In addition, it is quite appropriate for them to have a more "national" view on things so long as they had the basic knowledge and skills to negotiate a position – in our case Slovenian and EU interests strongly overlapped.

Interpretive validity

In evaluating interpretive validity we carefully consider whether or not we have correctly understood the insider perspectives of the participants. As discussed above, the BNIM interview is geared towards gaining that insider perspective. We are aware of the possibilities of omission, lying, manipulation, fallible memory, etc. However, given that our interviews were anonymous and our informants were willing to give their time in explaining the acknowledged opaque processes involved in the presidency, there would be little for them to gain strategically by purposefully giving misleading stories. Also, since our questions are designed to elicit narrative sections about the involvement of our informants in the unfolding of events, there is less room for the deliberate and spontaneous construction of a coherent false narrative.

Furthermore, while our informants had clearly different narrative styles, there was little or no contradiction in the narratives of the common events in which they all participated, which leads to enhanced confidence in the validity of our findings. After all, the narratives were quite descriptive and straightforward; and the narratives of our interlocutors often overlapped as they worked together on numerous projects. These narratives seem to complement and confirm each other.

We wish to single out two important aspects of BNIM analysis that aided us in minimising researcher bias. The first of these concerned the distinction made between lived stories and told stories, which involved compiling a time line of events of a person's biography (insofar as this is possible) as well as the key points of that person's biography as they are related during the course of the interview. Making the distinction between these two aids the researcher in maintaining a level of reflexivity concerning interpretation of life stories on the part of the narrator as well as on the part of the researcher (Wengraf 2001: 258-259).

The second concerns analysing interviews in a panel format so as minimise bias of any individual researcher. We analysed our interviews in tandem, and in order to make up for the small size of our panel, we discussed our findings with other officials familiar with the issues and processes under study.

Theoretical validity

In evaluating theoretical validity we consider whether or not there might be (significantly) better concepts or abstractions that could be used for constructing an account of the phenomenon. Although it would be impossible to entertain every other possible configuration of concepts, categories and abstractions that might be used in describing the phenomenon, we need only consider some various possible conceptual frameworks grounded elsewhere in the literature. According to Maxwell's framework, theoretical validity only comes into play when there is potential disagreement 'within the community of inquirers about the descriptive or interpretive terms used. Any challenge to the meaning of the terms, or the appropriateness of their application to a given phenomenon, shifts the validity issue from descriptive or interpretive to theoretical' (Maxwell, 2012: 141). Accordingly, we need only address potentially controversial categories and abstractions that have been used. However, we have deliberately used straightforward concepts, abstractions and categories, so we do not anticipate any major issues of theoretical validity in our results and conclusions. Nevertheless, we can discuss the likelihood of other plausible accounts in what follows.

Alternative hypotheses

In completing our consideration of threats to the validity of our results, we address possible plausible alternatives to our findings. Is there another substantively different and better account of phenomenon that was missed in our analysis of the available evidence? The most obvious alternative hypothesis to the active integration of Slovenia into the EU negotiating process through it national officials during the time of the Slovenian Presidency is that they were somehow either bypassed in the process or that those negotiations were actually directed or led by someone else. Since this possibility is clearly not reflected in the interviews, in order for that hypothesis to be viable, either our informants would have to be either consciously or unconsciously misleading in their stories, or most of the actual negotiations were carried out behind their backs. However, the detailed narratives of personal involvement in the events preclude the former since it would be difficult to produce coherent corroborating stories of fictional events and since the central role of the presiding country in negotiations would make the latter possibility highly unlikely. In addition, the narrated distinction made by our interlocutors between the descriptions of activities before and during the presidency seem to confirm rather than undermine the credibility of their accounts. This was an intense period of active negotiating with all of the main actors, as clearly expressed in the interview transcripts. It would not be possible for the 'real' negotiations to be running in a parallel process not known to the Slovene team, and therefore absent from their stories.

In addition, there were indeed a few narratives (noted above) concerning certain tasks and programs that the presidency did not take on and were consciously left to the next presidency. This demonstrates that while the Slovenian Presidency team was limited in resources, they were at the centre of deciding which dossiers would be handled under their watch – which makes it unlikely that they were sidelined from the process.

Summary of validity assessment

In summary, we can claim a high degree of validity within the circumscribed limits of our claims in this study, which means that we do not make claims on external validity. The validity we claim is that of a high degree epistemic objectivity for the ontologically subjective phenomena we researched.

Concluding remarks

This chapter was intended as an example of the use of realist biography to produce an account of a particular historically situated social phenomenon from the realist standpoint of its being acted out by particular people reflexively working through their own career trajectories.

On the basis of our analysis of the collected interviews, we could track a process of knowledge and experience accumulation as well as an intense process of socialization during the preparations for the Slovenian Presidency. Our informants narrated stories of numerous interactions with actors across the EU institutional framework both before and during the presidency, interactions that provide evidence of the inclusion of our informants into the legislative process, both formal and informal. Furthermore, the evidence suggests that they operated as active agents in these processes during the presidency itself, brokering policy negotiations on virtually all environmental dossiers that were on the docket during this six month period. These activities were related together with a high value placed on the EU's particular legislative process and an identification with the role accorded to our informants during the presidency process.

We find that our informants became fully participating members of the European institutions as national Eurocrats and played an active role as members of Slovenia's presidency team. In addition, the preparation for and implementation of the presidency played a key role in their integration as effective national Eurocrats whose positioning within the institutions are not only a result of their structural role but also of lived experience.

Since we recognise that any account is the product of the particular set of methods used, we gave necessary attention to threats to the validity of our account. We claim a high degree of validity in our findings, since we can directly follow the insider narratives of the processes involved in presiding over a key policy area. We do not make any claims of generality in our findings to other policy areas or to what should be expected from other national presidencies. Otherwise, the evidence we have put together along with our checks on threats to validity allow us to state with high confidence that our results are sound in terms of the Slovenian Presidency at that one particular important historical moment.

Works Cited

Bajuk Senčar, T. (2009). 'The integration of "East" and "West": Slovene "Eurocrats" and the politics of identity within the institutions of the European Union'. *Traditiones*, 38 (2), 153-166.

Best, E., Christiansen, T., and Settembri, P. (eds.) (2008). *The Institutions of the Enlarged European Union*. Cheltenham, UK: Edward Elgar.

Christiansen, T., Jørgensen, K. E., and Wiener, A. (eds.) (2001). *The Social Construction of Europe*. London: Sage.

Christiansen, T. and Larsson T. (eds.) (2007). *The role of committees in the policy-process of the European Union*, Cheltenham, UK: Edward Elgar.

Costa, O. (2009). 'Who decides EU foreign policy on climate change? Actors, alliances and institutions'. In P. G. Harris (ed.), *Climate Change and Foreign Policy: Case Studies from East to West*. New York: Routledge. pp. 134-147.

Creitaru, I. (2008). Environmental security seen from the European Union: The case of EU climate policy as a preventive security policy. *Europolis, Journal of Political Science and Theory*, 3, pp. 87-114.

Delanty, G. (2000). 'Social integration and Europeanization: The myth of cultural cohesion'. *Yearbook of European Studies*, 14, 221-238.

Geuijen, K., 'T Hart, P., Princen, S., and Yesilkagit, K. (2008). *The New Eurocrats: National Servants in EU Policy Making. Amsterdam*: Amsterdam University Press.

Häge, F. M. (2008). Who decides in the Council of the European Union? *Journal of Common Market Studies*, 46 (3), 533-558.

Harris, P. G. (ed.) (2007). *Europe and Global Climate Change: Politics, Foreign Policy and Regional Cooperation*. Cheltenham, UK: Edward Elgar.

Knill, C., and Liefferink, D. (2007). *Environmental Politics in the European Union.* Manchester, UK: Manchester University Press.

Maxwell, J.A. (2012). *A Realist Approach for Qualitative Research.* London: Sage.

Oberthür, S., and Roche Kelly, C. (2008). 'EU leadership in international climate policy: achievements and challenges'. *The International Spectator*, 43 (3), 35-50.

Shore, C. (2000). *Building Europe: the Cultural Politics of European Integration.* London and New York: Routledge.

Stevens, A., and Stevens, H. (2001). *Brussels Bureaucrats? The Administration of the European Union.* New York: Palgrave Press.

Thedvall, R. (2006). *Eurocrats at Work: Negotiating Transparency in Postnational Employment Policy.* Stockholm: Intellecta Docusys.

Van Schaik, L. G., and Egenhofer, C. (2005). 'Improving the climate: Will the new constitution strengthen the EU's performance in international climate negotiations?'. *CEPS Policy Briefs* (63).

Vogler, J. (2008). 'Climate change and EU foreign policy: the negotiation of burden-sharing'. *Working Paper* 08-11. UCD Dublin European Institute, July.

Vogler, J., and Stephan, H.R. (2007). 'The European Union in global environmental governance: Leadership in the making?'. *International Environmental Agreements* Vol. 7: pp. 389–413.

Wengraf, T. (2001). *Qualitative research Interviewing: Biographic Narratives and Semi-Structured Methods.* London: Sage.

Wengraf, T. (2008*). Life-histories, lived situations and ongoing personal experiencing. Biographic-narrative interpretive method: BNIM interviewing and interpretation: Short Guide and Detailed Manual.* Version 8.12j; Available from tom@tomwengraf.com.

8. Linking Structural and Agential Powers: A Realist Approach to Biographies, Careers and Reflexivity

Markieta Domecka & Adam Mrozowicki

Introduction

The discussion on the consequences of accelerated changes in the sphere of work for career patterns belongs to the central topics of the contemporary sociology of work. It is suggested that secure, coherent and linear occupational careers might be less and less available option in societies of "late", "radicalized", or "fluid" modernity (Bauman, 1999; Sennett, 2006). Existing research on occupational careers has been focused on testing these theoretical assertions (Gold and Fraser, 2002, Blockerhurst 2003; Fenton and Dermont, 2005). The goal of this article is different. It draws on the ongoing debate on agency-structure relations (Archer, 2003; Mouzelis, 1995) to reconstruct the mechanisms shaping the evolution of contemporary careers. According to the classical formulations of Chicago School sociologists, career refers to a person's course through life and especially through that portion of her/his life in which s/he works (Hughes, 1997: 389). Exploring career patterns, we make use of the notion of "realist biography" as a theoretical concept linking structural influences and agential powers of reflexivity. The concept of realist biography assumes that life stories are both influenced by actual life events and influence human practices and processes in the real world; and offer a privileged way to the analysis of the mechanism of reflexivity that mediates between social structures and human agency (Turk, Mrozowicki, *this volume*). As a theoretical concept, realist biography makes it possible to analyse both the effects of the mechanisms related to structurally defined opportunities and constraints and the mechanism of reflexivity that enables individuals to deal with structural powers in the light of individually and collectively constructed life projects.

The main feature of this chapter, setting it apart from the earlier studies, is the theoretical framework, which combines theoretical inspirations coming from critical social realism (Archer, 2003) with the tradition of biographical research (Schütze, 2008a; 2008b) and the Chicago School analysis of careers (Becker and Carper, 1956). Both the biographical method, as advanced by Schütze (1983), and critical realism, in particular its variety proposed by Archer (2007), share common roots in philosophical pragmatism, common interests in life histories, and similar analytical concepts, in particular biographical work and reflexivity exercised through the inner dialogue with oneself ("internal conversation", see Archer, 2003). For Archer (2007: 98), "a full understanding of how actors reflexively make their way through the world, dealing as they must with at least some of its social properties and powers, requires an exploration of their life and work histories." This theoretical assertion offers a link with the tradition of biographical research, which has not been fully utilised in the existing studies (Turk, 2007).

The body of the chapter demonstrates how the concept of realist biography can improve our understanding of the mechanisms underlying the structural and subjective dynamics of careers in a rapidly changing social and economic reality. We explore the case of Poland as an example of a country in which neoliberal restructuring at work proceeded in an accelerated pace in the 1990s leading to profound changes in structural mechanisms influencing career patterns. Based on the analysis of 290 biographical interviews with manual workers and managers in Poland, the empirical research reconstructs the impact of these changes on career patterns in two distinct social milieus. We present four types of careers: "construction", "anchor", "patchwork" and "dead end" and discuss the mechanisms underlying their emergence and people's mobility among them. In the final part of the chapter, theoretical and policy implications stemming from realist research on occupational careers are discussed.

Careers, agents and structures: a place for reflexivity

The concept of career provides a link between the level of structurally given opportunities and constraints and the level of individual choices, concerns and strategies of action. In accordance with Chicago School traditions (Barley, 1989; Hughes, 1997), the objective components of careers indicate the changes in one's participation in various organisations, a stream of more or less identifiable positions, offices, statuses, and situations (Strauss, 1977 [1959]). Their subjective components are in turn connected with "one's self, identity and transformation" (Becker and Carper, 1956: 289). The interrelated subjective and objective aspects of careers reflect the interwoven relationship between individual action and social structures. On the one hand, every career, like every biography, reveals the "limiting effect of socio-structural relations" (Bertaux and Kohli, 1984: 219). On the other hand, subjective career assumes biographical work, i.e. interpretative efforts "carried in the service of actor's biography, including its review, maintenance, repair and alternation" (Strauss, 1993: 98). The Chicago School understanding of careers is close to the critical realist approach by Archer, which emphasises the subjective and the reflexive. Archer (2003: 5) claims that in order to explain what people do we need to refer not only to existing structural conditions, but also to people's subjective and reflexive formulation of their personal projects.

Biographies offer an access to the causal mechanism of reflexivity which underlies human practices in the world as it mediates between social structures and human agency. As remarked by Archer (2007: 37), "reflexivity needs not to be consigned to the free-form construction, deconstruction and reconstruction of life narratives; it can be examined as the causally powerful relationship between deliberation and action in people's social lives". Confronted with structural powers, agents have the capacity to suspend them through their circumventory actions and adaptive ingenuity, thus, the agents are conditioned but not determined (Archer, 2007: 10). A similar assertion can be found in the field of biographical sociology by Fritz Schütze (2005; 2008a; 2008b). According to Schütze, social reality is not only experienced and bestowed with meaning by individuals, but "it is produced, is supported and kept in force, is endured with pain and suffered, is protested at and turned over or even destroyed as well as it is gradually changed by individual actors with their personal life histories and involved biographical development" (Schütze, 2008b: 2). Importantly, the analysis of people's careers as revealed in autobiographical narrations is not only a way to understand actions and to shed light on the working of structure, but it also demonstrates how the two levels are interconnected; how they get synchronized and how they get out of tune, depending on how people interpret their lives; what kind of opportunities and obstacles they see; what they define as their main concerns; what kind of decisions they take in their professional lives and how far they go in realising their plans.

Following Strauss (1993) we can say that the kinds of thought process and self-references, which are implied by the theory of reflexivity by Archer, assume an actor "working" on his or her biographical experiences. This process of biographical work can be translated substantively into descriptive language such as an actor "thought over", "struggled with", "fought out with himself", and "finally got a new slant on himself" (Strauss, 1993: 98). Such descriptive phrases imply self-interactive work as well as work with others. Some of this work is likely to involve personal and/or collective indecision, anguish, and suffering (cf. Riemann and Schütze, 1991). It is this type of work which is done by autobiographical recollection and reflection about alternative interpretations of one's life course. These are self-critical attempts of understanding one's own misconceptions of oneself and self-erected impediments as well as the impediments superimposed by others and by structural conditions. Thus, both biographical work and reflexivity denote an inner activity of mind constituted by conversation with significant others and oneself (cf. Schütze, 2008a; Archer, 2007).

The realist analysis of careers makes it possible to overcome the shortcomings of the alternative, structuralist and voluntaristic, approaches to career studies. On the one hand, structuralist research suggests that the possibility to define careers as reflexively planned projects is strongly dependent on the resources an individual can mobilize to cope with structurally-driven transitions (Fenton and Dermott, 2006; Li et al., 2002). On the other hand, the dominant discourses of career-making, including those to be found in the publications on occupational counselling (see for instance CBS Compendium, 2011), tend to be voluntaristic and solely focused on issues such as "career management skills", personal preferences, flexibility and creativity. The structuralist approaches say little about *how* structurally available career options are individually interpreted and weighted against people's main concerns. The voluntaristic discourse of occupational counselling underplays, in turn, the role of *real* and intersecting social inequalities, including those of class, gender, ethnicity and age, which set the initial conditions for the development of an individual career. By contrast to the structuralist and voluntaristic stances, the realist approach to careers explores them as the outcome of the interaction of two types of powers: the personal emergent powers of reflexivity and the structural (and cultural) emergent powers endowing individuals with resources which they might use to advance their careers. We maintain that this assertion can shed new light on the discussions on career patterns in the context of the global restructuring at work.

Careers and restructuring at work: the case of post-socialist transformation

The neoliberal turn, which has been taking place in the sphere of work since the late 1970s in the advanced Western capitalist economies and since the 1990s also in Eastern Europe, has renewed the discussion on careers. Institutional changes, which aimed at achieving new kinds of comparative advantages by labour market deregulation and flexibilisation, were accompanied by new discourses stressing the need for occupational mobility, versatility, entrepreneurship and continuous improvements of individual skills. The idea of a "new career" reflecting on the one hand the increasing fragmentation of career patterns, and on the other hand focusing on individual planning, reflexivity, and self-perception has been extensively discussed (Arthur and Rousseau, 1996; Gold and Fraser, 2002). The "new" forms would include "boundaryless career", as the opposite of "organizational career" unfolding in a single employment setting (Arthur and Rousseau,

1996) and portfolio career (Gold and Fraser, 2002) defined in opposition to organizationally "bounded" patterns. Still, the scope of the new careers does not seem to be extensive in Europe. According to the recent European Working Conditions Survey (EWCS, 2011), 80% of the interviewed employees in the EU27 were employed on indefinite contracts and around 40% of respondents have been there for 10 years or more in 2010. Simultaneously, 14% of the EU27 employees had temporary contracts in 2011 (*Eurostat* data*)*; the latter figure in Poland reaching the top EU level of 27%.

Systemic change in Poland (and other Eastern European countries) provides a particularly good context to analyse the interplay of structures and agency in shaping career patterns. Capitalist transformation has affected both objective and subjective aspects of careers, since the value of previously accumulated resources had to be reassessed and new types of capitals accumulated[1] (Eyal et al., 2000; Mach, 2005). At the beginning of transformation, new career possibilities were created by re-establishing the dominant value of cultural capital and economic capital, i.e. two capitals described by Bourdieu (1984) as decisive for the shape of capitalist social structure. However, the value of educational credentials proved to be less certain in the second decade after the end of state socialism. Excess supply of university graduates, whose number in Poland increased 5 times over 20 years, the expansion of temporary employment as a result of labour market deregulation and the mass migration abroad of around 2 million Poles after the EU enlargement were only some of structural processes which affected career patterns in the mid of 2000s. Their most important effect seems to be growing uncertainty about what kind of investments in which kind of resources can pay off in terms of "good jobs", the latter being identified with high wages, lack of stress and stable employment (Szafraniec, 2011). According to Archer (2012: 1-2), the absence of clear social guidelines about what to do in novel situations is an increasingly generic feature of late modern societies, which creates an "imperative to engage in reflexive deliberations." The most recent global economic and financial crisis has only increased this fundamental uncertainty about the value of resources confirming the causal powers of distant, macro- and mega-level social processes and structures vis-a-vis individual life projects.

In this chapter, we maintain that the analysis of occupational careers in Poland can help us to understand more *generic* types of coping with rapid changes in the sphere of work that are likely to be present also in other developed capitalist

---

[1] The link between the properties of career patterns and individual resources is explored by adapting Bourdieu's concept of capitals. Following Bourdieu (1986), we distinguish four kinds of capitals: (1) economic capital (overall material assets), (2) cultural capital, in the form of educational credentials and practical competences, (3) social capital made up of social networks and mutual obligations, and (4) symbolic capital, i.e. all forms of capitals "unrecognized as capital and recognized as legitimate competence" due to a privileged position of its possessors in power relations (Bourdieu, 1984: 137).

societies. In order to explore the role played by reflexivity and resources at one's disposal in shaping career patterns, we focus on two contrastive milieus, workers and management people, which differ from each other in terms of their social class positions. Objective cleavages between workers and managers and owners, viewed from the structuralist perspective, have been crystallised during the course of transformation constituting a divide between its "winners" and "losers", which reflected clear differences in terms of educational attainments, occupational ranks and incomes (Słomczyński et al., 2007). However, did such objective differentiation of "life chances" of workers and managers translate into sharp differences in the career patterns typical of them, as noted in the career studies carried out in the UK (e.g. Fenton and Dermott, 2006)? Or does reflexivity have an autonomous role in shaping career patters, which would then cut across the existing class and structural divisions?

Empirical research into career patterns of workers and business people in Poland

In order to explore the role of "internal conversation" in shaping career patters, we decided that it is the biographical method (Schütze, 1983; 1984) that will allow us not only to reconstruct the objective patterns of careers followed after the post-socialist transformation, but also to understand individual motives, interpretations, and meanings standing behind them. The biographical approach was combined with grounded theory methodology (Glaser and Strauss, 1967), which enabled us to elaborate upon the types of career patterns and link them with existing theoretical ideas in strict interrelation with empirical analysis during the course of research. In practice, we used the assumptions and practical procedures of Schütze's biographical method (Schütze, 1983) in the process of data collection and transcription, and the principles of grounded theory (Glaser and Strauss, 1967) for data analysis. In the years 2001-2004, in the south-western region of Poland, in Silesia, 290 biographical narrative interviews were conducted with manual workers, managers and entrepreneurs, in manufacturing, construction and services. Each interview included a complete life history, from the childhood up to the present moment, additional questions of clarifications and theoretical questions inspired by the first analytical steps. In both milieus, the sample was diversified along the dimensions such as age, gender, positions in organizational hierarchy, and types of work organizations[2].

---

[2] In workers' milieus the interviewees were hired employees occupying the lowest positions in organizational hierarchy and performing manual or routinized semi-manual tasks in industry, construction and services. Within business people's milieus, we interviewed entrepreneurs, presidents and managers of private production and service companies, as well as financial institutions.

The empirical data consists of 166 interviews with workers and 124 interviews with business people. We adopted a theoretical sampling strategy wherein the choice of subsequent cases was made on the basis of categories that emerged during the analysis of previous interviews (Glaser and Strauss, 1967). The theoretical sampling was guided by the process of data analysis, which consisted of two interwoven procedures. First, it involved open coding, done line-by-line "close reading" aimed at fracturing biographical data and conceptualizing observed regularities in the form of categories and their properties. Next, selective coding was conducted, during which the relationships between the career types and other categories that emerged were established (cf. Glaser, 1978: 56-72).

Selective data coding, focused on the ways of linking the subjective and objective dimensions of occupational careers in workers' life stories, made it possible to distinguish four main career patterns: anchor, bricolage, dead-end and patchwork. Their differentiation was made possible by crossing two continua of categories (see Figure 8.1). First, at the level of the objective shape of careers, the problem of career fragmentation was addressed. Exploring the patterns of occupational mobility in both milieus after the system change, a continuum was established of single-track careers, characterised by continuous employment in one company, and multi-track careers, involving intensified occupational mobility and/or simultaneous engagement in different occupational activities. Second, the

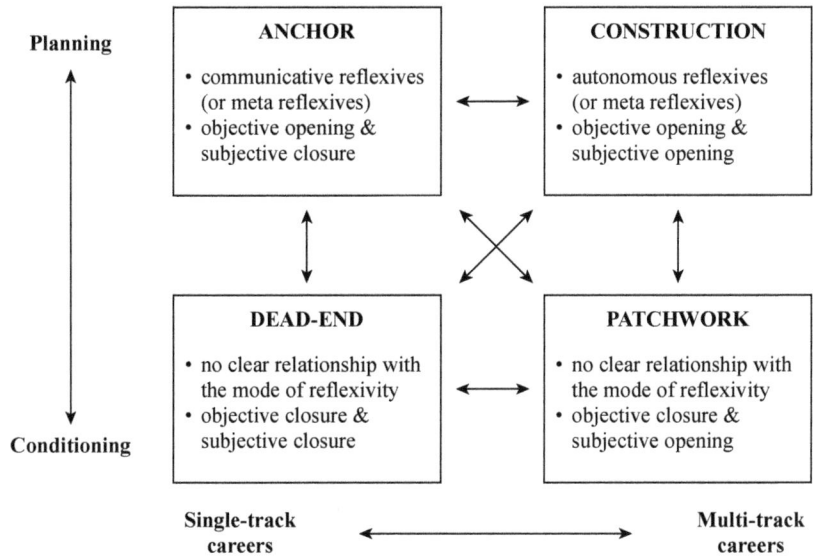

Figure 8.1 Career patterns in workers' and business milieus and the types of reflexivity
Source: Own research.

subjective aspects of career were located on the continuum of "planning" (intentional action schemes) and "conditioning" (conditioned action schemes), which was borrowed from the biographical sociology of Schütze (2005 [1984]: 306). "Planning" indicates a subjective perception of occupational life as an endeavour which can be controlled either at individual level ("work on resources") or by the collective means (coordinated actions). "Conditioning", in contrast, denotes a subjective definition of career in terms of limited control and overwhelming structural determination, which make individuals resemble "passive agents", i.e. those "to whom things simply happen" (Archer, 2007: 6).

Planning can be pursued in two forms reflecting two main types of reflexives distinguished by Archer (2007). In the case of communicative reflexives, internal conversation, through which career planning takes place, requires "completion and confirmation by others before resulting in the courses of action" (Archer, 2007: 93). Since this kind of reflexivity is founded on the actively endorsed continuity of action context, communicative reflexives tend to be grouped in the anchor type of career. By contrast, "autonomous reflexives" are those, who actively endorse contextual discontinuity and develop self-contained internal conversations (Archer, 2007: 93), which lead them to occupational mobility among various work contexts. Their natural locus is the construction type of career, based on the voluntary occupational mobility across different jobs and work organisations. The distorted link between internal conversations and actions is apparent in the single-track "dead end" careers and a multi-track "patchwork" careers. Those in the "conditioned" career types can also be (or become) "fractured reflexives", whose internal conversation does not provide them with instrumental guidance about what to do in practice (Archer, 2003: 299). However, the "fractured" self still can be mended if some effort of biographical work is undertaken and new resources are accumulated. The dominant mode of reflexivity is one of central factors determining which type of career will be chosen as a preferred means to overcome involuntary patchwork and dead-end[3].

As we applied in our study the strategy of theoretical sampling we cannot make any claims about representativeness in statistical terms. At the same time, our sample was big enough (290 life histories) to reach theoretical saturation

---

[3] In our study we did not find any cases of meta-reflexives, the fourth type distinguished by Archer (2007: 93; 2012), referring to those, who are "critically reflexive about their own internal conversations and critical about effective action in society". One of the reasons might be that workers and business people were involved first of all in advancing their pragmatic concerns and therefore did not dedicate themselves fully to non-pragmatic vocational ideals, as meta-reflexives tend to do. Nevertheless, it is difficult to say if the absence of meta-reflexives in our research is connected with the fact they are dramatically under-represented in business field and among workers or if it is simply an outcome of our sampling strategy. It also should be stressed that our goal was not to verify Archer's theory, but to make use of "theoretical codes" derived from it to understand the development of career patterns emerged from the analysis of biographical data.

and to allow us to formulate hypotheses about tendencies connected with the social distribution of the career types. By the concept of theoretical saturation we understand the stage of qualitative research where the continuation of sampling does not lead to the generation of any new conceptual insights. Instead of discovering new phenomena, the categories developed during the earlier stages of inquiry, appear again and again. Comparing at this stage the two social milieus, workers and managers we saw clear similarities and differences between them. The construction career type was more typical of business people as it is closely related to the level of resources possessed and the dominating discourse in this milieu. Typically, managers and owners felt a need to portray their experiences as the outcome of their strategic thinking and a matter of their own achievement even in the situations when there was a certain level of conditioning or contingency. Therefore, there was a tendency to perceive one's career as construction even if objectively it was closer to the patchwork pattern.

Another difference between the two milieus is the perception of the anchor career. As for workers it is often the most desirable career pattern, assuring financial stability and social continuity, in case of managers anchor, symbolizing the lack of mobility and perhaps also the lack of ambition, requires additional justification. This may explain why we have encountered so many argumentative segments in the interviews with business people whose careers resembled the anchor pattern. Managers and owners had a much stronger tendency than workers to picture their anchor careers as constructions. Dead-end careers differentiated strongly workers and business people. Being the outcome of "unhappy micro events" dead-end theoretically could happen to everybody. However, as for business people it symbolized only a temporary difficulty, which could be overcome on the basis of possessed economic, social and cultural capital, for workers dead-end was often becoming a long-term pattern which could not be changed on the basis of one's limited means. The similarity between the two milieus lies in the patchwork pattern being equally present in workers' and managers' biographies. This is the result of deep social change bringing previously unknown precariousness into the sphere of work and introducing discontinuities in all people's lives, which again can be bridged more successfully if one has a high level of biographical, social, economic and cultural resources at their disposal.

In line with biographical approach (Rosenthal, 2004), anchor, construction, dead-end, and patchwork conceptualize the types of relationships between the overall structure of told occupational biographies (*told story*) and objectively followed career paths (*lived life*). They may be considered also as independent patterns, with the possibility of "entering" and "leaving" them in different stages of occupational lives. Although the statistically non-representative character of our research sample makes it impossible to discuss the statistical distribution of the types, the differences between workers and business people in terms of the occurrence of the *dominant* career patterns in the narratives collected do not seem to be accidental. Anticipating the results presented further, it should also be emphasised that the fact that career types were observed, albeit in different forms and to a different extent, in both milieus offers strong empirical support for the theoretical argument about the central and autonomous role of reflexivity in shaping individual careers.

Anchor careers

Anchor careers are intentionally shaped single-track patterns, based on long-standing employment in a particular work organisation. This type of career is related to laboriously worked-out occupational statuses. People become "attached to positions by virtue of having done particularly well at them" (Strauss, 1975: 89), and this attachment leads them rather to self-limitation of aspirations than to the search for new career paths. Anchor careers are typical of communicative reflexives, whose ultimate concerns are inter-personal relations in their social milieus (Archer, 2003: 349). Their ability to keep their occupational position is linked to two kinds of capital. Firstly, seniority increases social capital, built around the networks of contacts and recognition at workplace. Secondly, cultural capital, in the form of practical knowledge acquired through work experiences, is constantly adapted to new organizational requirements.

Although in both milieus studied anchor careers are based on a very different level of objectively possessed resources, similar properties of this pattern in the case of workers and business people reflect a shared mode of reflexivity founded on single-track occupational experiences. In workers' milieus, the pattern expresses attempts to protect working-class identities against new economic threats and the devaluation of educational credentials, through reference to craftsmanship and emotional we-community. In the collected data, it was most typical of middle-aged, blue-collar workers considering themselves as "craftsmen":

> **Leszek:** "This factory is my whole life. I was connected with this factory throughout my whole life. I lived in a workers' hostel, I got hitched with a girl from the factory because she worked on injection moulding machines, and I worked in this big locksmith's department. (...) [Nowadays] they left only those, who're worth something, because those, you know, dimwits who cannot do anything and knock off trash, were kicked out" (a turner in machine industry, M, 49) [W-14][4]

---

[4] Labels contain: job description, gender, age and the code number of an interview

The life story of Leszek, a turner in his late forties, was shaped by the reality of a large, state-owned company he has been employed for the most of his career. An anchor career interlinks social capital (networks) and practical cultural capital (craft) with a specific organisational context. Since the latter is threatened, reflexive choices need to be taken to preserve individual occupational position. Profound social changes contribute to a situation in which the continuity of action context is not just involuntary given, but needs to be also agentially co-determined (Archer, 2003: 187) precluding any mechanical relationship between contexts and practices. The agential co-determination has its price. Under conditions of economic restructuring motivated by the minimisation of labour costs, maintaining an anchored career usually means accepting the reduction of economic benefits for the sake of employment security and non-instrumental social bonds since, as stated by one of the interviewees, "life isn't only about making money" [W-77].

While anchor-careers in workers' milieus are highly appreciated, they are much more problematic in a business milieu, where long-term employment in one firm is perceived as *per se* contradictory to "successful career-making" discourse. A lack of professional mobility requires some justification and frequently these are the emotional ties with a company and a strong embeddedness in a place which play such a justifying role. An anchor career, when followed by managers, is not accompanied by the "we-perspective" typical of workers. Instead, the justification of long-term anchoring in one firm proceeds on an individual level. On the one hand, objective advancement within an organization and extensive professional knowledge bonded with work performed are emphasized. On the other hand, the self-limitation of aspirations is stressed as a way to "do what one feels" and means to achieve a balance between workloads and family life. An example is Paulina, a branch director of a bank:

> **Paulina:** "It's absolutely sufficient for me to be a branch director, because I know how hard the work of the regional director is, who has to move around all branches. At this moment, it would collide too much with my family life. I'm ready for some sacrifices, but not to the extent [which would make me] to neglect my family. I've got a small child" (a branch director of a bank, F, 28) [B-111]

A pattern of self-limitation can also be found among entrepreneurs, who followed the path of establishing a small, family-owned business, step-by-step developed from the beginning of 90s or even from the state-socialist time. This becomes clear in an argument made by a female owner of a small, family-run sport shop, who juxtaposes "stunning careers" to "small regional success" [B-90], based on the ability to remain in business even in the time of economic recession. The presence of anchor careers in both milieus studied contradicts the liberal discourse, which emphasises endless flexibility and occupational mobility. Anchoring is not a result of personal failures or lack of marketable resources. Instead it expresses reflexive attempts to maintain continuity in occupational life; a conscious choice for the social or balanced life priorities.

Dead-end careers

Dead-end careers denote the pattern of "immobilisation" in a subjectively rejected work environment. At the objective level, these are single-track patterns, which assume limited job mobility in the period after the system change. At the level of subjective interpretations, they describe a durable or progressive loss of capacities to shape one's occupational career in a subjectively desirable manner. Instead, people "get stuck" in an organisational environment, which guarantees neither the economic nor social advantages expected. Dead-end illustrates also a broken career pattern where one stays out of employment against their will being unable to change the situation on the basis of one's own means only. No clear relationship between this career type and the mode of reflexivity was observed. Dead-end careers were encountered in the biographies of communicative reflexives, whose social milieus underwent disintegration during the course of systemic change, and autonomous reflexives, who at a certain stage of their occupational life encountered unsurpassable organisational obstacles that blocked their advancement within and between work organisations. In both milieus, dead-end careers reflected a more or less advanced distress of the mechanism of internal conversation and, in this sense, were also present in the narratives of "fractured reflexives" (Archer, 2003: 300). Long-term dead-end career results in a passive attitude of "taking things as they come", "working from day-to-day" and withdrawing to these spheres of live, which offer more stability and fulfilment (e.g. family life and friend circles).

Dead-end careers have sometimes been considered the most common career patterns in low-skilled, peripheral factions of workers' milieus (Thomas, 1989: 359). This is confirmed by the occurrence of the dead-end type in our sample, which was more common in the workers' milieu than in the case of business people. In case of older and middle-aged generations of workers, dead-end careers were accompanied by the development of "collective trajectories" (Schütze, 1992a: 192), characterised by the loss of autonomy in occupational life as a result of the restructuring and closure of old, ex-socialist manufacturing plants. Simultaneously, there is a new wave of dead-end careers in the youngest generation of workers, whose educational investments proved to be insufficient or misfit for changing labour market demands. An example is Weronika, employed as a low skilled worker in a printing shop:

> **Weronika**: "I decided to go to secondary school of economics, because in 2000...when I'd finished school, this field was a very...topical issue, you could've earned a lot of money (...) I intended to go for university studies, but I've...there was such a difficult financial situation, so I didn't. (...) In our region it's very difficult to find work, so I came to O-city (...) I began to work as a picker [in a print shop], at one of the machines, it's about picking up piles of paper from this machine...Well, this is very hard work [...] When I started school, I thought I'd work somewhere in an office, I didn't even think that I'd end up in O-city and I'd work as a picker" (an unskilled printing worker, F, 24) [W-86]

In the life stories of managers and owners, the dead-end phases of occupational biographies are considered rather as challenges to be overcome than impassable barriers. If constraints are encountered, they tend to be reinterpreted as impediments of idealized market situation. A "fossilized organization" [B-5] and "dismotivating" environment [B-9] are likely to be identified with work experiences in state-socialist firms. In other cases, the personalization of dead-end phases appears, which emphasizes uncontrollable events on the biographical level, such as illness or family problems. Rarely, dead-end is interpreted as a consequence of the general principles of the system's functioning, with the notable exception of some small entrepreneurs such as Bogusław:

> **Bogusław**: "I didn't develop the firm, so I'm an individual providing different kinds of services connected with electronics, working on my own (...). When it turns out that there are big undertakings, then I employ some people, but now there is less and less of these big undertakings. So, everything is getting blurred and I asses these occupational perspectives as very bad, it's a weak point that I can't move (...) I can't force myself now (...) to apply somewhere, although I know that maybe they wouldn't employ me, because I'm already, let's say, too old" (a self-employed, M, 50) [B-85]

A theme of "missed opportunities", typical of a dead-end pattern, is repeatedly interwoven with Bogusław's narration about his business activity. Anchored as a specialist in a state-owned firm during socialism, he decides to enter the business field too late, when the opportunities for "small entrepreneurship" are already much more limited. In the course of time, the profitability of his small service company gradually decreases and Bogusław finds himself trapped – on the one hand unable to develop his firm, due to the lack of significant economic capital and high competitiveness in the field, and on the other, reluctant and afraid of applying for a job in an organization. Although the dead-end in this case, as much as in other business people's narrations, is rather temporal than definite, its durability depends *both* on macroeconomic situation and reflexive abilities to mobilize already possessed resources.

Construction careers

While anchor careers reflect intentional attempts to preserve occupational stability and contextual continuity, which the concerns of communicative reflexives are founded on, construction careers are most typical of autonomous reflexives. Self-contained internal conversation becomes a generative mechanism fostering upward and inter-organisational mobility. Construction means moving among post, specialisations and organisations, experiencing various turning points and opening of new possibilities. There is a general framework assuming a long-term accumulation of all kinds of capital based on the capacity of risk-taking and resourcefulness. At the same time, even though structural conditions of "constructing" tend to be downplayed and replaced by the idea of self-determined planning, promoted by the liberal market discourse, the ways in which a construction career is actualized clearly depends on available resources, including economic capital (financial predictability), social capital (professionally useful social networks), and (marketable) educational credentials, of which a higher amount increases the freedom of experimenting with new career possibilities.

In the workers' milieu, in which the overall level of objectively possessed resources is generally lower than in the case of business people, construction careers rely mostly on reshaping and converting of the "resources at hand", which makes this career pattern resemble rather a "bricolage" than strictly planned design (cf. Baker and Nelson, 2005). Construction in one sphere of occupational life is often combined with anchoring in another as the "hybridised construction" of Maciej demonstrates:

> **Maciej**: "Although I work here, I also have a private business (...) Through some contacts, there was a bus for sale in the factory (...) And I started a business. In the afternoons, after coming back from work in the factory, sometimes till the morning, I was lying under [the bus], so in the morning it could go. (...) I worked for a year, I earned a bit, I didn't spend it, but I bought another bus, a better one. (...) It was working, working, and earned again. And

I bought another one." (a machine operator in household appliances factory, M, 45) [W-12]

Maciej combines anchor-pattern with construction career connected with establishing a small transportation firm. Hybridization maximizes economic profits by mobilizing available resources without losing advantages offered by permanent employment. The postponed consumption and hard work make it possible for Maciej to maintain a small company. The motive of sacrifice for future gains can also be observed in the case of young workers, who invest in the university weekend education. Construction careers constitute an active and innovative response to structural limitations. If structural constraints discourage a primary life project, which is often connected with a stable job in one company, the constructing logic and autonomous reflexivity lead people to "actively use their reflexivity to devise 'second' or 'third' best projects for themselves" (cf. Archer, 2007: 19).

The logic of construction was the most common pattern in the narratives of business people. It was often linked to the feeling of empowerment after the systemic change, which can be described as "the effect of spread wings". The beginning of the 1990s is idealized as the time when it was possible to start one's own business "from scratch" or become a member of higher management despite a scarcity of cultural capital. However, in the process of gradual structural closure, the role of initial economic assets and educational credentials has increased greatly. It explains why construction becomes a dominating pattern among the possessors of relatively higher amounts of all assets in business milieus, the members of higher and medium level management and the owners of big and medium private enterprises. An illustration can be found in the narrative of Eryk:

> **Eryk:** "Speaking about professional career, I'm really, really God's chosen one, because even when I was working in that socialist firm, even when I was the head of the team they didn't dare to come to me and persuade me to join the Party (…) Later on, the whole American adventure, extremely nice, and later the whole managerial career, after coming back from the States, it's a really fantastic experience…So, I'm a very happy man ((*laughing*)) but, but a bit busy… (…) I assess it… what happened… exactly in this way, as amazingly positive… with a deep conviction that I had a direct influence on it, that it's been created by me, worked out" (president of a printing house, M, 55) [B-80]

The career of Eryk, president of a printing house, entails a far-reaching contextual discontinuity, involving geographical mobility (a managerial career in the US) and occupational progression through many companies. Just like in other cases of autonomous reflexives, there is a strong belief that everyone must take personal responsibility for themselves. According to the rhetoric of success, the interrelated processes of self, biography, and career construction result in a deep conviction that one is at the same time "Gods' chosen one" and "the master of his own destiny". Another common motto, typical of construction careers in business milieu, is "I'm myself the helm, the ship and the sailor" [B-27, B-34, B-50]. A successful creation, not only of one's own career but also of new organizational rules, reinforces the feeling of the virtually unlimited possibilities of occupational development, which significantly differs from the hybridized construction-careers in workers' milieus.

Patchwork careers

Patchwork describes a multi-track career pattern which is more conditioned than intentionally planned. The pattern symbolises a torn career, made up of miscellaneous elements arranged at random without a clear larger design (cf. Alheit, 1995: 167). It consists of many semi-intentional or unintentional job changes interwoven with periods of unemployment and desperate job seeking. Expressing the chaotic aspects of social reality, patchwork is ruled rather by the logic of coincidence and necessity than the logic of purposeful planning of occupational life. It was most typical of autonomous reflexives, whose occupational projects were broken by market competition, insufficient resources and unhappy "micro events" at the level of individual and family life. However, it also emerged from the narratives of communicative reflexives, in particular workers, whose anchor careers were interrupted by uncontrollable organisational changes. Finally, patchwork was also encountered in narratives of "fractured reflexives" whose biographical problems and occupational problems overlapped magnifying distress and disorientation.

Patchwork is often, albeit not always, connected with "precarious", instable work (Standing, 2011) which represents the "dark" side of labour market flexibility. Both in the case of workers and business people, whom we interviewed, it tended to be presented as an "integral and unavoidable" element of modern economy: "we live in such times" [W-79], it is said with resignation, "this is how the reality looks like nowadays" [B-100]. In worker milieus, access to anchor-careers became limited in the course of capitalist transformation, especially for lower skilled, older workers, made redundant after restructuring of state-owned firms, and young employees entering a labour market defined by high unemployment and forced flexibility. An example of a young precarious worker experiencing a patchwork career is Aleksander:

Aleksander: "At the first job, my contract expired, they didn't want to prolong it, because I still worked as an apprentice (…) The second job, as I said, in this storehouse, [arranged] by an acquaintance of my father (…) He didn't pay for social security, which was crap, so I gave up this job. Afterwards there's a transportation firm. I worked there for a long time. I mean long, I'd worked for less than two years after I got there. And I had to go on the dole, 'cause the firm was closed. Then, a petrol station (…) And after military service, I sat firmly on these chairs for the unemployed and now I work here [in a supermarket] (*Question about the value of work*) I've learnt that I've never worked only for work…I did it for myself, because I liked it, I wanted to have money out of it." (a shop assistant in a hypermarket, M, 27) [W-28]

Aleksander, a young shop assistant, could not acquire meaningful occupational identity and valuable professional skills throughout his occupational career, which involved various and unrelated low-skilled jobs. Alexander's emphasis on "agency" contradicts the forced occupational mobility provoked by the low-regulated labour market. Both in the workers' milieu and business people's milieus the patchwork pattern is accompanied by the feeling of a "lone struggle" expressed as a conviction that "one has to manage on his own" [B-100], without relying on other people and institutions. Work intensification combined with readiness to take any available job ("I'm not afraid of any work" [W-3]) becomes the main strategy to preserve the minimal level of economic stability.

In the business milieu, patchwork careers were typical of small and medium firm owners, who were not able to accumulate significant economic resources in the starting phase of economic transformation and who later were facing increasing market competition and bureaucratic obstacles in their business development. Multifaceted defensive strategies used for saving one's firm from bankruptcy are illustrated in the narrative of Mirosław:

Mirosław: "One needs to stay somehow on the market. Now [2003], there's a crash (…) and one cannot foresee what will happen. Me too, I changed the profile of my business many times. I had some commerce, a tax consulting company, I had pawnshops, second-hand shops, electronics commerce, construction business, many things, catering. Now, we're looking for some solution to maintain what we already got, to have some money at hand" (an owner of a construction company, M, 45) [B-34]

During the years of his activity in the business field Mirosław has frequently changed not only the profile of his business, but also its organization and style of management, coming from partnership to individual ownership. None of those changes, though, was a result of careful long term planning. It was rather a response to the changing context, like falling demand, low profitability and a lack of consensus among the partners. Importantly, Mirosław – following himself the patchwork pattern – perpetuates it by the practice of flexible employment, according to season and current economic situation. This indicates a possible link between the career patterns followed by entrepreneurs and the workers they employ. Torn occupational biographies in the business milieu are translated into workers' fragmented careers, and in both milieus the normalization of patchwork pattern perpetuates the inconsistency of institutional rules, which at the same time promote self-directedness and increase structural constraints on autonomous actions in the sphere of work.

Conclusions

In this chapter we proposed a realist approach to the study of careers, which linked some assumptions of the traditions of the Chicago School and the realist social theory of Margaret Archer. The notion of "realist biography" allowed us to explore the occupational experiences as the result of both the individual placement in the distribution of resources and the agential attempts to reflexively deal with structural powers. It is worth emphasizing that the emerged career types transcend the boundaries of milieus traditionally considered as different social classes: individuals occupying the lowest and highest positions in organizational hierarchies. This similarity of career patterns despite persistent class inequalities cannot be explained without accepting the proposition that careers are shaped by similar modes of reflexivity, which cannot be reduced to mere reactions to the objective structural conditions of people's actions. Simultaneously, as remarked by Adams (2006: 524), it is necessary to understand "what comes 'after' the moment of reflexive awareness, in which choices are resourced or otherwise". This suggestion is confirmed by our study. Even though movements between career patterns are possible, not all of them are equally feasible for workers and business people. It was often not due to the lack of reflexivity, but limited material resources that careers were "blocked" or "torn". Nevertheless, as individuals attempt to change their unfavourable occupational situation, reflexivity becomes the core mechanism of "getting out" from conditioned career patterns. Resources are necessary means to advance individual careers, but their efficiency depends on the mode of reflexivity developed during the course of earlier life events and career stages.

The realist approach to the analysis of careers, as elaborated in this chapter, makes it possible to transcend one-sided approaches which emphasise the far-reaching structural determination of occupational trajectories (see e.g. Bourdieu, 1984) or, contrastingly, create an illusion of open opportunities which only need to be seized through the development of adequate "career management skills" (see for instance CBS Compendium, 2011). The approach proposed in this chapter puts an equal emphasis on the causal role of social structures and individual reflexivity in shaping career patterns. In this respect, some of our empirical observations suggest that career patterns are not only influenced, but they might also (cumulatively) influence structural and organisational conditions. On the one hand, the "desirable" models of occupational lives in late capitalist societies, such as the multi-track construction patterns, are mapped onto persons demanding re-adaptation of their careers. On the other hand, however, these models encounter the limits of possessed resources and personal attempts to reflexively shape occupational identities in line with earlier biographical commitments and future-oriented life projects. In consequence, career choices not only conform to the new logic of "boundaryless careers", but they can also contribute to the emergence (and, more likely, reproduction) of organisational rules which support the continuity of anchor careers, especially for the "core", highly valued and better skilled employees.

The research presented in this chapter can also have some pertinent policy implications. Two possible areas, in which the realist approach to career analysis can be practically used, include occupational counselling and related active labour market policies. The relevance of the biographical method for occupational counselling has been already stressed in the existing research (see Betts, Griffiths, Schütze, Straus, *no date*), which suggested that the identification of biographical resources accumulated in earlier career stages is central for the counselling practice. Based on our approach, it can be added that the analysis of the types of reflexivity needs also to be undertaken as a part of career advisory work. For instance, anchor careers might be especially desirable for "communicative reflexives" who value reliable social networks, good relations with their colleagues and well-defined area of occupational skills and expectations, which all favour more contextual continuity than change. By contrast, construction careers are often the most desirable patterns among those practicing an "autonomous" type of reflexivity. Although the construction career might seem to be very desirable, the biographical costs of advancing it are often underestimated until the point when one's personal and family situation becomes "impossible to deal with" and some alternatives need to be sought. In the course of biographical work a certain level of awareness is achieved of high biographical costs[5]

---

[5] For more insights about biographical costs of corporate careers see Kaźmierska et al (2012) and biographical costs of mobility see Spanò et al in this volume.

paid as a result of one's career pattern. This is a point where career counselling may be crucial for finding more balanced and self-preserving solutions. In case of "conditioned" patterns, occupational advisory work should be focused on stimulating biographical work aimed at strengthening action capacities and personal autonomy of individuals experiencing career fragmentation (patchwork) and dead-end situations, which all quite often require quite radical biographical decisions. The question should be asked which of two career types (anchor or construction) would match best the concerns of the individuals involved given the mode of their reflexivity.

However, in contradistinction to voluntarism putting the whole responsibility for occupational development on individuals, the realist approach also suggests that efficient coping with patchwork and dead-end careers requires a great deal of institutional work aimed at the creation of more secure and enriching jobs. As argued by the recent report by European Foundation for Improvement of Working and Living Conditions, "the policy agenda should promote sustainable work over the entire length of careers: in other words, the ability or all involved in paid employment to maintain their engagement in paid work over their professional career" (EWCS, 2011: 9). Similar conclusions follow from the International Labour Organisation analysis, which suggest the need to develop "an approach that recognizes the importance of placing jobs at the top of the policy agenda and the need for coherence among macroeconomic, employment and social policies." (ILO, 2012: xi). The realist analysis of careers makes it possible to combine such macro-level recommendations with those centred on and sensitive to individual concerns, which might be very different from the currently dominant discourse of disembedded, endlessly flexible and boundaryless careers. It can be helpful to detect what kind of institutional arrangements are needed to fit into the needs of communicative, autonomous and meta-reflexives. In this respect, the analysis in this chapter can be considered just a tentative contribution to such a larger project aimed at (re)linking the macro-policy agenda in Europe (and elsewhere) to the differentiated concerns of the workers.

Literature

Adams, M. (2006). 'Hybridizing Habitus and Reflexivity: Towards an Understanding of Contemporary Identity?'. *Sociology-the Journal of the British Sociological Association*, 40(3), pp. 511-528.

Alheit, P. (1995). "'Patchworkers': Biographical constructions and professional attitudes. Study motivation of adult education students". In P. Alheit, A. Bron-Wojciechowska, and E. Brugger (eds.), *The Biographical Approach in European Adult Education*. Wien: Verband Wiener Volksbildung, pp. 151-171.

Archer, M. (2003). *Structure, Agency and the Internal Conversation*. Cambridge: Cambridge University Press.

Archer, M. (2007). *Making our Way through the World: Human Reflexivity and Social Mobility.* Cambridge: Cambridge University Press.
Archer, M. (2012). *The Reflexive Imperative in Late Modernity.* Cambridge: Cambridge University Press.
Arthur, M. B., Khapova, S. N., Wilderom, C. (2005). 'Career success in a boundaryless career world'. *Journal of Organizational Behavior*, Vol. 26, pp. 177-202.
Arthur, M., Rousseau, D. (eds.) (1996). *The Boundaryless Career: A New Employment Principle for a New Organizational Era.* Oxford: Oxford University Press.
Baker, T., Nelson, R. E. (2005). 'Creating Something from Nothing: Resource Construction through Entrepreneurial Bricolage'. *Administrative Science Quarterly, 50*, pp. 329-366.
Barley, S. R. (1989). 'Careers, Identities, and Institutions: the Legacy of the Chicago School of Sociology'. In Arthur, M.B., Hall, D.T., and Lawrence, B.S. (eds.), *Handbook of Career Theory.* Cambridge: Cambridge University Press, pp. 41-65.
Bateson, M. C. (1989). *Composing a Life.* New York: Grove Press.
Bauman, Z. (1999). *Work, Consumerism and the New Poor.* Buckingham: Open University Press.
Becker, H. S., and Carper, J. W. (1956). 'The Development of Identification with an Occupation'. *American Journal of Sociology, 61*(4), pp. 289-298.
Betts, S., Griffiths, A., Schütze, F., Straus, P. (no date) *Biographical Counselling: an Introduction*, available at: http://www.uni-magdeburg.de/zsm/node/544 (accessed on 07.06.2012).
Bertaux, D., and Kohli, M. (1984). 'The Life Story Approach: A Continental View'. *Annual Review of Sociology, 10*, pp. 215-237.
Bourdieu, P. (1984 [1990]). *Distinction. A Social Critique of the Judgement of Taste.* Cambridge, Massachusetts: Harvard University Press.
Bourdieu, P. (1986). 'The forms of capital'. In J. G. Richardson (ed.), *Handbook of Theory and Research for the Sociology of Education.* New York: Greenwood Press.
CBS Compedium (2011). *Compendium: Innovative Tools and Methods in Career Guidance and Counselling, Euroguidance*, available at: http://www.npk.hu/public/tanacsadoknak/konferencia_2011/COMPENDIUM.pdf
Eyal, G., Szelényi, I., and Townsley, E. (2000). *Making Capitalism Without Capitalists. The New Ruling Elites in Eastern Europe.* London, New York: Verso.
EWCS (2011). *Fifth European Working Conditions Survey. An Overview Report.* Dublin: Eurofound, available at: http://www.eurofound.europa.eu/pubdocs/2011/82/en/1/EF1182EN.pdf
Fenton, S., and Dermott, E. (2006). 'Fragmented Careers? Winners and Losers in Young Adult Labour Markets'. *Work Employment and Society, 20*(2), pp. 205-221.
Glaser, B. (1978). *Theoretical Sensitivity. Advances in the Methodology of Grounded Theory.* Mill Valley: Sociology Press.
Glaser, B., and Strauss, A. (1967). *The Discovery of Grounded Theory. Strategies for Qualitative Research.* Chicago: Aldine Publishing Company.
Gold, M., and Fraser, J. (2002). 'Managing Self-Management: Successful Transitions to Portfolio Careers'. *Work Employment and Society, 16*(4), pp. 579-597.
Hughes, E. C. (1997). 'Careers'. *Qualitative Sociology, 20*: 389-397.
ILO (2012). *World of Work Report 2012: Better Jobs for a Better Economy.* Geneva: International Labour Office, International Institute for Labour Studies.

Kaźmierska, K., Piotrowski, A., and Waniek, K. (2012). 'Transnational Work in the Biographical Experiences of Traditional Professions and Corporate Executives: Analysis of Two Cases', in Miller, R. (ed.) *The Evolution of European Identities. Biographical Approaches*, Palgrave Macmillan, pp. 76-101.

Li, Y. J., Bechhofer, F., Stewart, R., Mccrone, D., Anderson, M., and Jamieson, L. (2002). 'A Divided Working Class? Planning and Career Perception in the Service and Working Classes'. *Work Employment and Society* (16)4: 617-636.

Mach, B. W. (2005). *Transformacja systemu a trajektorie życiowe młodych pokoleń.* Warszawa: IFiS PAN.

Mouzelis, N. (1995). *Sociological Theory. What Went Wrong? Diagnosis and Remedies.* London: Routledge.

Riemann, G., Schütze, F. (1991). '"Trajectory' as a basic theoretical concept for analyzing suffering and disorderly social processes". in Maines, D. R. (ed.) *Social Organization and Social Process. Essays in Honor of Anselm Strauss*. New York, Walter de Gruyer.

Rosenthal, G. (2004). 'Biographical research'. In Seale, C., Gobo, G., Gubrium, J.F., and Silverman, D. (eds.), *Qualitative Research Practice*. London: Sage, pp. 48-64.

Schütze, F. (1983). 'Biographieforschung und narratives Interview'. *Neue Praxis, 3*, pp. 283-293.

Schütze, F. (1992). 'Pressure and Guilt – War Experiences of a Young German Soldier and Their Biographical Implications'. *International Sociology, 7* (2), pp. 187-208.

Schütze, F. (2005 [1984]). 'Cognitive Figures of Autobiographical Extempore Narration'. in Miller, R., (ed.) *Biographical Research Methods*, SAGE Publications, Vol. II, pp. 289-338.

Schütze, F. (2008a). 'Biography analysis on the empirical base of the autobiographical narratives: How to analyse autobiographical narrative interviews', *Part I, INVITE – Biographical Counselling in Rehabilitative Vocational Training*. Further Educational Curriculum. EU Leonardo da Vinci Programme. www.biographicalcounselling.com/download/B2.1.pdf

Schütze, F. (2008b). 'Biography Analysis on the Empirical Base of the Autobiographical Narratives: How to Analyse Autobiographical Narrative Interviews', *Part II, INVITE – Biographical Counselling in Rehabilitative Vocational Training.* Further Educational Curriculum. EU Leonardo da Vinci Programme. www.biographicalcounselling.com/download/B2.2.pdf

Słomczyński, K. M., Janicka, K., Shabad, G., and Tomescu-Dubrow, I. (2007). 'Changes in Class Structure in Poland, 1988–2003: Crystallization of the Winners—Losers' Divide'. *Polish Sociological Review, 157*(1), pp. 45-64.

Spanò, A, Domecka, M., and Perone, E. (2012). 'Biographical Costs of Mobility and Trans-nationalisation in European space' in this volume.

Standing, G. (2011). *The Precariat. The New Dangerous Class*, London: Bloomsbury.

Strauss, A. L. (1977 [1969]). *Mirrors and Masks. The Search for Identity*. London: Robertson and Co.

Strauss, A. (1975). *Profession, Work and Careers*. New Brunswick: Transaction Publishers.

Strauss, A. (1993). *Continual Permutations of Action*. New York: Aldine.

Szafraniec, K. (2011). *Młodzi 2011.* Warszawa: Kancelaria Prezesa Rady Ministrów.

Thomas, R. J. (1989). 'Blue-Collar Careers: Meaning and Choice in a World of Constraints'. In Arthur, M.B., Hall, D.T., and Lawrence, B.S. (eds.), *Handbook of Career Theory*. Cambridge: Cambridge University Press. pp. 354-379.

Turk, J. D. (2007). 'Interpretive economics in Slovenia: A useful approach for green economics?'. *International Journal of Green Economics, 1*(3-4), pp. 494-512.

Contributors

Tatiana Bajuk Senčar, PhD, is an anthropologist currently working as a Research Fellow at the Scientific Research Centre of the Slovenian Academy of Sciences and Arts, Institute of Slovenian Ethnology. Her research interests cover several areas. One is transition and post socialist studies, in which she has focused on the social roles of economists and economic knowledge during Slovenia's transition process as well as on the development of socialist entrepreneurship – the latter being a project based on the collection of biographical narratives of socialist managers. In addition, she has also collaborated on Europe-level research that shed light on post-socialist developments in organized labour movements in selected new EU-member states using biographical narratives. The second research area concerns the links between tourism, sustainable development and heritage studies, in which she has published ethnographic research on the relationship between the local and global in tourist development and is currently working on a project concerning sustainable development and state bureaucratization of heritage practices in the protected area of Triglav National Park in Slovenia. Her third research area concerns the European Union and the construction of transnational identity. Her recent research in this area includes study of the integration of the first generation of Slovene Eurocrats and the construction of identity within the EU institutions, research that is based on an ethnographically grounded analysis of collected biographical and career narratives.

Bob Carter is Professor of Sociology at the University of Leicester. He is the author of *Realism and Racism: Concepts of Race in Sociological Research* (2000) and is the co-author of *Applied Linguistics as Social Science* (with Alison Sealey 2004). He has published extensively on the topics of racism and ethnicity and on realist social theory and social research. His most recent publications have been *Nature, Society and Environmental Crisis* (2010) and *Humans and Other Animals* (2011), both co-edited with Nickie Charles.

Prue Chamberlayne has extensive experience of teaching comparative social policy and of using biographical methods in research. She has used biographical methods in a range of research and policy settings and has applied such methods to professional training and evaluation work. She co-directed (with Michael Rustin) the *Sostris* project on *'Social Strategies in Risk Society'* (1996-9) and has co-authored and co-edited several seminal books on biographical approaches in social science: *Welfare and Culture in Europe: Towards a New Paradigm in Social Policy* (1999), *Cultures of Care: Biographies of Carers in Britain and the two Germanies* (2000), *The Turn to Biographical Methods in Social Science:*

Comparative Issues and Examples (2000), *Biography and Social Exclusion in Europe: Experiences and Life Journeys* (2002) and *Biographical Methods and Professional Practice: An International Perspective* (2004). Retired from the Faculty of Health and Social Care at the Open University, she now writes poetry, and is involved in a community development project in Uganda.

Markieta Domecka is an independent researcher collaborating with the University of Naples, Federico II, Department of Sociology'. She has worked at Queen's University Belfast in the FP7 project *EUROIDENTITIES – 'The Evolution of European Identity: Using biographical methods to study the development of European identity'*. Previously she worked in the Sociology of Work and Organization research group at the Catholic University of Leuven doing her doctoral research on the relationship between post-socialist transformation and career patterns in business field. Her research interests refer to the problems of identity and belonging, relationships between agency and structure and the application of different biographical narrative methods in social sciences.

Norbert Kluge, PhD, is coordinator and adviser for the European Works Council of ThyssenKrupp AG. He was formerly Senior Researcher at the European Trade Union Institute (ETUI) in Brussels for 8 years. His main areas of expertise at the ETUI were worker participation, the European Company (SE-Societas Europaea) and corporate governance. During his last 2 years at the ETUI he also set up the EWPCC (European Worker Participation Competence Centre) providing support for workers' representatives in boardrooms of European Companies. He was also head of the *SEEUROPE* project, which studied worker participation at the board level in European Companies. As a social scientist with a doctorate from the University of Kassel, he was during 1988–2002 an expert on co-determination at the Hans Böckler Foundation in Düsseldorf.

Adam Mrozowicki, PhD in Social Sciences (Catholic University of Leuven, 2009), is lecturer at the Institute of Sociology, University of Wroclaw. His expertise lies in the areas of the sociology of work, comparative employment relations and qualitative methodology. He has also longstanding interest in biographical methods developed in his PhD research on the life strategies of workers in Poland and his current research on the biographical experiences of trade union activists in Central and Eastern Europe. In the years 2009-2011 he was post-doctoral research fellow of the Foundation for Polish Science (Homing Programme) coordinating research on trade union revitalisation in Poland, Romania, Estonia and Slovenia. He cooperates with European Trade Union Insitute. He has published in Work, Employment and Society, European Journal of Industrial Relations, Qualitative Sociology Review, Economic and Industrial Democracy and EMECON.

Lyudmila Nurse, (née Koklyagina), PhD, is a sociologist and a director of Oxford XXI – a strategic think tank and development support organisation which generates innovative research on economic, social, cultural and related issues and a director of Hart Group, UK. She studied Sociology at the Institute of Sociological Research of the USSR Academy of Sciences in Moscow and at the University of Manchester in the UK. She was a visiting research fellow at the Universities of Warwick and the City University of London. She was a senior researcher, head of a research centre at the Institute of Sociology of the Russian Academy of Sciences in Moscow until 1996, where she did her PhD dissertation in 1987. In 1982-1992 she worked in the longitudinal project "Paths of generations" focusing on the on the comparative, intergenerational analysis of life courses of the 1980-s age cohorts in Russia and the former Soviet republics and later continued her study using biographical methods. She continued developing mixed methods, comparative approaches in research and consultancy projects. She was a partner in the EC FP7 *ENRI-EAST: Interplay of European, National and Regional identities: Nations Between the States Along the New Eastern Borders of the European Union*. She designed and led the *Cultural Identities and Music* study and was a designer of the biographical study in the ENRI-East project. Since 2011 Lyudmila has been a member of the European Cultural Parliament. She is author of more than 50 academic publications and international analytical reports on life courses, the transition from education to employment, cultural reproduction, cultural identities and ethnic minority studies in the inter-generational and comparative perspective.

Elisabetta Perone, PhD in Sociology and Social Research (University Federico II of Naples), has in the recent past worked as Research Assistant in the FP7 project *EUROIDENTITIES – 'The Evolution of European Identity: Using biographical methods to study the development of European identity'*. Her main research interests concern biographical courses in the sphere of education and work. One of her latest works refers to the trajectories of inclusion at school of the second generation of migrants in Italy and their processes of belonging/identifications in the host country.

Valeria Pulignano is Professor of Sociology of Labour and Industrial Relations at the Centre for Sociological Research at KU Leuven and Fellow at the Industrial Relations Research Unit (IRRU), Warwick University (UK) and at CEPS/INSTEAD (Luxembourg). She is also researcher of the "Interuniversity Research Center on Globalisation and Work" (CRIMT) at the University of Montréal (Canada). Her research interests include more broadly comparative European industrial relations, with a particular focus on trade unions and systems of workplace representations both at the national and European level, employees' participation, employment relations within multinational companies, company restructuring, labour flexibility and change in the labour markets in a comparative European perspective. She has been participating in several projects led by the EU Social Partners and funded by the European Commission on restructuring, social dialogue and local authorities. She is currently working on two large projects founded by the Bezonderonderzoekfond in KUL and the Federal Weteschappen Onderzoefond (FWO) on labour flexibility and work security within multinationals in a comparative perspective in Europe. She is partner in a recently founded Marie Curie Initial Training Networks Programme (ITN) – *FP7-PEOPLE-2012-ITN*. She was a partner in the EU FP6 project *The European Socio-Economic Models of a Knowledge Based Society* within the FP6 Framework of the European Commission), and was the project coordinator of a *TRACE* (ETUI-REHS) project on *"Trade Unions Managing and Anticipating Change in Europe"* (Art.6 European Social Fund). She is editor of *Flexibility at Work: Recent Development in the International Automobile Industry* (2006).

Antonella Spanò is Associate Professor of Sociology at University of Naples Federico II. She has carried out biographical research for over a decade, mainly in the areas of social exclusion. Scientist in charge of the Italian team in the FP7 project *EUROIDENTITIES – 'The Evolution of European Identity: Using biographical methods to study the development of European identity'*, has previous experience of European Research, as scientific consultant of the Italian team in Sostris Social Strategies in Risk Societies, IV Framework Programme. Her main research interests include social exclusion, unemployment, gender, migration, youth and social policy, with a peculiar focus on biographical methods as tools for evaluating social interventions and for identify people's coping strategies. Recently her research interest concerned Second Generations of migrants, their forms of identifications, coping strategies and processes of integration.

Jeffrey David Turk is a Research Fellow at the Scientific Research Centre of the Slovenian Academy of Sciences and Arts, currently located at the Centre for Sociological Research, KU Leuven. He earned his first doctorate in experimental elementary particle physics at Yale University in 1994. After working as a Physicist at the European Laboratory for Particle Physics (CERN), he earned his MA in Transition Economics at the Central European University in Budapest (1997) and then a DPhil in Contemporary European Studies from the University of Sussex (2003). He specialises in realist research methods in the social sciences with a focus on European policy studies.

Tom Wengraf, formerly Senior Lecturer in Sociology and Social Research Methods at Middlesex University, and Honorary Research Fellow at the Birkbeck Institute for Social Research, University of London, was co-editor of *The Turn to Biographical Methods in Social Science* (2000), and his *Qualitative Research Interviewing: Biographic Narrative and Semi-Structured Methods* was published in 2001. Previously on the editorial board of *New Left Review* and a founding member of the Conference of Socialist Economists, he was involved in the EU-funded *Sostris* project on *'Social Strategies in Risk Society'* (1996-9) and the follow-up research study (separately funded) of the 'Bromley-by-Bow Centre' (East London). He has also researched university performance indicators of staff consultation, empowerment and satisfaction (*PISCES*). He runs training courses in London and elsewhere by request in the Biographic-Narrative Interpretive Method (BNIM). He is a member of the UK Psychosocial Studies Network and the International Research Group in Psychosocietal Analysis. A free update of his *BNIM Short Guide and Detailed Manual* is always available on request.

Index

abduction 21
accumulation of experience 177
actor-network theory 43
actor-sensitive research 35
Adcock, Robert 33
agency of collectivities 47
agent-self 22
alternative explanations 25
alternative hypotheses, validity and 186
analytical dualism 37, 43, 49, 57, 59
  and emergence 44
  and sociological realism 44
anthropology 167, 172
Archer, Margaret S. 13, 14, 17, 22, 23, 24, 44, 66, 94, 109, 116, 126, 146
  and careers 192
  and morphogenetic model 45
  three-stage model of human action 23
articulating social interests in a multi-national governance system 153
Austria 55, 56
Austrian Presidency of the (Council of the) European Union 181
Aventis 157
aviation emissions 181
Bajuk Senčar, Tatiana 34, 37, 38, 167, 215
Baltic States 121, 132
Belarus 121, 126, 127, 128
Belgium 53, 116, 149, 150, 157
Bennett, Jane 43
Berlin 75, 76, 103, 104
Bertaux, Daniel 26, 27, 28, 192
Bhaskar, Roy 24, 27, 44, 63, 67, 70, 94
bias, measurement 33
biographical case reconstruction 30
biographical costs 209
  and career counselling 209
  and mobility 93
biographical methods 13, 37, 64, 75, 88
  as compatible with realism 15

biographical narratives 115, 116, 120, 122, 124, 130, 175
biographical research
  methodological debates within 26
  tradition of 25
biographical resource 58, 112, 116, 126, 133, 209
biographical work 13, 31, 32, 82, 93, 109, 192, 198, 209
Biographic-Narrative Interpretive Method. *See* BNIM
biographic narratives
  as reflecting internal conversation 14
BNIM 30, 58, 63, 73, 168, 175, 185
borderlands, EU-non-EU 117
Bosch 156
Brussels 42, 167, 169, 170, 172, 175, 177, 178, 182, 183
Brussels way of thinking 178
business people 196, 198
  and anchor careers 199, 200
  and career patterns 196, 199, 208
  and construction careers 199, 204, 205
  and dead-end careers 199, 202, 204
  and patchwork careers 206, 207
  interviews with 197
Byrne, David 50
capitalist regimes 37
career
  anchor 192, 197, 198, 199, 200, 204, 205, 206, 209, 210
  construction 204
  dead-end 197, 198, 199, 202, 210
  multi-track 197, 198, 206, 209
  occupational 191, 192, 195, 197
  patchwork 100, 111, 192, 197, 198, 199, 206, 210
  single-track 197, 198, 200, 202
career patterns 36, 191, 194, 196, 197, 202, 208, 209
Carter, Bob 14, 15, 37, 43, 45, 115, 215

222 INDEX

case-based strategies and realist approaches 50
case-oriented research 149
case studies, narrative-based 149
Catholic Church, Roman 122, 130, 131, 132
causal explanation 43, 50, 51
causality 50, 172
causal mechanisms 24, 37, 50, 51, 54, 55, 59
   identification of 51
causal processes, probing of 25
Central and Eastern Europe 157
chains of narration 28
Chamberlayne, Prue 14, 25, 30, 36, 38, 58, 63, 65, 75, 82, 119, 175, 215
Chicago School analysis of careers 191, 208
Chicago School tradition 25
climate change 37, 168, 169, 171
Climate-Energy legislative package 167, 168, 169, 171, 180, 181, 183
coda 29
codecision 171
co-determination 141, 147, 152, 155, 156, 201
collective bargaining 141, 143, 145
collective intentionality 18, 23
Collier, David 33
Commission for Social Affairs 152
Committee of Permanent Representatives of the Member States (COREPER) 169
comparative institutional analysis 35
compliance regimes 147
concept-dependence 51
constraints
   communicative 28
   institutional 161
   of rationality 22
   of realism 18
   social 24, 35, 46, 56, 66, 87, 88, 110, 116, 143, 146, 191, 192, 203
   structural 205, 208
   thematic 115
constructivism 15, 27, 37, 49
contextual discontinuity 55, 198, 205

contiguity 173, 174, 180, 183
contiguity-based solidarity 174
Copenhagen 180, 183
corporate governance 144, 152
Council Secretariat 169, 176, 178, 180
critical realism 13, 25, 37, 70, 83, 89, 167, 192
   methodological commitments of 37
cross-border mergers 151
cultural emergent property 45, 46
data acquisition 14, 18, 19, 20, 21, 22, 23, 24
decision-making, European 34, 118, 161, 169, 170, 177
Delanty, Gerard 173
descriptive statistics 17
DG Environment 171, 181
Directive 2002/14/EC on the national rights for information and consultation 152
discursive penetration 44
doing realist research 51
Domecka, Markieta 13, 36, 38, 93, 160, 191, 216
Eastern Europe 107, 115, 116, 117, 118, 121, 134, 136, 150, 194, 195
   in the 19th century 55
Economic and Monetary Union (EMU) 142
economic integration 142
economics 15, 16, 18, 19, 75, 203
Edwards, Paul 141, 146
Elder-Vass, Dave 46
emergence
   and analytical dualism 44, 45
   and generative mechanisms 50
   and sociological realism 43
   diachronic 54
   genealogical histories of 51, 54
   in critical realism 37
   of institutional arrangements in Europe 35
   of institutions and social structures 35
   of organisational rules 209
emergent property 45, 49, 50, 55, 57
   irreducibility of 45

second and third-order/level 45, 51
emotional bonds 95
emotional costs 94
emotional needs 95
emotional pendulum 106, 108
emotional ties 106, 201
emotions 97, 98, 99, 110, 116
   and we-community 200
empiricism 14, 34, 37, 53
   research strategies and observable data 50
employee inolvement 143
employee involvement 141, 144, 145, 146, 147, 148, 150, 152, 153, 154, 161
   and European law 161
   and social dialogue 156
   at the European level 150
   creation of space for 146
   EU directives on 151
   EU legislation for 151
   Europeanization and 143
   European space for 147
   European structure for 150
   macro-institutional initiatives involving 150
   macro-institutional structures for 154
   rights at the supervisory board 158
   rules and provisions for 151
   statutory representative forms of 149
employee representatives 141, 142, 145, 147, 149, 150, 151, 152, 155, 156, 157, 158, 159, 160, 161
enablements, social 24, 66
England 68, 122, 135, 138
ENRI-EAST 38, 116
ENRI-Values and Identities Survey 117
entrepreneurs 58, 196, 201, 203, 208
environmental policy negotiation 168, 183
environmental policy structure 176
epistemic fallacy 27
Erasmus programme 108
escaping strategy 95
essentialism 173
Estonia 120, 121
ethnic grouping 115, 116

ethnicity 38, 72, 194
   as a biographical resource 52
   as biographical resource 43, 53
   assumptions in research 52
   in western and northern Europe 52
   lay definitions of 53
   realist study of 51
   systems of naming 53
ethnic minority 52, 65, 115
ethnic solidarity 53
ethnographic description 176
ethnographic study 168
Euroidentities 36, 38
European Company Statute 151, 152
European Company Statute Directive 151
European Foundation for the Improvement of Living and Working Conditions 155
European Framework Agreements 143
European integration 14, 15, 144, 145, 168, 182
European Metalworkers' Federation 157
European opportunity structure 93, 96
European Parliament 171, 184
European policy studies 13, 14, 15, 34, 35, 39
European social dialogue 37, 38, 153
European stories 176
European studies 14, 15, 35, 36, 37, 38, 145
   methodological issues 37
European Union
   and global climate change 168
   and social dialogue 38
   and social integration 142
   Climate-Energy legislation 167
   Climate-Energy legislative package 183
   climate negotiations 180, 183
   committees 34, 174
   Council committees 170
   Council of the 168, 169, 170
   decision-making 34
   economic integration 143
   Emissions Trading System 181

enlargement of 34, 37, 116, 118, 147, 148, 168, 169, 170, 195
environmental policy negotiation 169
institutions 34, 167, 169
integration discourses 172
legislative process 179
permanent officials 167
policies 35, 36, 37
policy processes 14, 34
research sponsorship 74
rotating presidency of the Council 168, 169, 170, 180
social dimension 142
transnational experience 36
troika 171
European Working Conditions Survey 195
European Works Councils 141, 146, 157, 159, 160, 162
and corporate identity 158
based on commonalities and joint interests 155, 157, 159
based on regime competition 155, 156
Directive (94/45/EC) 150, 151, 152
experiences 153
proactive 155, 158, 159
Recast 2009 Directive 151, 159
structures for employee representation 153
faith 118, 127, 130, 132
Featherstone, Kevin 143
Ferejohn, John A. 149
feudal social forms, remnants of in 19th century Poland 55
Fifth Directive 151, 152
Fleetwood, Steve 141, 146
four domains. *See* Froggett, Lynn
France 53, 65, 108, 147, 149, 150
French Presidency of the (Council of the) European Union 181
Froggett, Lynn 71
future-blind approach 75, 76, 79, 80, 81
gender 65, 72, 93, 95, 97, 102, 104, 105, 112, 116, 117, 118, 127, 133, 194, 196, 200
General Secretariat of the Council 171

generative mechanisms 50
Georgakakis, Didier 36
Goertz, Gary 149
governance
  contemporary models of 54
grounded theory 196
groupness of ethnic minorities 116
Hacking, Ian 52
Haraway, Donna, J. 43
Hoggett, Paul 68
Holland. *See* Netherlands
Hollway, Wendy 67
human reflexivity 36
human resource management 141
Hume, David 24, 27
Hungary 56, 117, 136, 139, 149, 150
ICE regulations 153
identities under transformation 36
identity development 38, 111, 120, 136
identity management 116, 133
imagined community 121, 124, 128
immigration 121, 132
industrial relations 38, 141, 161
Information and Consultation of Employees Directive 151
innovative social agencies 65, 75, 82, 83
institutional work 35, 210
instrumental rationality, as classical model 22
integration, assessing 172
integration experiences 167
intentionality
  not bypassing 25
intentionality, collective 22, 33
internal and external worlds. *See* separate worlds
internal conversation 13, 14, 23, 32, 88, 192, 196, 198, 202, 204
  as causal mechanism 14
internal explanations 149
international relations theory 37
interviews
  biographical 120, 136, 138
  biographic-narrative 65, 84
  open-ended 50, 115, 150, 162
  open-narrative 175
  semi-structured 115, 136, 150, 162

unstructured 115
intrinsic properties 18
Ireland 99
Italy
   Northern 105
   Southern 97, 100
Jacobi, Otto 144
job enrichment programmes 141
joint decision making 141
KBC bank 157
kin-nation 118
Kluge, Norbert 37, 38, 141, 145, 155, 160, 216
Kotthoff, Helga 159
labour market regulation 144
language
   as cultural emergent property 45
language of worship 129
Latour, Bruno 43, 50
Latvia 120, 121, 127
Law, John 43, 50
Lawrence, Thomas B. 35
Lawson, Tony 54
Layder, Derek 49
Leca, Bernard 35
life course documents 120
Lithuania 116, 117, 120
liturgical tradition 132
Ljubljana 167, 172
London 64, 72, 82, 86, 97, 98, 109, 110
Maastricht Treaty 142
macro institutional structures 154
macro-level institutions 144
Mahoney, James 149
managers
   and anchor careers 199, 201
   and career patterns 38, 192, 196, 199
   and construction careers 199
   and dead-end careers 203
   and employee involvement 142, 161
   and patchwork careers 199
   interviews with 150, 196
Marginson, Paul 143, 144, 145, 147, 148, 149
Mari, Luca 19, 20
Marxism 49
Maszkienice, Poland 54, 55, 56, 57, 58

material semiotics 43
mathematical modelling 18
Matthew effect 112
Maxwell, Joseph A. 24, 32, 33, 149, 172, 173, 174, 177, 183, 184, 186
measurement 16, 33, 38, 50, 52
   model-based 19, 20
   realist 16
   truth-based 19, 20
metamorphosis 30
metamorphosis, biographical 93, 95, 104, 105, 110, 111
micro effectiveness 142
migration
   as Sostris category 65
   as source of betterment 55
   from Poland 54, 55, 57, 195
   personal project of 56
migration culture 56
Ministry of the Environment and Spatial Planning of the Republic of Slovenia 172, 182
models and beliefs, checking through data 13
models in science 20
mode of existence
   implications for measurement 16
MOL (Hungarian company) 157, 158
money, as ontologically subjective 16
Morawska, Ewa 54
morphogenesis 44, 57
   double 44, 48
   morphogenetic cycle 48, 57
Mrozowicki, Adam 13, 36, 38, 160, 191, 216
multinational corporations 161
myth of cultural cohesion 173, 188
Naples 99, 102, 103, 104
narrative analysis 176
narrative bias 185
national Eurocrats 167, 188
negotiating skills 177
neo-institutionalism 146
Netherlands 53, 98
newly independent states 116, 118
new nationalism 116, 118, 136

non-linear character of the social world 50
numerical data 17
Nurse, Lyudmila 36, 38, 115, 120, 217
objectivity, ontological vs epistemic 15
occupational counselling 36, 194, 209
occupational mobility 194, 197, 198, 202, 207
Old Believers 121, 127, 132
ontological subjectivity, as source of uncertainty 33
ontology 15, 37, 43, 50, 59, 143
   objective vs subjective 16, 33
   stratified social 45, 51, 53
open-endedness, of realism 50, 115
open-narrative questioning 175
open world, explanation in 45
organisation theory 35
Orthodox Church, Russian 121, 132
O'Sullivan, John 115
overlapping subjectivities 33
owners 196, 199, 203, 205, 207
panel interpretation, future-blind 80
Park, Robert 26
Parliamentary Committee on Environment, Public Health and Food Safety, EU 181
participants, in policy processes 37
particle physics, as model for realist science 15, 16, 17, 20
Pawson, Ray 50, 54
Peirce, Charles S. 21
Pennsylvania 56
performativity 43
Permanent Representation of Slovenia in Brussels 167
Perone, Elisabetta 36, 38, 93, 160, 217
personal documents 120
physical science 20, 33
Poland 38, 54, 121, 124, 125, 129, 131, 134, 135, 192, 195, 196
Poles, ethnic, in Vilnius 120
Porpora, Douglas 46
postmodernism 14, 15, 37
post-socialist countries 168
practical human rationality 22
pragmatic refraction 29

pragmatism 31
Prague 157
pre-coda 30
probing social phenomena 16
process-tracing 24, 25
psycho-social psychologism and critical realist sociologism 65
psycho-societal realism 63
Pulignano, Valeria 37, 38, 39, 141, 145, 147, 157, 159, 160, 217
qualitative social science studies 119
quantitative indicators 36
quantitative methods 49
quantitative studies 36
Radaelli, Claudio M. 143
rational actor theory 22
Realist biography and European policy workshop 37
realist biography as scientific method 17
realist empirical research 50
realist framework 13, 14, 15, 37, 38, 39, 141
realist social theory 13
reality check
   on knowledge claims 18
reality check, measurement as 17, 18
reflexivity 26, 102, 103
   as personal emergent power 23
   as personal emergent property 46
   autonomous 95, 102, 103, 109, 111, 196, 198, 200, 202, 204, 205, 206, 208, 209, 210
   communicative 97, 99
   fractured 95, 96
   methodological 52
regime competition 144, 154, 159
reliability
   of measurement 33
retrodiction 51
retroduction 51, 54
Riessman, Catherine Kohler 27, 28
right to information and consultation 156
risk
   individuals at 65, 74, 75, 83, 204
Rosenthal, Gabriele 13, 14, 21, 26, 28, 30, 75
rubber-stamping 178

Russia 102, 120, 121, 125, 126, 127, 132, 133
Russians, ethnic, in Vilnius 120
Sanofi-Aventis group 157
Sanofi-Synthelabo 157
Sayer, Andrew 50
Schütze, Fritz 13, 14, 26, 28, 29, 75, 83, 93, 94, 119, 192, 193, 196, 198
science
 component levels of 13
 physical vs social 16
 realist concecptualisation 20
Searle, John R. 15, 18, 20, 33
self-assessments of national identity 137
self-identification, ethnic 115, 124, 125, 126, 128, 136, 137
separate worlds 69, 70
Shaw, Clifford R. 26
shock of enlargement 34
Siemens 156
Siemens Employee Committee 157
Silesia 196
Single European Act 142, 152
Sisson, Keith 143, 145, 154
Slaughter, Anne-Marie 170
šlekta 121
Slovakia 136
Slovenia 38, 167
Slovenian Presidency of the (Council of the) European Union
 and environmental policy negotiation 38, 168, 169, 171, 176, 180
 and permanent representation 167
 experiences 176, 179, 180, 181, 183, 184, 185, 187, 188
 historical juncture 168, 170, 172, 188
 lines of authority 172
 preparation for 178, 179, 180, 181, 187, 188
 symbolic importance of 168
 trio partners 180
small-N studies 149
social dialogue 38, 142, 145, 146, 148, 153, 156, 159, 160, 161
social-economic phenomenon 141
Social Europe 142
social field 141, 145, 146

social hydraulics 17
social integration, European 142, 170
social psychology 68, 119
social structure, as not reified entity 44
sociological realism 43, 44, 45, 115
Somers, Margaret R. 51
Sostris 38, 65, 75, 76, 81, 82
Soviet Union 116, 121, 124, 125, 126, 127, 132
Spanò, Antonella 36, 38, 93, 95, 96, 112, 160, 209, 218
statistical correlations 25
statistical techniques, as appropriate but insufficient 17
statistical uncertainty 18
statutory forms of representative employee involvement 142
Strauss, Anselm 31, 212
Streeck, Wolfgang 146, 147, 150, 151
structuration 44, 54, 74
structure and agency
 and analytical dualism 44, 45
 interplay 44
structured interviews 115
structured social relations 43, 44, 45
Stubbs, Paul 35
subjective personal identity 134
subjectivity, ontological vs epistemic 15
Suddaby, Roy 35
Sweden 65, 135
systematic uncertainty 18, 33
Telekom 157, 158
telling of the told story 30, 78, 79, 88
temporal priority of structure 46
Tenth Directive, dealing with cross-border mergers of limited liability companies 151
Texas 106
Thelen, Kathleen 146
thematic analysis 30
thematic-based dialogue 120
Tilly, Charles 58
trade union representatives 150
trade unions 38, 72, 147, 149, 150, 151, 152, 153, 155, 156, 158, 161
trajectories of experience accumulation 176

trajectories of suffering 30
transliteration of surnames 130
transnational mobility 38, 93, 94, 95, 96, 110
trio, German-Portuguese-Slovenian 180
true values 17, 19, 20
Turk, Jeffrey D. 13, 14, 20, 34, 37, 38, 63, 167, 170, 172, 191, 192, 218
twin-track procedure 75, 76, 79, 83
UNFCCC 169
United Kingdom 149, 150
United States of America 106, 109, 158, 205
    employment agents from 56
    migration to 55, 56, 57, 58
unobservable nature of causal mechanisms 50
validity 32, 33, 38, 168, 177, 186, 188
    as encompassing term 33, 34
    as epistemic objectivity 33
    assessment of 183
    descriptive 34, 183, 184
    interpretive 34, 184, 185
    shared standards 33
    theoretical 34, 184, 186
variable-based research strategies 50
varieties of capitalism 37
Vilnius 116, 120
Vredeling Directive 151, 152
waste disposal and processing 181

Weisbein, Julien 36
welfare policies, European 36
Wengraf, Tom 14, 25, 30, 36, 38, 39, 58, 63, 65, 70, 71, 72, 73, 74, 75, 76, 81, 82, 83, 84, 85, 119, 160, 175, 185, 219
worker cooperatives 141
worker involvement. *See* employee involvement
workers 198
    and anchor careers 199, 200, 201
    and career patterns 38, 192, 196, 197, 199, 208
    and construction careers 204, 205, 206
    and dead-end careers 199, 202
    and European Works Councils 158
    and patchwork careers 199, 206, 207, 208
    blue-collar 200
    in declining industries 65
    in public administration 100
    interviews with 196, 197
    involvement in management 141
    migrant 56
    representatives 151
Working Group on International Environmental Issues 169
Working Party on the Environment (WPE) 171

www.ingramcontent.com/pod-product-compliance
Ingram Content Group UK Ltd.
Pitfield, Milton Keynes, MK11 3LW, UK
UKHW021838210426
53221PUK00021B/359